FUNDAMENTALS OF THE U.S. FEDERAL REPUBLIC

Jack M. Bernardo

County College of Morris

Kendall Hunt
publishing company

Image of ship © 2012 JupiterImages Corp.
Cover design courtesy of Jose Rouco.

Kendall Hunt
publishing company

www.kendallhunt.com
Send all inquiries to:
4050 Westmark Drive
Dubuque, IA 52004-1840

Printed in the United States of America
10 9 8 7 6 5 4 3 2 1

CONTENTS

LIST OF FIGURES & TABLES

SECTION THREE: POLITICAL CIRCUMSTANCE   113

ACKNOWLEDGMENTS

The author wants to acknowledge all those who made this project possible, most notably his family, friends; and faculty colleagues over the years, particularly those at the County College of Morris; all those who taught him about politics and government, particularly Dr. Robert Cunningham; all the authors of all the textbooks who provided the means for him to teach—and learn—across the last two decades; and Sue and Sarah at Kendall Hunt, who kept him on track.

Jack Bernardo
July 2012

PREFACE

This book is primarily intended to serve as a textbook to introduce lower-division college students to the basics of U.S. government and politics in a single, 15-week semester. Some professors might also find it useful as a refresher text for upper-division or graduate courses in U.S. government and politics, intergovernmental relations, or federalism. A number of my academic colleagues, particularly those who have spent a lifetime in specialized study of any of the topics covered herein, will undoubtedly find parts of my presentation incomplete and/or oversimplified. I admit that is the case, but hope those readers will understand my goal of preparing a complete but compact overview of the very complex phenomena that government and politics in the United States are today—and have been since 1776. Some form(s) of supplemental material will be needed to provide students with a complete, contemporary picture of our political system; my personal plan is to use an e-reader and current events websites.

Anyone who has taught introductory American government knows that one must expect a wide range of student interest. The reality is that most students will be taking the course simply to fulfill some requirement for their degrees. There will be a handful, however, who bring a genuine interest in government and politics to their studies, along with, hopefully, a few for whom the course will awaken a sincere interest in those subjects. This book was designed to meet the needs of all of those students. It focuses on the basics throughout, but also provides some groundwork for further study in key areas. References to the literature of political science are limited and, for the most part, provided in footnotes for those atypical students. Hopefully, the book will instill in all students an appreciation for the very special nature of the U.S. political system, and help them to be at least a bit better citizens than they would otherwise have been.

In writing about the fundamentals of the structure and operation of the U.S. Federal Republic, I draw upon over four decades of studying, working in, and teaching about government and public affairs. I am presenting here relevant highlights of my experiences because my personal story is a component of the methodology of this monograph. I feel that I actually "lived" U.S. federalism during most of my 24-year public service career, which mostly involved working in the federal grants arena. Having public administration as the core of my political science training left me with a deep respect for the *verstehen*[1] type of learning that comes only from direct experience. That career included teaching a range of introductory political science courses as an adjunct for the last ten years, which provided me with a "participant-as-observer"[2] perspective to which relatively few have had access. Teaching full-time the last five years has immersed me in the subject as nothing else does, moreover.

I am a first-generation American, the son of a man who initially came to the United States illegally (more than once), but pursued citizenship and became a citizen as soon as possible. Dad also volunteered to serve in World War II, although his age and marital status made it unlikely he would have been drafted. He taught me a deep love of this country. With the Vietnam War dominating my youth, and growing up in the media smorgasbord of New York City, I was easily drawn to politics. Like most Americans at that time, I strongly supported the Vietnam War at first.

Being blessed with parents who pushed education, I was able to choose my high school

after graduating (quite incidentally) from the same grammar school as Supreme Court justice Sonia Sotomayor. The one I chose (which, again incidentally, includes a Supreme Court justice, Antonin Scalia, among its alumni) required participation in the Army Junior Reserve Officer Training Corps, which I took to, leading to selection for officer candidate school and a cadet commission. So, I decided to try for West Point.

I succeeded in getting a nomination from my congressman, but was not good enough to beat my competition for admission. A New York State scholarship led to supplemental offers from a few universities, giving me opportunities that most of my peers envied. My choice of Syracuse University can be considered the "precipitating event" that eventually led to this book, because being involved in the political turmoil that occurred there in the late1960s led to my majoring in political science.

At that time, every Syracuse liberal arts student was required to take a year-long "Introduction to Public Affairs" course, which proved to be just that for me. Hundreds of us would assemble in Hendricks Chapel each Monday to listen to, and ask questions of, notable faculty members or guest speakers. We would then discuss whatever we had heard in small classes later that week. My clearest memory about that course is of being awakened to the reality that racism was "not just a Southern problem" by NAACP president Floyd McKissick, but the Vietnam War was at least talked about every week.

While I was still interested in pursuing a military commission and career, as a Junior ROTC graduate I could skip the first year of the college program. I took that option so I could focus on my other courses to ensure that I kept my scholarships—and to experience what life was like as "a civilian." It certainly was different.

---

[1] The *Online Dictionary of the Social Sciences* produced by the International Consortium for the Advancement of Academic Publication (ICAAP) tells us: "Verstehen refers to understanding the meaning of action from the actor's point of view." Its methodological contribution is elegantly described by Stephen Wasby in *Political Science—The Discipline and its Dimensions* (New York: Charles Scribner's Sons, 1970, 22): "While intuition and *Verstehen* should not be used as substitutes for empirical work in data collection, they can, particularly if 'educated' or 'informed' on the basis of long exposure to a particular research problem, provide a 'grasp' of a problem not available from tests of hypotheses alone."

[2] Nicholas Babchuk, "The Role of the Researcher as Participant-Observer and Participant-as-Observer in the Field Situation," *Human Organization*, 21 (1962), 225–228. Wasby (see Note 1) nicely summarized the differences between the two on p. 182.

Like most young people on their own for the first time, I tried new things like growing my hair and a beard, and opened my mind to new ideas. I attended several "teach-ins" by antiwar activists and listened to many debates, and came away with the realization that the issue was much more complicated than I had thought it was.

Unlike most of my peers, I did not turn against the war, however. My exploration and soul-searching did leave me skeptical about all simplistic "solutions" that could be reduced to short slogans (what we now call "sound bites"). I rejected "My country, right or wrong" patriotism, but my conclusion was that our leaders deserved the benefit of the doubt. I felt I owed something to the United States just for giving me the freedom and opportunity to make up my own mind—especially compared to our Cold War adversaries. In late 1967, however, most college campuses—and the nation—were not tolerant of those wanting to walk a middle path (sound familiar?), and I knew I had to choose a side.

So, for spring 1968 I enrolled in both Army ROTC and my first political science course (American Government—I still have that textbook[3]), having no idea that year would bring the series of events that led *ABC News* to label it "A Crack in Time" in a television special decades later. I was not directly involved much in political action (which ROTC discouraged), but several times found myself the target of anti-ROTC protests, and did participate in a few Young Americans for Freedom (conservative youth) activities. My most vivid memories are of guarding the American flag flying on "the Quad" with some fellow cadets during a few antiwar demonstrations, and fleeing the campus when students protesting the invasion of Cambodia in May 1970 set a fire at the construction site for a new campus Geology building.

Despite basically daily ridicule by other students and outright contempt openly expressed to me by some faculty, I went on to complete my political science degree with honors and earn a Regular Army commission as a Distinguished Graduate of ROTC. They had stopped sending "green" lieutenants to Vietnam at that point, so my request for an overseas short tour led to my first assignment being Korea, after a few months of training in Oklahoma. Driving cross-country in my first car introduced me to the beauty and expanse of the United States; and getting to know people from the Midwest, South, and Southwest, where most of the soldiers I served with came from, was a very broadening experience for me.

Korea was no picnic, but it wasn't Vietnam. As I stated in a guest editorial published just before the Iraq War,[4] "I'm no war hero—never saw combat . . . . I did get shot at a few times by snipers and our South Korean allies while on night missions near the DMZ—and you don't have to hear bullets whiz by your head too many times to truly experience the risk every soldier faces." One thing I did experience there that only a small number of people can claim, I believe, was doing periodic 12-hour shifts monitoring one of two "red phones" that were part of the system for authorizing the use of nuclear weapons. The most memorable experience was commanding U.S. soldiers. I am proud of many things I have done, but that remains my proudest achievement. My focus on decision making is likely rooted in these formative military experiences.

---

[3] Karl M. Schmidt, ed., *American National Government in Action* (Belmont, CA: Dickenson, 1965).

[4] "America owes disabled vets better care," *The Star-Ledger*, 11/11/2002, 11.

My military career lasted only a few years, due to a back injury incurred during a readiness inspection not long after I returned to the United States, and I used my limited "GI Bill" benefits to help fund my graduate studies at the University of Tennessee, Knoxville. Those studies included my first government experiences. A full-time, eight-month internship with the Tennessee Department of Public Health's Office of Policy Planning in Nashville was my introduction to the realities of U.S. federalism, and a year as a research assistant to the 1978 Knoxville-Knox County Metropolitan Charter Commission was my introduction to the realities of local government.

I also did my first political science teaching back in Knoxville while completing my Ph.D. coursework, taught full-time and coordinated Washington, DC, internships for a New Jersey state college for two years while working on my dissertation, and then took a year off to complete it. All these experiences had combined to produce in me a deep appreciation of the interplay between theory and practice. Theory does provide a useful starting point for action when you are facing your first big decisions and new or unusual situations as an experienced practitioner. Practical experience gives you what I call the "operational knowledge" (elaborated in Chapter 7) that is an essential ingredient for success in public affairs.

I clearly recall debating with myself what the next step in my career should be. Since the most professional and successful individuals I had encountered in both areas in the decade since leaving Syracuse had *both* solid theoretical preparation and ample "operational knowledge," I decided I needed more government experience to be truly prepared to confidently teach public policy and administration, my specialty field. So,

I obtained an entry-level staff position in county government, and quickly discovered that I enjoyed *doing* public administration as much as the analytical side of it. The openness of the communication process and the variety of the work, particularly compared to the military, captivated me. One could also make a difference in people's lives.

That first position introduced me to the world of government grants, setting the stage for the core of my public service career. Among my first assignments were assisting a committee that distributed social services grants and the quasi-independent office that administered the Community Development Block Grant (CDBG) and other U.S. Department of Housing and Urban Development (HUD) programs. Having been swayed by the "New Public Administration" literature[5] encountered during my graduate studies to be a "change agent" whenever possible, I sought out opportunities to improve both the efficiency and effectiveness of programs.

Learning the realities of government budgeting was my next lesson. Creating change—even greater efficiency—usually requires resources. It did not take long to find out that those who have or control resources tend to be extremely reluctant to part with them. Annual budgets are one of the major constraints that all public administrators must deal with; supplemental funding is rare. So, my desire to enhance or expand worthwhile activities quickly led me to the pursuit of new resources. If you want to get policymakers to approve something new

---

[5] Frank Marini, ed., *Toward a New Public Administration: The Minnowbrook Perspective* (San Francisco: Chandler, 1971), the proceedings of the 1968 Minnowbrook Conference at Syracuse University. Ironically, I was at Syracuse when the conference occurred, although I did not learn about it until starting my graduate studies years later.

or expand existing services, you need to "show them the money."

During half of the next 24 years I was director of county grants departments at the community development office of a neighboring county and the community college where I now teach, and in both cases I was very active in the related statewide associations, being elected president and vice president, respectively. I also worked for a small nonprofit organization created by another county to carry out state grant–funded projects, and as a member of project consulting teams for a few other counties and a number of municipalities and housing authorities. One of my most interesting posts was as project specialist with the state Purchase Bureau for 18 months, bidding out high-profile contracts. I also worked directly for two community nonprofits under short-term contracts.

This wide range of experience allowed me to see both the best and worst of U.S. federalism in action. The best was watching local communities accomplish some of their dream projects that provided both immediate and long-term direct benefit to residents using national (HUD), state, and local funds under our county administrative umbrella. I can still recall the beaming smile on one little girl's face as she enjoyed a new "pocket park" playground that I do not think would have been built if not for some refinements to the selection process that I had initiated and gotten approved. The worst was finding millions of dollars sitting unused in phantom and mismanaged project accounts by an urban county political machine while residents were going homeless. Our consulting team was able to get them to put that money to work by "reprograming" it.

I always envisioned myself returning to teaching, and was given the opportunity to adjunct in 1995 at another community college in New Jersey. As I had hoped, my government experience enriched my courses, and it was not long before I envisioned capping my public service career by returning to full-time teaching. My adjunct career lasted the decade covering my last three practitioner positions, providing me with the rare, "participant-as-observer" experience I noted at the beginning.

One of the most useful nuggets of wisdom that I ever encountered in my public service career was "Miles Law," which goes, "Where you stand depends on where you sit."[6] The lesson it seeks to convey is that peoples' perspective in all decision-making situations is shaped by their position and its role in the process. I thought it useful to relate the highlights of my very mixed career experiences to lend credence to the descriptions and observations about the U.S. political system that are presented in this monograph. The many places I have "sat" have allowed me to see that system from many diverse perspectives, and led me to appreciate its very "gestalt" nature, in that term's most basic sense. To this political scientist, "the whole" of the U.S. political system is truly greater than the sum of its parts.

This monograph portrays that system as a mosaic, a set of intricately intertwined parts, overlaid "subsystems" that both compete and cooperate, with the U.S. Federal Republic (a mosaic of "subsystems" itself) as its core structure. Moreover, there may be a rhythm to its operation. Although not easy to portray, one visualization of it is as a latticework of pulsating organizational fields driven by ideological struggle. What this political scientist sees is a "dialectical dance" between coalitions that desire more government protection and ones desiring

---

6 Rufus E. Miles, Jr., "The Origin and Meaning of Miles Law," *Public Administration Review*, 38 (1978), 5, 399–403.

personal freedom that manifests itself at times as downright fear of government intrusion. But that is part of its secret to success:[7]

> *What makes U.S. political culture unrivaled is its peaceful dynamism. There are always competing patriotic forces arguing for their vision of America. Hamiltonian's done you wrong for eight years? Cast your vote for the Jeffersonians for a change.*

The most useful visual image of how it operates, based on student response over the past 15 years, is to depict the system as a complex set of ongoing "tugs-of-war" among its various parts, allowing each of the two desires to compete for control. So, both core values are continuously represented somewhere in the public policy arena, with dominance by one of them occasionally achieved while always being countered in some way. Therefore, "control" is always circumscribed, and is actually shared by the two competing core "factions." To this political scientist, James Madison and his fellow Founders succeeded brilliantly.

Hopefully, the manner in which this mosaic is presented will help all readers learn the fundamentals of how the U.S. political system works, and some to appreciate its intricacies enough to want to learn more. If that is the case, its purpose will have been fulfilled.

---

[7] *Newsweek,* June 8, 2009, 18, reviewing Simon Schama's *The American Future* (New York: HarperCollins, 2009).

Introduction: A "Good Ship"—The U.S. Federal Republic

WHAT YOU ARE ABOUT TO STUDY

Before we begin our journey through the U.S. political system, we need to cover some preliminary matters. For many of you, this is your very first course in political science, so we need to establish what you are about to study and how we are basically going to go about it.

First, is political science really a science?[1] The word science comes from the Latin noun *scientia*, which means knowledge. Today, however, when we think of science we mean a very special type of knowledge that has been developed using "the scientific method." To most people, the essence of science is controlled experimentation that can be replicated. That is what provides the verification that allows knowledge to be labeled "scientific." Applying that criterion, political science does not qualify. It will never be able to achieve the level of certainty that physics, chemistry, and biology can achieve, because the most rigorous types of experiments cannot be performed.[2]

The research efforts of political scientists are like those of astronomers. We observe and collect information about political phenomena like astronomers study celestial phenomena. They differentiate and categorize what they observe (e.g., stars, planets, comets) by applying definitions they create and refine for use in further analysis. For example, the recent redesignation of Pluto involved differentiating "dwarf planets" from "planets." We do the same regarding politics, and also share the same goals—understanding and explanation—but must deal with a more "fickle universe":[3]

We political scientists envy astronomers . . . . They speak with assurance, because they can usually trust heavenly bodies to obey the laws of

---

[1] For those interested in exploring this further, there is a wealth of writings on social science theory. The works that most influenced my thinking in this matter were *The Conduct of Inquiry* by Abraham Kaplan (San Francisco: Chandler, 1964), *The Structure of Scientific Revolutions* by Thomas S. Kuhn (Chicago: University of Chicago, 1970), and *Patterns of Discovery in the Social Sciences* by Paul Deising (New York: Aldine-Atherton, 1971).

[2] While they are possible, most people would condemn them as unethical. See, for example, "Uproar by pols over 'cruel' test of city homeless," New York *Daily News*, 10/1/10, 4.

[3] John J. Pitney, Jr., "The Study of a Fickle Political Universe," *The Chronicle of Higher Education*, 12/15/95, A52.

celestial mechanics and follow regular courses.... Nearly every time we think we have found a durable pattern of behavior, something changes.

Next, please understand that there are a number of ways to study or to teach about politics and government, and that what is presented here is not "absolute truth." Those of you who choose to continue studying them in the future need to be aware that other authors and professors will likely present these subjects in different ways. This is the case in all of the "social sciences"— even the ones that do include "experiments" and controlled comparisons—and is one of the things that makes them so interesting.

These differences are due in part to the variety of "approaches"[4] that are used. Social scientists select a focus for their observations and analysis. They base their selections on their personal intellectual objectives and what their early studies and experiences lead them to conclude will be most useful in helping them understand their subjects. Most tend to adopt a general approach to their field and specific approaches for particular research efforts. Approaches usually involve "an organizing concept or set of concepts"[5] that primarily offer guidance and/or direction.

One's general approach is an umbrella strategy for study, an orienting device. For example, today many political scientists focus on communications, which is very understandable given the important role that it plays. Others argue that politics is so closely tied to economics

that you cannot separate the two for purposes of study and research. As computers improved our ability to collect and analyze quantitative data, that drew increasing attention, and some think "polimetrics"[6] is the wave of the future.

The general approach underlying our journey will be "systems theory":[7]

In general, then, we can say that every system has three characteristic components: identifiable elements, relationships among the elements, and boundaries. In addition, most systems will have subsystems. That is, the elements and relationships of a system will, in effect, break themselves into smaller systems.

Why? "The political system idea serves to keep us attuned to the broad implications of political acts and institutions, and to the interrelatedness of events."[8] Moreover, "it is natural to think of phenomena as parts of wholes."[9] Our journey through the U.S. political system will be an analytical one. The word "analysis" comes from the Greek word meaning "to break up." As in many other sciences, political scientists study their subject by "dissecting" it. Various "parts" of the U.S. political system will be discussed individually, as pieces of a puzzle. Keeping a system orientation in the back of your mind throughout the journey will hopefully help you put the puzzle together at the end, giving you the

---

[4] Chapter 9 of *Scope and Methods of Political Science* by Alan C. Isaak (Homewood, IL: Dorsey Press, 1975) directly addresses "Approaches to the study of politics," and the book discusses seven types of them. Oran Young uses five categories in *Systems of Political Science* (Englewood Cliffs, NJ: Prentice-Hall, 1968).

[5] Isaak, 156.

[6] Gary King, "On Political Methodology," *Political Analysis*, 2 (1991), 1–30. The quantitative approach to politics should not be confused with a new subfield proposed in a 2008 special issue of *Environmental Fluid Mechanics*.

[7] Isaak, 215. The first proponent of the systems approach to political analysis was David Easton in *The Political System* (New York: Knopf, 1953) and subsequent articles and books. We will return to his work below.

[8] Stephen Wasby, *Political Science–The Discipline and its Dimensions* (New York: Charles Scribner's Sons, 1970), 109.

[9] Isaak, 213.

comprehensive basic introduction this work is intended to be.

WHAT IS POLITICS?

Politics is a very complex set of phenomena. When most Americans think about politics, they tend to focus on elections or government activity, but it involves so much more. Since one of the goals of this book is to introduce you to the study of politics as a social science, we must deal with this complexity to some extent. We will do this by introducing three (3) "levels" of definition that have been found useful in conveying that complexity:[10]

1. *"Nuts and Bolts":* What is the most basic behavior that you would want to observe? Probably the most concise definition of basic politics ever formulated was "who gets what, when, and how,"[11] because this is what public issues[12] at all levels are basically about on a day-to-day basis. Which states will receive what amounts of federal funds for what purposes? Which interest groups will get more of what they want in

new legislation? Which level of government will prevail in a court case? When change to the process itself is involved, the "how" comes into play. It should be noted that politics deals specifically with community support for ideas and the allocation of public resources that are extracted from and supported by private economic activity, so I would refine that classic definition into: *Who gets and pays for what, when and how, with respect to public resources and support.*

2. *"Operational Concept":* What bundles or clusters of measurable, concrete phenomena should be focused on when observing this basic behavior? Of the hundreds of operational definitions of politics available, the one this political scientist has found most useful is:[13]

   Reduced to its universal elements, then, politics is a social process characterized by activity involving rivalry and cooperation in the exercise of power, and culminating in the making of (authoritative) decisions for a group.

   Take a few minutes to consider the components of this definition. It tells us that we are going to be studying "a social process," which means people interacting. It specifies what type of activity we want to examine, "the exercise of power," a term used throughout this book in its most basic sense of the ability to get what you want accomplished. Furthermore, this definition even provides a very specific focus for our attention, a culmination point, "the making of (authoritative) decisions." Why the word in parentheses was added is explained below. One can examine

---

[10] These correspond to the three levels of social science theory-building first elaborated by Robert Merton in *Social Theory and Social Structure* (New York: Free Press, 1957). Wasby (see Note 8) provides an excellent summary description on p. 63, and Isaak (see Note 4) thoroughly discusses theory-building, its applications, and uses.

[11] Harold Lasswell, *Who Gets What, When, and How* (New York: McGraw-Hill, 1936).

[12] The distinction between "public" and "private" used throughout this monograph is based on the classic formulation by philosopher John Dewey in *The Public and Its Problems* (1927), nicely summarized by Wasby (see Note 8), 13: "actions were public when they had indirect consequences, that is, consequences which spread beyond the individuals or groups immediately or directly involved in the actions." See also *The Collected Works of John Dewey,* Jo Ann Boydston, ed., 37 volumes (Carbondale: Southern Illinois University Press, 1967–1991).

[13] William Bluhm, *Theories of the Political System* (Englewood Cliffs, NJ: Prentice-Hall, 1965), 5, with parentheses added by this author.

what leads up to an authoritative decision and what follows from it.

3. *"Theoretical"*: What abstract, high-level generalizations capture and convey the most important knowledge we have observed? If the observations have been carefully made and analyzed, these will reflect the essential realities of the phenomena. This is called empirical social science, and is contrasted with normative analysis, which deals with what should be rather than what exists, and is usually labeled political philosophy.[14] With many to choose from again, the theoretical definition of politics that most clearly conveys its essence to this political scientist, since all decisions reflect underlying value judgments by the people involved in making them, is:[15]

Politics is the authoritative allocation of values within a society, for the society as a whole, backed by the ultimate use of a monopoly of physical force.

That definition was, interestingly, formulated by the originator of the systems approach to political analysis, David Easton, and one of his contemporaries provided the final link to the specific approach that will underlie our analytical journey:[16]

Now if, as Easton asserts, politics is the authoritative allocation of values and if, as I interpret it, "allocation" refers not to a physical process but to the social process of deciding how a physical process shall be carried out,

then the subject studied by political scientists is decision-making.

It would be difficult to continuously deal with all three of these definitions as we proceed through our analytical journey, although they will be recalled at times. By choosing these definitions, the specific approach for our journey has been selected, but needs some clarification. We are moving towards a handy definition that incorporates some elements of all three levels of thinking. Let's explore some linkages:

- Considered individually, what behavior do the words "who," "what," "when," and "how" describe? Choosing something!
- When a choice is made deliberately, it is called a decision.
- Deliberate choices reflect priorities. What is more valued at that time?
- The qualifier "authoritative" from the theoretical definition was added to "decisions" in the operational concept because all decisions are not received equally by the people in a community. The acceptance of decisions is based on the perceived authority and ability of the decision makers to carry them out.
- The idea "public" was introduced above to distinguish the issues that politics deals with, meaning those that can be anticipated to have notable impacts well beyond the people directly involved.
- This political scientist prefers the term "community" to "group" or "society," since that term implies some level of cooperation, and it can be applied to any size collective of people from a small village to the entire world.
- Both communities and the values that communities widely share, which tend to be the ones that politics applies, change over time.

---

[14] Again, social science theory covers this in an array of ways. Isaak (see Note 4) summarizes the distinction quite well on page 136 and discusses it at some length in his first chapter.

[15] David Easton, "An Approach to the Analysis of Political Systems," *World Politics*, 9 (1957), 383–400.

[16] William Riker, *The Theory of Political Coalitions* (New Haven, CT: Yale University Press, 1962), 10.

Applying these linkages and clarifications, we arrive at a concise answer to the question "What is politics?" that can be readily applied throughout our journey:

> *Politics is the process of making authoritative decisions to deal with public issues for a community that reflect the prevailing values of that community at that time.*

TWO OTHER BASIC CONCEPTS WE WILL USE

Having defined the most basic concept we will use, two related concepts need to be introduced. It was mentioned above that most people tend to think about politics as something related to "government," and rightfully so. A logical question to consider next would be how government relates to our definition of politics. Applying the selected approach, a focus on authoritative decision making, provides us with this very useful definition of government:

> *Governments are the social structures, both formal and informal, through which the authoritative decisions are made that address public issues and allocate values in communities.*

Please note that "social structures" does not refer to physical things, but rather to the "patterned, but not necessarily formalized regular behavior"[17] of people. One of the themes that

will emerge throughout our journey is the need to look at both formal (that is, specifically authorized in some legal or otherwise "official" manner) and informal (allowed and accepted, but not specifically authorized in any formal way) behavior in order to fully understand the operation of the U.S. political system—or any social system.

The third basic concept we will use on our journey is "public policy." That term has been used in political discussion for a long time, but as the quantitative approach gained momentum in political science in the second half of the twentieth century, it spawned a new subfield, "policy analysis," and an extensive debate over how to define it. One recent definition ties public policy directly to our selected specific approach, if one accepts that governments are authoritative structures for communities: "Public policy is whatever the government decides to do or not to do."[18]

Although many of you may never have encountered the term "nondecision"[19] before, you have certainly made one, and likely more. We have all avoided and/or postponed choices we needed to make, and most governing bodies spend much more time formulating and debating alternatives than actually choosing which ones to adopt. Another tie to our chain of definition is that the political scientists who

---

[17] Wasby (see Note 8), 98. He provides this definition as part of an excellent summary discussion of structural-functionalism as a broad "frame of reference" for political science. Patterns of human activity are tied to their "relevant consequences," that is, function(s). Structural-functionalism was developed, and continues to be an important general approach, within the fields of Anthropology and Sociology.

[18] J. M. Shatfritz, E. W. Russell and C. P. Borick, *Introducing Public Administration* (New York: Longman, 2007), 42. This is a derivative of Thomas R. Dye's now classic definition from *Understanding Public Policy* (Englewood Cliffs, NJ: Prentice-Hall, 1980), "Public policy is whatever government does or does not do."

[19] Peter Bachrach and Morton S. Baratz, "Decisions and Nondecisions: An Analytical Framework," *The American Political Science Review*, 57(3) (1962), 632–642. See "Nondecision-Making," *International Encyclopedia of the Social Sciences* at Encyclopedia.com for a brief introduction to the topic.

originated the concept were analyzing the exercise of political power, and wanted to clarify that it often involves stopping certain decisions from being made. Adding that terminology to that of our selected specific approach yields the following definition:

> *Public policies are the authoritative decisions (including nondecisions) made for a community regarding public issues and conflicts that arise.*

This trio of concepts meshes together quite nicely, providing a convenient way to think and talk about the basics of how political systems operate:

- Politics is *the process* of making authoritative decisions on public issues.
- Governments are *the structures* through which those decisions are made.
- Public policies are *the products* of that process, the decisions themselves.

DECISION-MAKING STRUCTURES

There is a rich body of social science literature on decision making reaching back to the 1950s – too rich to attempt to summarize here. One comprehensive analysis of social systems that places "political rationality" within the broader social context portrays it as "the rationality of decision-making structures."[20]

---

[20] Paul Deising, *Reason in Society: Five Types of Decisions and Their Social Conditions* (Urbana: University of Illinois Press, 1962 [rpt. Greenwood, 1973]), 170. The five types of rationality are technical, economic, social, legal, and political. In "Paul Diesing and Social Science: A Career Review Essay," Richard Hartwig states, "He would have added ecological rationality, had this paradigm been well developed in 1962," based on a 1984 interview with Deising. http://www.tamuk.edu/geo/urbana/Fall03/Articles03/Diesing.doc.

The political structure of a group is the organization of forces which determines how its decisions are made, that is, its decision-making structure. Political science is the study of decision-making structures.

In addition to endorsing our selected approach to studying politics, this work is being noted because its explanation of decision-making structures inspired the outline for our analytical journey through the U.S. political system. We begin our breakdown of the U.S. decision-making structure by identifying three basic components:

1. *Political Culture*: "a set of beliefs and values, more or less held in common by participating members. These define the kind of ideas that can seriously be considered during discussion and decision."[21] This includes "the system of empirical beliefs, expressive symbols, and values which define the situation in which political action takes place."[22] A community's political culture primarily shapes political *roles* (the expected and allowable behaviors by members filling all the various decision-making positions), but also impacts political *rules* (the basic operational parameters for authoritative community decision making), both formal (legal or otherwise "official") and informal (adopted norms).

2. *Political Configuration*: The operational framework and basic processes within which authoritative decision making takes

---

[21] Deising, 170–172.
[22] Sydney Verba, "Comparative Political Culture," in Lucien Pye and Sydney Verba, eds., *Political Culture and Political Development* (Princeton, NJ: Princeton University Press, 1965), 513.

place. A community's political configuration primarily shapes political rules, but also impacts political roles.

3. *Political Circumstance*: "The sum of determining factors beyond willful control."[23] Political circumstance particularly includes "the commitments already accepted by a [community] and the courses of action in which it is already engaged. All decisions have to be made in an actual context of actions and commitments resulting from previous decisions."[24]

A quick look at this book's Contents list will reveal that these three components serve as the basis for its three main sections, and each will be further explained at the beginning of those sections. The Contents list also tells the reader what aspects of the U.S. political system fall under each component. In the Conclusion we will review all the pieces of the puzzle and provide this political scientist's picture of how they fit together. It will be portrayed as a mosaic, a set of intricately intertwined subsystems that both compete and cooperate, with the U.S. Federal Republic as its core structure.

A rather positive view of the system as a whole will be presented, but it is not perfect. As with all human inventions, it has flaws. To this political scientist, the greatest strength of the U.S. political system is its capability for self-correction based upon its openness, adaptability, and resilience. Americans often forget how many very important changes have been made to our authoritative decision-making structure

since its establishment over two and a quarter centuries ago. These have often come in bursts of innovation, and have always been accompanied by resistance. For example, what twenty-five year period in U.S. history is this writer describing?

There came in America during this period certain changes in government, certain legislative, political, and judicial innovations. Whether these are all enrichments is a subject of debate, as the changes in science and industry are not. Some would refuse to concede that all the changes in government were advances. In any event they were innovations, the fundamental importance of which warrants almost any superlative.

From that description, this could be almost any period in U.S. history. Perhaps listing a few of the "most important" will help identify it:[25]

- "The *Direct Election of United States Senators*," which "increased the control of the people over the selection of their representatives."
- "The *Graduated Income Tax*," which "was an extension of the power of the Federal Government over private property."
- *National Woman Suffrage*.

The footnote tells you that period was 1900 to 1925, but it should be noted that some of those changes had begun percolating through the political system much earlier.

Other extremely important changes had been made previously, most notably adoption of the Bill of Rights and the Civil War Amendments, which abolished slavery, formally ended race as a voting requirement (for men), and extended the reach of the Bill of Rights to state and local governments

---

[23] *The American Heritage Dictionary*, 2nd College Edition (New York: Houghton-Mifflin, 1982), 275.
[24] Deising, 171–172, with modification by this author in brackets.

[25] Mark Sullivan, *Our Times: The United States 1900–1925* (New York: Charles Scribner's Sons, 1926), 65–66.

and private activity regulated by law. Change continued in the twentieth century, with a term limit placed on the presidency and extension of the right to vote to 18-year-old citizens.

And these are just the *most formal* changes that have been made—constitutional amendments. Some of the other "most important" changes made about a hundred years ago were accomplished by changes in state laws ("The *Direct Primary*," which "gave the people increased control over the selection of their officials; and greatly reduced the power of party machines"), or by informal means ("*Conservation*," which "reversed the government's previous policy of expediting the transfer of public lands into private ownership . . . an extension of the power of the executive branch of the government by [Theodore] Roosevelt, who established the precedent that the President can do whatever he is not expressly forbidden to do by the Constitution or the laws").[26]

To this political scientist, the political history of the United States has been a great dialectical dance—one that continues to this day. It began with those who wanted to work things out with the British debating those who argued for independence. As soon as that issue was resolved, the role of the central government took its place. It is not uncommon to have this debate presented as a competition between the "Hamiltonians," who "although they had been strongly opposed to the central government of England, came out in favor of a strong central government in the United States for compelling practical reasons," and the "Jeffersonians," who had "fear and dislike of the central government" as their "first principle."[27]

Those two "factions," using James Madison's classic terminology, went down in history as the Federalists and Anti-Federalists. That debate boiled over into our Civil War over slavery, continued as we responded to the Industrial Revolution and its intermittent economic crises (especially the Great Depression), was revived by the twentieth century Civil Rights Movement, and spawned both the "New Federalism" reaction to it and the current century's Tea Party Movement. Even a respected mid-twentieth century commentator who was not a political scientist saw the pattern:[28]

> *The Americans down to the present day have jumped back and forth between the doctrines of Hamilton and those of Jefferson according to which doctrine each one thought most advantageous to the political purposes he might have in mind.*

The author of a much more detailed contemporary discussion about the U.S. political system aptly characterizes Americans as "ambivalent about government in general," helping to foster "a deep ambivalence . . . across a wide range of issues."[29] This dialectical dance has at times endangered the system's very existence, including the Civil War and the delayed response to the Great Depression. Since we are still responding to the rise of international terrorism and the Great Recession of the early twenty-first century as this is being written, it is not possible to determine the relative danger we are in or how well the system will respond.

While that dance between competing ideological principles (Ideology will be defined and

---

[26] Sullivan, 65. Brackets added by the author for clarity.
[27] David Cushman Coyle, *The United States Political System and How It Works* (New York: Signet, 1954), 121.

[28] Coyle, 121.
[29] Cal Jillson, *American Government: Political Development and Institutional Change* (New York: Routledge, 2011), 104–105.

discussed in Chapter 4.) is important, it is only one part of the puzzle. Let's close out this introduction by returning to our general approach and discussing some different descriptive metaphors. In addition to the "three characteristic components: identifiable elements, relationships among the elements, and boundaries .... every system has an environment—there are always other systems 'on the outside,' so to speak."[30] In fact, the first application of the systems approach to politics was:[31]

> *primarily concerned with portraying the relationships between a system and the environment in which it was located. . .[and]. . .directed attention to the boundary between politics and other aspects of social life and postulated the existence of a close relationship between system and environment.*

It is important to understand that this applies to subsystems as well, with the larger system being the environment for its subsystems. While it oversimplifies things, as most metaphors do, the best way to visualize this is to picture one of those Russian matryoshka, or babushka, "nesting" dolls. To capture the dynamics of a social system, however, one must picture one with moving parts on its multiple levels.

Sailing has been used as a metaphor for many, many things, including life itself. To this author, it is particularly useful for considering the capabilities of political systems, although I must confess to very limited experience with sailing, particularly compared to my decades of dealing with government and politics. That limited experience made me very fearful the few times when the ships I was a passenger on seemed about to keel over, but those experiences taught me that a "good ship" with an able crew running it can survive just about any storm or other circumstance that arises. That is the image of the U.S. Federal Republic my mind conjures up from everything I have learned.

Having been observing quite closely as it sailed through the turbulent waters of the second half of the twentieth century and the beginning of the twenty-first, I remain confident about our future. Sometimes due to the sheer turbulence it was facing, and other times due to crew error, there were occasions when it "tacked" so close to the water that I feared it would capsize. But the "good ship" United States of America survived, has provided a good life for me and millions of others, and should continue to do so for the foreseeable future. Some of you may see things differently at the end of our journey, but I hope the trip will at least tell you what repairs are needed. Let's begin.

---

[30] Isaak (see Note 4), 215.
[31] Wasby (see Note 8), 109; brackets added.

SECTION ONE
Our Political Culture

The term "political culture" was presented in the Introduction as one of the three basic components of a community's decision-making structure, and it was described as "a set of beliefs and values, more or less held in common by participating members. These define the kind of ideas that can seriously be considered during discussion and decision."[1] This is a concise expression of an idea that was traced back to the ancient Greek philosopher Plato by the noted social scientists who first made it an important operational concept in political science.[2]

They explained that a political culture includes "the system of empirical beliefs, expressive symbols, and values which define the situation in which political action takes place."[3] Their operational definition, which is still used today (especially in comparative political research), identified several dimensions of the concept:

- A sense of national identity
- Attitudes about all the members of a political community, including oneself
- Attitudes and expectations about governmental performance
- Attitudes about the political decision-making process

[1] Paul Deising, *Reason in Society: Five Types of Decisions and Their Social Conditions* (Urbana: University of Illinois Press, 1962 [rpt. Greenwood, 1973], pp. 170–172.
[2] Gabriel Almond, "The Intellectual History of the Civic Culture Concept," in Gabriel Almond and Sydney Verba, *The Civic Culture Revisited* (Boston: Little, Brown, 1980), 1.

[3] Sydney Verba, "Comparative Political Culture," in Lucien Pye and Sydney Verba, eds., *Political Culture and Political Development* (Princeton, NJ: Princeton University Press, 1965), 513.

A number of you are probably first-generation Americans, like this author. Our idea of "being American" is different from those of you whose family has lived here a long time and those of you who only recently immigrated here. Our political socialization (basically, how we learn about politics and government) produced these different "senses of national identity." We all learned our senses of national identity through our personal histories, and different histories produce different outcomes.

There are some core notions about "being American" that we all share, however, including some having to do with politics. The U.S. political culture is that *set of shared values regarding politics and government that predominates across our nation*. This also applies to other political communities, and these values underlie the beliefs and attitudes that motivate political behavior. Just as we learned our senses of national identity through our personal histories, the U.S. political culture was "learned" by the nation over the course of its history. Two historical examples illustrate this.

Should 18-year-olds have the right to vote? They were considered too young and immature when this author was that age. That was changed as a by-product of the Anti–Vietnam War Movement in the 1960s, which convinced most of the nation that if you are old enough to die for your country, then you are old enough to vote. This appeal to the widely shared American value of fairness changed the majority of people's attitudes about who should be allowed to vote.

The second example is the Watergate scandal. Watching it unfold on television and culminate in the only resignation of a president in U.S. history caused the majority of people's attitudes toward the national government to plummet, as measured by a variety of public opinion tracking polls. And it has never recovered, except briefly following the 2001 terrorist attack. Watergate was one of the important "steps" in the "dialectical dance" discussed near the end of the Introduction.

A community's political culture is important because it clearly shapes how we anticipate both average citizens and authoritative decision makers to behave, from those who only vote to those who fill the highest positions. What most community members expect, and will tolerate, from themselves and other members, especially public officials, have been labeled "political *roles*" by political scientists, who borrowed the term from Sociology. It also impacts political *rules*, the basic operational parameters for authoritative community decision making, both formal (legal or otherwise "official") and informal (adopted norms), by setting expectations and limitations for governments and other structures that make up the configuration of a political system.

We will begin by looking at what "democracy," "republic," and "federalism" mean, and how they apply to the U.S. political system. Chapter 1 concludes with a list of "ideal principles" that are the core values we share–a synopsis of our political culture. Next we take a condensed look at the U.S. Constitution of 1787, covering the basics of its development and ratification, a summary of its key elements, how we change it (both formally and informally) and the fundamental principles of governance it enshrined. Chapter 3 presents introductory overviews of civil liberties and civil rights in the United States, and Chapter 4 introduces the concepts of political socialization and political ideology, including a closer look at the concept of political culture and our initial look at the political functions and impacts of the mass media in the United States today.

CHAPTER 1

Our "Democratic Federal Republic"

BASIC TYPES OF GOVERNMENTS

In the Introduction it was noted that political scientists observe and collect information about political phenomena, then differentiate and categorize that information for further analysis. Social scientists usually call these categorizations typologies, sets of types, and debating and refining types and typologies are among their core activities.

Most phenomena do not fit exactly into basic types, because the characteristic(s) compared actually vary along a range in which categories are not obvious. How does one differentiate between "tall," "medium," and "short" people? One has to operationally define each term, and some people will still fall right at the chosen break points. So, one useful way to portray a typology is along a continuum.

We will begin our introductory journey through the U.S. political system by briefly comparing our government to others using a typology (see Figure 1-1) often applied in political science that differentiates them based on the degree of power exercised over people.

Numerous definitions of these five basic types of government have been offered over thousands of years. The following ones provide elementary contrasts and combine ideas from too many scholars to attempt to acknowledge:

Anarchy means no government, no formal social structure authorized to tell people what they can and cannot do and to enforce those rules. Some who advocate radical change to the current "world order" call themselves anarchists, but the essence of anarchism is the belief that all forms of governmental authority are unnecessary and undesirable.

Let's briefly consider that proposition. What would life be like with no government? With human nature what it is, it would likely get very risky very quickly. Even those of you

---

| No Power | .... | Total Power |

Anarchy---------Democracy-----------Republic-------Authoritarian--------Totalitarian

FIGURE 1-1: A Continuum of Government Power

who have paid little attention to politics until now have probably heard about the problems in Somalia, which has not had an effective national government in decades. Trouble like that tends to spread beyond the immediate area, moreover. It is not a coincidence that piracy has enjoyed a modern revival recently just off the coast of Somalia.

A more directly relevant analogy for most of you is driving. That is the most dangerous thing (with respect to risking serious injury or death) that most Americans regularly do. How much more dangerous would it be if there were no traffic controls (lights, signs, road markings, speed limits, etc.) and some means to enforce them? Even most people who really dislike government will grudgingly admit that it is a "necessary evil." The most complete short explanation of how government benefits everyone that this author has ever encountered is:[1]

> *Governments are the mechanisms that human groups employ to protect themselves from internal and external threats and to establish the policies that will provide the most favorable conditions for pursuing their lives.*

Let's return to the typology:

Democracies are governments which derive their authority from the people. The term originated in Greek by combining the words for "the people" (*demos*) and "authority" (*kratos*). Two basic subtypes are *direct* democracy, in which the people actually take part in authoritative decision making, and *indirect* democracy, in which communities choose some of their members to make decisions on public matters for them.

Republics are governments designed to serve the communities who created them. The term originated in Latin by combining the words for "thing" (*res*) and "people" (*publica*) to describe a government that would use its authority and power to "do the people's thing."

Authoritarian governments use their authority and power (at times including the overt or covert use of force) to maintain control of the political process, and usually only interfere in other aspects of people's lives if they find that control threatened by that activity.

Totalitarian governments use their authority and power (including the overt or covert use of force) to try to control all aspects of people's lives–even down to the way they think.

Where does the U.S. government fit on this continuum? The title of this book calls it a republic, and most readers have heard it called a democracy. This political scientist places it between the two, but closer to Republic than Democracy. The people do participate in authoritative decision making, and ultimately steer public policy in the direction they desire, but this is accomplished through a complex structure that is not entirely democratic. Other political scientists have different views, and those of you who pursue further studies in this area will find a wide array of positions and supporting arguments to consider. Our next step, however, is to describe this "democratic republic." We will leave historical details to the historians throughout our journey, while summarizing key developments and occasionally taking note of, or providing references for, details that illustrate or help to explain what was presented.

The United States of America was created when the original colonies declared and then won their independence from the British

---

[1] Max J. Skidmore and Marshall Carter Tripp, *American Government: A Brief Introduction.* 5th ed. (New York: St. Martin's Press, 1989), 1.

Empire for a variety of reasons that historians still debate. From the political perspective, the colonists wanted a system of government that would serve their needs and desires, not those of that Empire or its king. They wanted some form of republic, and that implied that political authority ultimately had to reside in the people. This was, literally, a revolutionary idea at that time, when monarchy or other forms of absolute rule prevailed in the world. Political scientists labeled that idea "popular sovereignty" because it shifted authority from an individual "sovereign" (often the leader of a family, clan, or army) to the people.

Seeds of democracy had been planted very early in U.S. history, moreover. Anyone who has studied that early history at all knows that the stark realities of separation by the Atlantic Ocean in that preindustrial era made control by the British government very difficult, if not impossible. Both direct (e.g., New England's "town meetings") and indirect (e.g., Virginia's House of Burgesses) democratic practices took root, but it needs to be remembered that participation in authoritative decision making was very limited at first, and remained that way for decade after decade after decade.

Our Founders were mostly members of the elite of that time, the landed gentry and successful merchants. There was little sympathy for "democracy," as evidenced by the undemocratic structures and processes they continued or created. In addition to the most obvious ones like slavery and extremely limited rights and roles for women, there were property requirements to both vote and hold office, and in many places religious tests as well. Many of the Founders feared that "democracy" would become mob rule, in part because most people at that time were not just uneducated, they were illiterate.

Of course, historical context must be taken into consideration. Just as Athens is still recognized for pioneering direct democracy in spite of the small percentage of its population that actually got to participate, our Founders should be credited with introducing a set of ground-breaking, even radical,[2] political ideas to the world.

"Democracy" is a concept that has been argued about by both political scientists and political philosophers for centuries. Two notable contrasting views of its essence in U.S. history are Jefferson's "government by consent of the governed" and Lincoln's "government of the people, by the people, and for the people." E. E. Schattschneider succinctly but thoroughly analyzed those two basic views as he sought an operational definition of democracy that could be applied to a modern nation-state, and argued:[3]

> *The classical definition of democracy as government by the people is predemocratic in its origins, based on notions about democracy developed by philosophers who never had an opportunity to see an operating democratic system....*

---

[2] See, for example, Gordon S. Wood, *The Radicalism of the American Revolution* (New York: Random House, 1991).
[3] E. E. Schattschneider, *The Semi-Sovereign People: A Realist's View of Democracy in America* (Hinesdale, IL: Dryden, 1975), 127 and 131. It was David Adamany's Introduction that pointed this author to the Jefferson/Lincoln contrast. Adamany summarizes Schattschneider's view thusly: "Hence, there is a need to redefine democracy, making it consistent with what the people are able and willing to do and to know in the complex modern world." Jefferson's model of "government by consent of the governed" is much more realistic in such a world than is the classical definition of "government by the people" (xvii). He cites Schattschneider's *Two Hundred Million Americans in Search of a Government* (New York: Holt, Rinehart and Winston, 1969), 5 (now out of print).

Is it possible to reformulate the question in terms of democratic concepts other than the primitive notions derived from the ancients?

Applying our specific approach to studying politics, the critical question becomes, "To what extent are the people involved in authoritative decision making?" His answer:[4]

The people are involved in public affairs by the conflict system. Conflicts open up questions for public intervention. Out of conflict the alternatives of public policy arise. Conflict is the occasion for political organization and leadership.

Recall that we defined the most basic political behavior as "who gets what, when, and how," then characterized that as "rivalry." That may have been a bit too polite, but Schattschneider's "conflict system" is a bit of an overstatement also. His reality-based assessment eventually leads him to conclude that "competition" is the key variable, and to base his resulting modern definition of democracy on it:[5]

Above everything, the people are powerless if the political enterprise is not competitive. It is the competition of political organizations that provides the people with the opportunity to make a choice. Without this opportunity popular sovereignty amounts to nothing....

Democracy is a competitive political system in which competing leaders and organizations define the alternatives of public policy in such a way that the public can participate in the decision-making process.

We will return to the issue of participation in Section Three, and take a closer look at the issue of competition at the conclusion of our journey. At this point, we will assume that the U.S. has sufficient levels of both to be classified as a "democratic republic," since the people very actively use political organizations and elect "leaders" and others to make our major authoritative decisions and appoint the officials who make the rest of them, while expecting those decisions to serve their needs and preferences. This brief analysis argues that the United States has always been a limited, indirect democracy, relying on our elites to lead us in the early days and on political organizations and elected leaders and representatives in modern times.

The question of whether or not the people's needs and preferences are being met takes us back to the very essence of politics–value judgments. Recall the "great dialectical dance" metaphor presented at the end of the Introduction regarding the issue of how strong our central government should be. The two opposing viewpoints have actually stretched to encompass the broader issue of "how much" government we want, creating the two basic ideological blocs that compete for the people's support today. In very simplified terms, those who tend to favor "more government" are "liberals," while those who tend to favor "less government" are "conservatives." These, along with a few other political "ideologies," will be discussed in more detail in Chapter 4.

As our journey unfolds, you will learn that the focus of this unending debate over what the government should be doing is primarily carried on to attract those who do not have a clear preference, but choose a side based on the circumstances they and their communities are facing. The debate's very existence as an ongoing competition among political leaders and organizations for the people's attention and support tells

---

[4] Schattschneider, *The Semi-Sovereign People* (see Note 3), 135.
[5] Schattschneider, *The Semi-Sovereign People* (see Note 3), 137 and 138.

us that we have what most political scientists would classify as a "democratic republic."

THE INVENTION OF FEDERALISM

At this point we need to examine the final basic characteristic of our core political structure, federalism, beginning with some brief history. Although they were "united" in their opposition to the British, very few of the Founders–and the general public of the day–considered themselves "Americans." Whatever political loyalty most people had at the time was directed toward their state.

It is often underappreciated, even overlooked by some, that it was the states that actually joined together–and only grudgingly–to create the United States. William Penn had proposed a union of the colonies as early as 1697, and Ben Franklin began promoting that idea during the 1750s, even providing a draft constitution for a colonial union to the Second Continental Congress–that was ignored. That draft eventually served as the basis for the first U.S. constitution, the 1781 "Articles of Confederation and Perpetual Union."[6] Our Founders first attempt to create a national government is often neglected because it did fail, but it was a critical building block of the United States as a nation.

While The Articles did not provide a formal structure capable of dealing with new national problems that emerged, they did provide the framework for the states to deal with many issues that the Revolution intensified. Their ratification, which took over three years, involved the resolution of many state boundary disputes and land claims, and the new Confederation

Congress did accomplish several noteworthy things. These included establishing a national postal system and national standards for weights and measures, and adopting The Northwest Ordinance. That innovative law established the mechanism for new states to join the United States and injected two rather radical ideas into the national political debate: the prohibition of slavery and support for public education.

Each of the 13 original states considered itself an independent political entity, and the colonial experience had ingrained in those first "Americans" a fear–even hatred–of strong, centralized government power that endures in the hearts of many today. For these reasons The Articles provided no national executive or judicial structures at all, and deliberately avoided giving the Confederation Congress the power to tax or regulate interstate trade. This absence of what are now recognized as vital capabilities for a central government led to economic and political problems that threatened to undermine the social order. The Shays Rebellion in Massachusetts is often cited as epitomizing that threat and precipitating the Annapolis Convention of 1786, which petitioned Congress to convene a Constitutional Convention the next year. That Convention produced what "is perhaps the most striking of all American inventions in government"[7]–federalism. We will outline how that happened in the next chapter on the U.S. Constitution.

BASIC FORMS OF GOVERNMENT

One of the reasons why social scientists use typologies is that it is often easier to define something by contrasting it with other similar

---

[6] Thomas Wendel, "The Articles of Confederation," *National Review*, 7/10/81, 768–770.

[7] S. E. Finer, *The History of Government From the Earliest Times*, Volume III (New York: Oxford, 1999), 1514.

phenomena. That is the case here. The simplest way to define "federalism" is to briefly visit the political science subfield of comparative government and borrow one of its basic typologies. It deals with what many political scientists call the "basic forms" of government, and distinguishes them based on how the exercise of power is channeled between or among whatever levels its formal structure has. Every government can be classified using the following three categories:

1. *Unitary*: All formal authoritative decision-making power resides in a central government. Where levels exist, subnational governments (states, provinces, etc.) will typically have only those powers granted to them by the central government.
2. *Confederation*: All formal authoritative decision-making power is retained by the subnational governments (states, provinces, etc.), and the central government typically has only those powers granted to it by the lower level(s).
3. *Federation*: Formal authoritative decision-making power is shared between or among the national and subnational levels of government, and each government has some distinct powers that the other government(s) cannot override.

The key distinction to remember about the basic forms of government is how the power is allocated. In *unitary* political systems, all formal power is *centralized* in one entity (e.g., Japan). In *confederations*, while there is some sort of unifying framework, power is *decentralized*, residing in the subnational governments (e.g., the United States under The Articles). In *federal* systems, power is *shared* among the various levels of government, with the specific structures and functions of each established by the system's

"constitution" or other recognized formal authorization method.

Recall that the basic *types* of government discussed above (democracy, republic, etc.) were portrayed on a continuum to illustrate that many "in between" versions exist. That is because most governments can change the degree of power they choose to exercise over their people relatively easily by changing public policies. While there is also significant variation within basic *forms* (e.g., in the degree of power centralization for federations[8]), these categories are more distinct and less flexible. Significant changes to formal structures usually require rather elaborate formal procedures, or involve rather radical changes in circumstances. In actual practice, power most likely shifts back and forth between or among levels due to changes in policies and behavior patterns in response to fluctuations in political circumstances as they occur. We will summarize the rather complex "evolution" of U.S. federalism in Chapter 5.

The distinction between a confederation and a federation is clearly illustrated by comparing the 1781 Articles and the Constitution of 1787 that created the U.S. Federal Republic. The earlier document included:

> *Article 2. Each State retains its sovereignty, freedom, and independence, and every power, jurisdiction, and right, which is not by this confederation expressly delegated to the United States, in Congress assembled.*

The simple idea of formally agreeing to share political power, the essence of federalism, was a completely new idea in the 1780s, which was still a time when empires and rulers competed to amass as much political power as they could.

---

[8] See, for example, Gregory S. Mahler, *Comparative Government*, 5th ed. (Upper Saddle River, NJ: Pearson, 2008), 30.

The structural sharing of power between the national and state governments was accomplished in the U.S. Constitution of 1787 by listing the lawmaking powers granted to the new national Congress. That is, through our Constitution the states delegated authority to the new national government to make certain decisions. Although this may seem to be what confederations do, other constitutional provisions (most importantly the Supremacy Clause) that will be discussed in the next chapter made it different.

Some of the most prominent leaders of our Revolution (e.g., Patrick Henry) feared that this mechanism of "enumerated powers" would not be sufficient to limit what the new national government could do (justifiably so, as our journey will reveal). At first those who wanted to preserve the power of the states became "Anti-Federalists" and fought the ratification of the Constitution. When that effort failed, they joined with those who demanded that explicit guarantees for individual liberties (a written "Bill of Rights") be added to the new Constitution, and succeeded in having "reserved powers" for the states included. The language used clearly contrasts with what was in The Articles:

> *Amendment 10. The powers not delegated to the United States by the Constitution, nor prohibited by it to the States, are reserved to the States respectively, or to the people.*

SOME ADVANTAGES AND DISADVANTAGES OF FEDERALISM

We will continue the discussion of how the Constitution shares power between our national and state governments in the next chapter, but at this point will consider what benefits and problems come with having a federal structure as the framework for a political system. Some *major advantages* that political scientists have identified are:[9]

- *Dividing government power helps protect liberty.* Having power allocated among different levels of government makes it more difficult for any individual or group to gain control over the entire authoritative decision-making structure. This is particularly beneficial in systems that value personal liberty.
- *Federalism maximizes the opportunities for meaningful participation.* With important decisions being made at different levels, more people can, and tend to, get involved. This is particularly beneficial in systems that value democracy.
- *Public programs can be tailored to local conditions.* For example, to reduce our dependence on oil, we need to encourage the use of alternative energy sources. Natural gas will be "the best" (considering availability, cost, safety, etc.) option for some states/regions, while wind power may work better for the coastal areas and solar power for the plains states. National incentives can be provided for projects developed by individual states or regional coalitions that promote all three.

---

[9] An excellent comprehensive but brief treatment of U.S. federalism in theory and operation is *American Federalism: A Concise Introduction* (Armonk, NY: M. E. Sharpe, 2007) by Larry N. Gerston. The most thorough theoretical work on federalism currently available is *The Robust Federation: Principles of Design* (New York: Cambridge University Press, 2009) by Jenna Bednar. The latest scholarly research on federalism is available through *Publius: The Journal of Federalism* at http://publius.oxfordjournals.org/content/current.

- *Subnational* (state and local in the United States) *governments serve as training grounds* for national politicians *and as "laboratories"* in which new public policies can be tested. Experience gained at lower levels of government is often an important factor in getting elected or appointed to national office, and in how well prepared individuals are for their responsibilities. Two examples of policy "experimentation" are national "welfare reform" in the 1990s and the recent "health care reform" effort. Many elements included in both were first tried in a number of states.

- *Federalism promotes diversity within political systems* by providing a mechanism through which different political subcultures can work together. This is a "value" variable that some people will disagree with, but from a systems perspective it is an advantage. The ability to effectively incorporate multiple different sources of information into a decision-making structure increases its capacity, which usually generates better (that is, more useful) results.

Political scientists have also identified some *major disadvantages*:

- *Federalism makes it difficult to pursue national policies.* The greatest failure of U.S. federalism was the persistence of segregation and legal discrimination by several states for over 100 years after the Civil War Amendments were ratified. It should be noted, however, that federalism was also the solution—eventually—when the national government stepped in using its full authority in response to the Civil Rights Movement of the mid-twentieth century.

- *Federalism can be "undemocratic"* with respect to *"majority rule"* at times. Some Americans remain upset about the 2000 presidential election (when George W. Bush won in the Electoral College although his opponent had won the popular vote), but this problem can, and does, manifest itself in other ways. A policy proposal overwhelmingly favored by the people of 24 states can be blocked by slim majorities in the other 26 getting their Senators to vote against it. Depending on the specific populations and numbers of supporters in the states comprising the opposing blocs, a small minority could prevail. Using data from the 2000 Census, one political scientist calculated that if that scenario involved the 26 smallest states versus the 24 largest, 18 percent of the population would be able to prevail over the other 82 percent.[10]

- *Overlapping authority can generate confusion or "spillover effects"*, which can lead to ineffective, inefficient public policies and programs. This author considers the botched response to Hurricane Katrina the greatest failure in the history of U.S. public administration. Another example of this problem that has widespread impact is how limited regulation of gun sales by some states leads to increases in violent crime in others across the nation.

- *Federalism can lead to harmful competition.* Two examples are competition for natural resources like water, notably in the Southwest, and to attract businesses and jobs by states and cities across the United States that generates economic disruption and avoidable environmental problems. It should be noted that some analysts of federalism view

---

[10] S. R. Shalom, *Which Side Are You On? An Introduction to Politics* (London: Longman, 2003), 171.

competition more as an advantage than a disadvantage.[11]

THE IDEAL PRINCIPLES OF OUR DEMOCRATIC FEDERAL REPUBLIC

At the very beginning of our discussion about politics it was stated that it was a very complex set of phenomena. Government is one of them, and is rather complex itself. The brief overview of basic types and basic forms above is intended for people taking their first "scientific" look at this subject, and presents extremely abbreviated versions of centuries of research and analysis. Even so, it has likely left some of you wondering whether you understand it. The primary purpose of the overview was to provide a rationale for why most political scientists classify the U.S. government as a "democratic federal republic" by providing basic explanations for each of those terms. These three important structural characteristics (recall how we defined government!) shape the authoritative decision-making process.

So why were they presented to introduce the "Political Culture" section? Each of them also has an important values aspect. It was stated above that the essence of federalism is the sharing of power, which reflects a value judgment. The process of sharing is evaluated as its most important feature. The overview also discussed how others favor one level of government more than the other. These are also value judgments.

The essence of being a republic is valuing the needs and preferences of the community as a whole, the general public, over those of any particular members of the community, especially the authoritative decision makers themselves. In the United States, the people's specific concern about this is reflected by how temporary the grants of authority we give public officials are. Very few of us actually enjoy election campaigns, but they are conducted frequently. We value popular sovereignty more than longer periods without being bombarded with political advertising and the other annoying aspects of campaigns.

That leaves democracy. Again, its definition has been argued about for centuries, so there is no agreed-upon list among political scientists of what values democracy must include. So, we will consider what values have become attached to that term over the course of U.S. political history. The following is this author's compilation, and draws from many sources encountered over several decades, but it was particularly inspired by the ideas presented in a more comprehensive work on American Government written by a team of excellent contemporary scholars:[12]

- *Personal Liberty* means that the political system should foster the greatest freedom for individuals which is consistent with the freedom of others. We place individual rights above the aspirations–even the needs–of the community. This inevitably leads to conflicts when historical norms are challenged and when collective opinion clashes with individual desires. Some observers see the United

---

[11] See, for example, Thomas R. Dye, *American Federalism: Competition among Governments* (Lexington, MA: D. C. Heath, 1990) and a range of scholarly papers by The American Enterprise Institute at http://www.aei.org.

[12] Chapter 1 of *American Government and Politics Today*, 13th ed. (Mason, OH: Thomson Wadsworth, 2008) by Steffen W. Schmidt, Mark C. Shelley, and Barbara Bardes.

States as too individualistic, but this is clearly one of the cornerstone values we share.

- *Equality* is another one of those ideas that has been argued about for centuries, and is the most complex value on this list. While in reality it is unachievable in its fullest sense, we owe it to the world to keep pursuing it as an ideal principle since we were the political community that first declared it a "self-evident truth." With respect to how people are treated, the best we can hope to attain is maximizing equal opportunity and minimizing discrimination through public policy. We can also use government as the role model of evenhanded treatment for all.

- *Popular Sovereignty* means that ultimate political authority rests with the people. As noted above, modern realities make us more dependent on indirect means of exercising that authority, which will be discussed toward the end of our journey. It will be fascinating to see how the explosion of communications technology will impact the expression of the popular will as the twenty-first century unfolds.

- *Majority Rule* means that authoritative decisions should reflect what most community members want at any given time, but with controls incorporated into the decision-making process to prevent what James Madison labeled the "tyranny of the majority" (see below). This is a much more complex matter than it seems, particularly in multilayered systems like our Federal Republic.[13] We apply this value in different

ways for different types of authoritative decisions, at times requiring "supermajorities" for those we consider more far-reaching.

- *Minority Rights* are an outgrowth of personal liberty and striving for equality, and they counterbalance majority rule. They are important for those reasons and because history tells us most major innovations that are eventually adopted are initiated by a few brave souls who challenge majority thinking. Most of you have likely experienced the "tyranny of the majority" at some point. It was, hopefully, regarding some minor and temporary aspect of your life. Imagine what it would be like living in a political system that did not make any effort to control it.

- *Universal Voting Rights* has been the ideal in democratic theory for a long time, and the United States is now very close to achieving this. Except for full access to voting for persons with disabilities and the issue of whether rehabilitated felons should be able to regain their voting rights (some states now allow this), in formal terms we have. Informal practices aimed at preventing fraud that some claim amount to targeted suppression of voting will likely come under closer scrutiny in the future.

- *Free, Competitive Elections* are clearly vital for a functioning indirect democracy. For the most part we have achieved this with respect to basic formal operating rules and procedures. The issue that this author and many others now fear threatens our democracy is how money seems to have become the critical ingredient needed for both access to the ballot and electoral success.

- *Property Rights* are directly recognized in the Bill of Rights and clearly respected by a vast majority of Americans with respect to

---

[13] The most comprehensive analysis in both actual and theoretical terms of majority rule that this author has ever encountered is in Robert A. Dahl's *A Preface to Democratic Theory* (Chicago: University of Chicago Press, 1956).

private ownership. One of the most interesting political changes in this author's lifetime has been a growing recognition of "common property" rights. This term is derived from a classic essay entitled "The Tragedy of the Commons" by Garrett Hardin.[14] It warned about the eventual loss or destruction of public assets from deterioration caused by overuse by private parties. Recognition of the public's right to clean air and water are very basic examples of "common property" rights. Today, most people do not realize how limited environmental regulation was before the 1970s.

- *Free Enterprise* is an outgrowth of both personal liberty and property rights. Most Americans respect the rights of individuals and business organizations to engage in economic activity that does not harm others. Prevention of harm to others implies that there must be a functioning legal framework to monitor and enforce contracts, along with reasonable regulation of economic activity that clearly has the potential for direct or indirect injury or damage.

We will close this discussion with some points to keep in mind about these values. While the list does represent direct (by the author) and indirect (by others) empirical political science "observations," this discussion has a strong philosophical aspect to it. As the heading states, these are *ideal* principles, representing what most Americans think *should be*, not necessarily what exists. We strive to achieve all of them, but it is doubtful that the United States (or any) political system can ever fully realize them.

Why? First, because some of them compete against each other, and achieving one in absolute terms would diminish, if not defeat, the other. Many valid public opinion surveys have documented a willingness by a majority of Americans to curtail personal liberties in exchange for greater security. Public policy based solely on majority rule can easily result in the "tyranny" that Madison feared—and it has, at times, in our history. Second, while most of us share these values, some of us do not, and some even actively work against them, which is their right! In some cases they apply a different view of the world, and in others they think circumstances require that other priorities prevail. For this political scientist, the essence of democratic politics is people agreeing to disagree while still working together to deal with public issues. Last, the complexity of public issues precludes pure and simple results, which the achievement of ideals would be. Yes, complexity permeates politics—especially democratic politics.

So, given all these constraints, how have we come as far as we have? How did thirteen bickering independent states become the most powerful and prosperous nation that has ever existed? It all began when they chose to truly unite, and then created the first democratic federal republic with an excellent design that enabled it to work. That is the next stop on our journey, the U.S. Constitution.

---

[14] *Science*, 12/13/68.

CHAPTER 2

The U.S. Constitution

A BIT MORE BACKGROUND

One of the ingredients of the development of our Federal Republic mentioned in Chapter 1 was that some "democratic" institutions were established from the very early days of the American Colonies. This was not intentional on the part of the British, but occurred due to the realities of geography in that preindustrial age. Since it was basically impossible for the imperial government in London to direct the public affairs of the colonists, self-government sprouted in a variety of forms. These experiences accumulated into an expectation among many of the colonists that they would be able to continue being active participants, at the very least, in the authoritative decision-making processes for their communities.

When the British attempted to assert greater control using imperial authority as their primary justification, they met resistance. The British response to that resistance was a combination of commercial controls and military occupation. As history tells us, things spun out of control leading to armed revolt against the perceived repression by George III, leading to the colonies' joint Declaration of Independence. These highlights of our Colonial experience are noted because they left two important legacies. The first was that deep desire for self-government. The second was an attitude of extreme opposition–even hatred–toward strong central authority. These feelings set the stage for the first attempt to create the United States of America.

The Articles of Confederation probably deserve more respect than they are generally accorded, but the reality is that they did fail to provide an authoritative decision-making structure capable of dealing with the problems the new nation faced. The "league of friendship" (Article 3) that they created had no executive structure to implement policy and no judicial structure. States could petition the Congress of the Confederation to adjudicate disputes between them, but its powers were severely limited. Among the major weaknesses the new "national government" had were:

- No power to compel the states to pay their share of any operating costs, or to provide men for military service, leading to the disbanding of the army

- No power to tax citizens or businesses; it had to sell land for revenue
- No power to regulate state currencies, which led to economic chaos
- No power to regulate interstate commerce, leading to interstate "trade wars"

Proposals to strengthen the Confederation went nowhere because they required a unanimous vote in Congress and confirmation by every state legislature. Government powers at the state level were also diminished in various ways due to the anti-executive power climate, and armed rebellions sprang up. The social order was threatened. The Shays Rebellion in Massachusetts in the summer of 1786 is often cited as epitomizing that threat and precipitating the Annapolis Convention in September, which petitioned Congress to convene a general convention to address the problem. Congress approved the convention in February 1787, "for the sole and express purpose of revising the Articles of Confederation."

THE BASIC PROCESS

When that convention opened in Philadelphia, it was immediately faced with the reality that negotiating changes to the Articles was impossible because Rhode Island had refused to send a delegation. Recall that amendments required confirmation by every state legislature. In addition, the Virginia delegation arrived early and began promoting the need for a genuine, strong national government, including drafting a complete set of resolutions to be considered, primarily authored by James Madison.

That "Virginia Plan" favored the large states by proposing a bicameral (two-chamber)

Congress with votes in both allocated based on population or contributions. This new Congress would elect a national executive, appoint judges, and have broad legislative power, including the authority to void any state laws considered detrimental to the national interest. The representatives would have been chosen by a combination of direct and indirect elections. One chamber would have been elected by the people of each state, with the smaller "upper" chamber members chosen by the directly elected chamber based on nominations made by the state legislatures.

Delegates from the smaller states, led by William Paterson of New Jersey, put together a counter proposal that would retain "one state, one vote" in a single-chamber Congress with only limited, but critical, additional powers. That "New Jersey Plan" would have authorized Congress to impose taxes and regulate trade, elect several executive officials, and appoint a Supreme Court with narrow jurisdiction. It promoted the basic retention of maximum state sovereignty, but did introduce the idea of the "supremacy" of national laws and treaties over state laws.

THE BASIC ISSUES

The differences in the two plans proposed and debated at what became known as the Constitutional Convention point us to most of the basic issues that had to be worked out if a "new and improved" United States of America was going to happen. Recalling our discussion of "What is politics?" in the Introduction, we can see elements from all three levels of social science analysis involved. Who would wind up with what? The exercise of power was clearly involved, and would be reflected in how authority to make what decisions was allocated. In the end, would the common interests of the nation–of all states and the American people– be valued more than those of different regions or individual states? A matter not mentioned in either the Virginia or New Jersey Plans that became entangled with several that were– slavery–was unmistakably value laden. Finally, how and when would these issues get resolved?

In summary terms, the basic issues were:

1. The basic power relationship between a re-designed central government and the state governments
2. The basis for representation in the national legislature, which quickly became a power contest between the large and small states
3. The power to tax, including any restrictions on that power
4. The regulation of interstate commerce, in-cluding the value of currencies
5. The continuation of slavery, including their "representation" and importation
6. The form, powers, and selection method for a national government executive
7. The form, powers, and selection method for a national government judiciary

Several of these issues in addition to slavery were intertwined, of course. For example, there was clear consensus that Congress would be the center of power, so changing how it was selected and operated would impact the power relation-ship between the two levels of government:[1]

"One state, one vote" was not simply an equalizer for tiny Delaware and imposing

New York; it was a confirmation that the basic political unit remained the state even if the political forum changed. The Virginia Plan weakened this political premise. It cre-ated a forum in which state identity was so transfigured that a state's interests were no longer expressed in one voice but in many. The implications of this were not yet clear. But to many delegates they were worrisome indeed.

All of the basic issues were the subjects of detailed, serious debates over 115 days. Roger Sherman's "Great Compromise" or "Connect-icut Plan" on congressional representation is usually credited as the breakthrough that en-abled the Convention to succeed. While that is an oversimplification, "The Great Com-promise" was undoubtedly a critical point in U.S. history. Agreeing to have the House of Representatives elected based on population and equal representation in the Senate epito-mizes the pragmatic strategy that the Found-ers used to complete their task. This also set the precedent for how authoritative decision making needs to be done in a political com-munity marked by diversities of power and perspective.

The authors of the Constitution wanted to combine a central government strong enough to maintain order with strong state govern-ments. This was achieved through a series of compromises within the basic framework put forth by James Madison. This *"Madisonian Model of Government"* can be summarized as follows:[2]

---

[1] Carol Berkin, *A Brilliant Solution: Inventing the Con-stitution* (New York: Harcourt, 2002), 75. This is an excellent and very readable concise history of the Con-stitutional Convention for students.

[2] It should be noted that historians and political scien-tists include and/or emphasize different components. Many of Madison's writings discuss these ideas; the key sources usually cited are *Federalist Papers #51* and *#10*.

Separation of Powers: Independent legislative, executive, and judicial branches

+

Checks and Balances created by this independence and strengthened with specified counterbalancing controls (e.g., bicameralism, executive veto, judicial review)

+

Federalism: Sharing of power between the levels of government (central and state)

=

A government designed to control its people–and itself!

Each of these components will be covered in some detail in Section Two. Some additional points about federalism should be made here, however. In our discussion of basic forms of government, the topic of "enumerated powers" was introduced. The method proposed by Madison for limiting the new national government's power was to specify them in its authorizing charter. That sounds like a confederation, as defined in Chapter 1, since the central government would have "only those powers granted to it" by the states. How would this new arrangement be different?

Three other aspects of the new Constitution made it something new:

1. *The necessary and proper clause*: In addition to the seventeen specific powers listed in Article 1, Section 8, Congress was authorized:

   > *To make all laws which shall be necessary and proper for carrying into execution the foregoing powers, and all other powers vested by this Constitution in the government of the United States, or in any department or officer thereof.*

2. *Changes in how certain key decisions would be made*: The requirement for the unanimous consent of the states for ratification and for amendments was abandoned. Our discussion of U.S. democratic values mentioned that majority rule is applied in different ways for different types of authoritative decisions. The term "supermajority" is often used to describe the specific instances in which either two-thirds or three-fourths majorities are required. Both were included in the amendment process for the Constitution (discussed below), and Congress was authorized to override any presidential veto by a two-thirds majority vote.

3. *The "Supremacy Clause"*:

   > *Article 6. This Constitution, and the Laws of the United States which shall be made in Pursuance thereof; and all Treaties made, or which shall be made, under the Authority of the United States, shall be the supreme Law of the Land; and the Judges in every State shall be bound thereby, any Thing in the Constitution or Laws of any State to the Contrary notwithstanding.*

For this political scientist, it was the inclusion of the Supremacy Clause in the Constitution that created the U.S. Federal Republic. Recall that this idea was originally part of the New Jersey Plan. Madison's proposal to give the new national legislature the authority to override state laws was quickly rejected. Acceptance of the small states' proposal regarding the power of the central government was part of the bargaining process among the delegates. It appears that it was William Paterson who first clearly stated during the Convention that both Plans would have given the central government authority over individual citizens, moreover. Acceptance of this sharing of sovereignty by two levels of government by the delegates was the birth of modern federalism.[3]

This substantial change in authoritative decision making, particularly when paired with the Supremacy Clause, was highly significant. Some states and their citizens would, at some future time, have to live under national laws that they objected to, and may even have formally rejected. Add the "necessary and proper clause," and you clearly have a rebalanced decision-making structure. Those who wanted to preserve maximum power for the states did not give up after this reshaping of what federalism meant by the Constitution. As noted earlier, an "Anti-Federalist" movement took shape.

The ratification process will be summarized shortly, but one very specific future incident is worth noting here. Recall the contrast between the second of The Articles of Confederation and the Tenth Amendment presented in Chapter 1. During the debates in the first session of the House of Representatives that led to the Bill of Rights:[4]

> *[Thomas] Tucker [of South Carolina] wanted to place the word "expressly" in what would become the Tenth Amendment to confirm that the Federal government was one of limited powers.... The Tucker amendment would have greatly diminished congressional authority under the "necessary and proper" clause, which had granted Congress substantial discretion to carry out their responsibilities assigned by the Constitution.*

That this addition was defeated by an almost two-to-one margin by the full House tells us that there was rather broad support for this new form of "compound republic" among U.S. political leaders of that time. Tucker and his supporters would likely take comfort from the fact that the "necessary and proper" clause would become the subject of debate over its application that continues to this day, as we shall see in Section Two. Many, many scholarly efforts have analyzed the work of the Constitutional Convention in addition to the few footnoted in this chapter. The document itself should be the first thing read by anyone interested in the details about how the basic issues were resolved. Table 2-1 provides a useful summary for newcomers to the topic.

THE RATIFICATION "BATTLE"

Madison's proposal to use special conventions in each state as the ratification mechanism for the proposed Constitution was adopted, and unleashed a whirlwind of political activity.

[3] S. E. Finer, *The History of Government from the Earliest Times*, Volume III (New York: Oxford, 1999), 1514-1516. Do note that the term "federal" was used throughout the debates to describe what we call confederation.

[4] Richard Labunski, *James Madison and the Struggle for the Bill of Rights* (New York: Oxford Press, 2006), 230.

Power relationship between National and State levels of government	Federalism w/Supremacy Clause + "The Great Compromise" + other Checks and Balances
Representation and State Power: Large vs. Small	"The Great Compromise" + "The 3/5ths Compromise"
Power to Tax	Congress authorized to "lay and collect taxes, duties, imposts and excises," but no "direct tax" on individuals and no duties on exports or vessels traveling to interstate ports
Regulation of Commerce and Currencies	Congress authorized to regulate foreign and interstate commerce + coin and regulate the value of money
Slavery	Importing of slaves could not be banned until 1808, but $10 tax authorized; escaped slaves cannot be freed and must be returned if claimed; slaves counted as 3/5ths of a person in each national census
Form, Powers, and Selection of a National Executive	Individual President with full powers, elected through the Electoral College
Form, Creation, and Powers of a National Judiciary	Supreme Court with national and interstate jurisdiction + inferior courts if authorized by Congress

TABLE 2-1: Summary of Basic Issues and How They Were Resolved by the Constitutional Convention of 1787

In what one noted Constitutional scholar calls "an extraordinary act of democracy," each state held elections for delegates to a convention called for the sole purpose of debating and voting on whether that state would accept it. "In a yearlong process, up and down the continent, for the first time in history, people were invited to vote."[5] The new decision-making rule of a three-fourths supermajority (9 of 13 states) was used for the ratification process, moreover. A new political reality was taking shape.

That "battle" over the Constitution conceived our first two national political "factions" and spawned the ideological divide that remains at the root of our two-plus party system to this day. The supporters of ratification were labeled "Federalists," since they advocated for the new power sharing structure; the opponents became known as "Anti-Federalists." Although some violence took place, for the most part this process was a war of words and political maneuvers. The most remembered publications today are *The Federalist Papers*, a series of newspaper columns written to persuade the public to accept the proposed new government. While the Anti-Federalists did respond, they were not as successful in swaying public opinion.

The most debated issue will sound familiar–the fear of centralized power–but an issue that

---

[5] Akhil R. Amar, being quoted from a lecture delivered at St. Elizabeth's College, Convent Station, NJ, in "A revolutionary act of democracy" by Fran Wood, *The Star-Ledger*, 9/17/08, 15. This author heard Dr. Amar use similar language to describe the ratification process at the National Constitution Center in Philadelphia, PA, in July 2007, and he elaborates this idea in *America's Constitution: A Biography* (New York: Random House, 2005).

had concerned a number of the delegates, yet had been sidestepped by the Convention, reemerged– explicit protection for individual rights. Several of the states had such provisions in their constitutions, but attempts to add a "bill of rights" was unanimously rejected by all 12 state delegations as the Convention concluded:[6]

> *Fatigue was certainly a factor. The delegates had been hard at work for four months creating the Constitution. They were eager to go home to tend to personal and business matters and to report the results of their work. Some were concerned that instead of a few hours being required to prepare a list of rights, as [George] Mason had predicted, It could take days or weeks and could lead to the unraveling of precarious compromises reached in other sections of the document.... But the primary objection to adding a bill of rights to the original constitution was that the government to be formed under it would be one of limited powers.*

The Anti-Federalists took up this cause, hoping it would be the issue that would block ratification of the Constitution. While it did not, the problem "would soon become its most conspicuous flaw, and one that supporters would be unable to successfully defend."[7] The argument that the innovative arrangement of specified powers with "checks and balances" provided sufficient protection for individual liberties would fail. We will return to the Bill of Rights in the next chapter, but it is appropriate to take note here of the debt that all Americans owe to the Anti-Federalists for its existence.[8]

---

[6] Labunski (see Note 4), 9.
[7] Ibid.
[8] David J. Siemers, *The Anti–Federalists: Men of Great Faith and Forbearance* (New York: Alfred A. Knopf, 2001).

Elections for the special conventions began, yielding two waves of ratifications during the winter of 1787–1788 and the spring of 1788. The five earliest conventions showed strong support for the Constitution, but half of the spring conventions were battlegrounds. It won approval in Massachusetts and New Hampshire with 52.7 percent and 54.8 percent of delegate votes, respectively. Technically, the Constitution had been ratified, and this was recognized by the Congress of the Confederation in early July of 1788.

Virginia and New York were crucial, however. Together they were home to 40 percent of the U.S. population at the time, New York was the commercial center of the nation, and Virginia was recognized as the political leader among the states. Virginia's approval in late June, which came only after the Federalists at that convention agreed to pursue a bill of rights, helped secure New York's the following month; in both states the margin of success was under 53 percent. North Carolina declined to ratify until the autumn of 1789, after amendments on the protection of individual rights were being considered in the first session of the House of Representatives, and Rhode Island finally joined the new Republic in the spring of 1790– only after the new Congress had cut off trade with it!

KEY ELEMENTS

The U.S. Constitution of 1787 is a carefully crafted document representing intellectual innovation, political compromise, and moral contradiction. How do you reconcile the Declaration of Independence with its continuation of slavery? Most political scientists accept that without "The 3/5ths Compromise" the Constitution would not have been completed and

Article 1	*Legislative Branch*: The structure, election, powers, and limitations of *Congress*; qualifications; the legislative process; and "Denied" powers
Article 2	*Executive Branch*: The qualifications, election, term, powers, duties and oath of an individual *President & Vice-President*; impeachment criteria
Article 3	*Judicial Branch*: Establishment and jurisdiction of one *Supreme Court*; authorization of others by Congress; trial by jury; definition of treason
Article 4	*Interstate Relations*; admission of new states; fugitive slaves; public lands
Article 5	*Formal Amendment process*
Article 6	*Supremacy Clause*; oath with no religious test for office; debts recognized
Article 7	*Ratification process* - by elected special conventions of nine States

TABLE 2-2: Key Elements of the Constitution of 1787

ratified; others do not. That is a question historians still debate.[9] Again, any of you who have not read the complete document should do so, particularly those who envision themselves continuing to study American government. Table 2-2 summarizes the key elements in each article, providing a concise overview of what the Constitution says.

CHANGING THE CONSTITUTION

The greatest strength of the U.S. political system is its capability for self-correction. One thing that gives it that capability is its openness to adaptation, which includes the flexibility built into the Constitution by the Founders. They recognized that they could not possibly foresee all the circumstances that future Americans would face. Although it "is the most legalistic constitution in the entire world,"[10] it is also rather vague in key areas, as its critics argued and we shall see as we proceed on our journey. The most obvious

evidence that the Founders understood changes would be needed was that they included a *formal amendment process*. This involves two basic steps:

- *Proposal* by 2/3rds vote in each chamber of Congress (House and Senate) *or* by a national convention called by Congress in response to requests from 2/3 of the states, which has never been used. Recently, time limits for ratification of amendments have usually been included in proposed ones by Congress.
- *Ratification* by 3/4ths of state legislatures *or* special conventions (specified in the amendment); state conventions have been used only once (Twenty-first Amendment)

While over 11,000 proposed amendments have been formally considered by Congress, only 33 have been submitted to the states after being approved, and only 27 have been ratified since 1789. Since the first ten were all adopted in 1791 (the Bill of Rights), formally changing the Constitution has been a rare event. This small number of constitutional amendments would seem to counter any claim of flexibility, but the reality is that it has been changed many times–informally. This occurs through the basic act of governing.

[9] See, for example, Paul Finkelman, *Slavery and the Founders: Race and Liberty in the Age of Jefferson*, 2e, (Armonk, NY: M.E. Sharpe, 2001).
[10] S. E. Finer (see Note 3), 1516.

When key authoritative decision makers carrying out their constitutional functions establish precedents that are not challenged, or survive any political or legal challenges, they are, in effect, changing the Constitution by elaborating its provisions.

Although this is another point of contention among constitutional scholars, most political scientists accept the position "that the founders intended it to be only a framework for the new government, to be interpreted by succeeding generations."[11] Precedent plays an important role in the U.S. legal system, and therefore in its politics. One historian has even argued that endorsement of unprecedented policies by the people in decisive elections has twice created new eras in U.S. constitutional history.[12]

The basic *informal methods of changing the Constitution* are:

1. *Judicial Review*: Using their power to ensure that legislative, executive, and state and local government actions are constitutional, the federal courts, particularly the Supreme Court, establish how the Constitution applies and what it means in specific circumstances, establishing precedents that must then be followed. A clear example of this was the establishment of a "right to privacy" for Americans, which will be discussed in the next chapter.

2. *Congressional Legislation*: Every time Congress passes a law that gives the president new responsibilities, they are in essence embellishing the Constitution. For example, the Employment Act of 1946 added responsibility "to maintain employment, production, and purchasing power" to the president's duties.

3. *Presidential Action*: When presidents take executive action that breaks new ground in public policy, they can change the course of constitutional law. The controversy over "affirmative action," initiated with Executive Orders 10925 and 11246 issued by presidents Kennedy and Lyndon Johnson, is a prime example.

4. *Usage and Custom*: The Constitution says nothing about political parties (in fact, the Founders feared them), but they evolved from the factions competing to control the direction the new central government would take, and became very central elements of our political process. What works tends to be repeated, and repetition often generates custom, a soft, but very effective, source of authority.

Even informal actions such as personal decisions can have significant impact. One example was Washington's rejection of a third presidential term. That precedent became a custom which was followed (with reinforcement by the political parties) for over 140 years. When Franklin D. Roosevelt broke that custom, strong negative reaction generated a movement that eventually led to formalization of the two-term limit for presidents in the Twenty-second Amendment. So, we see how informal and formal political activity can intersect at times. That is true adaptability.

---

[11] Steffen W. Schmidt, Mark C. Shelley, and Barbara Bardes, *American Government and Politics Today*, 13th ed., (Mason, OH: Thomson Wadsworth, 2008), 48. This discussion draws from their section, "Informal Methods of Constitutional Change," 51-55. A noteworthy scholarly treatment of this topic is Howard Gillman's "The Collapse of Constitutional Originalism and the Rise of the Notion of the 'Living Constitution' in the Course of American State-Building," *Studies in American Political Development*, 11 (Fall 1997), 191-247.

[12] Bruce Ackerman, *We The People: Foundations* (Cambridge, MA: Harvard University Press, 1991), 40-57, referring to Congressional Reconstruction policy (1866) and Franklin D. Roosevelt's New Deal (1936).

FUNDAMENTAL PRINCIPLES

We end our overview of the U.S. Constitution with a list of fundamental principles dealing with both structural and value aspects of governance that it embodies:

- *Limited Government*: This fundamental law grants, allocates, and restrains the power to make authoritative decisions for our community, reflecting our values.

- *Representative Government*: The people choose representatives to make authoritative decisions for them with ongoing direct and indirect input from them.

- *Separation of Powers*: Independent branches create competing roles and rules.

- *Federalism*: Shared power among levels attaches added layers of competition.

- *Checks and Balances*: Competing roles and rules produce counterbalanced power.

CHAPTER 3

Civil Liberties and Civil Rights

The next stop on our journey will be an overview of two topics that are clearly related to our community values—Civil Liberties and Civil Rights. Americans take great pride in the fact that our nation has always been associated with freedom and equality. The discussion of equality as one of the shared values attached to U.S. democracy noted that we were the nation that declared it to be a "self-evident" truth. It was the first great debate of our political history as the United States of America, that "extraordinary act of democracy" leading to ratification of the Constitution that revealed the people's insistence that written guarantees protecting individual liberty be added as one of the first orders of business of the first U.S. Congress. Those are the roots of these two very important aspects of the U.S. political culture. We begin by resuming our discussion of the Bill of Rights.

THE BILL OF RIGHTS

Recall that it was the legacy of fear of government power that almost derailed the bold political experiment that creating the United States of America was. The Articles of Confederation had

been written to reflect that fear as its paramount value, creating a national government that was simply too weak to deal with the realities of a diverse, competitive political community. In the summary of the struggle to correct that, we discussed how the Constitutional Convention ended with the delegates sidestepping the issue of a bill of rights due to fatigue and concern that reopening debate could cause the bargains that had been carefully crafted to unravel.

But the issue of written guarantees of personal liberty would simply not go away. It became the dominant issue in the debate over ratification, and even those who had argued most vehemently that the intricately crafted Constitution would neither repeal existing guarantees in state constitutions, nor create a central government that would threaten personal liberties were forced to change sides. Many Federalists, most notably James Madison, were forced to accept the need for adding written limitations on the new central government to the document.

Madison became so convinced that addressing this issue was critical to the success of the new republic that he made it his personal quest to have amendments protecting liberty approved by the first session of the new Congress. Having finessed Patrick Henry's maneuvers to prevent his election to it, he announced to the House of Representatives within weeks of its opening session that he would be introducing amendments, and secured the support of President Washington. He had to fend off a competing drive to call a second constitutional convention for that purpose, and was frustrated by several postponements deemed necessary to take care of the basic tasks required for setting up a new government, but Madison persevered.[1]

As soon as possible, he introduced a set of 19 amendments which he had distilled from 75 distinctive ideas contained in over 200 proposals submitted by five different states. Interestingly, about half the states had no bills of rights, and among those that did, "none had a comprehensive list of guarantees."[2] Madison devised his amendments to provide an all-inclusive set of rights, but also to command broad support and minimize opposition. After debating an assortment of procedural matters, the House voted to refer the proposed amendments to a select committee.

That committee replaced some of Madison's words with phrases that would echo through our history ("freedom of speech, and of the press"), composed most of what would become the Ninth Amendment, made other significant changes, and accepted Madison's recommendation that the states be prohibited from infringing on certain rights along with the national government.[3] His original proposal had appeared in newspapers after Madison had introduced it, and had been circulated by letter,

leading to "lively debate…among his colleagues, their friends, and constituents."[4] About 100 days after he had announced that he would be introducing amendments, the House began "an extraordinary debate" over them.[5] The issue that had been raised at the Constitutional Convention and carried forward to the state ratifying conventions had finally reached the actual authoritative decision-making stage.

Madison's original proposal had been formulated so that the amendments would be incorporated into the body of the Constitution, not added at the end. This issue was more than procedural, since altering the original language could have complicated the process of gaining two-thirds approval in both chambers of Congress to the point of jeopardizing its success. Just debating this specific point took up significant time. Roger Sherman, further demonstrating that he is one of the more underappreciated Founders, "convinced the House, with Madison's grudging acceptance, to place the amendments at the end of the Constitution,"[6] creating the Bill of Rights we all know and revere.

Twelve amendments were eventually approved by both the House and Senate and sent to the states for ratification. The original first amendment that would have enlarged the House to better represent a diverse, dispersed population failed, and the original second amendment has a unique history that led to its becoming the twenty-seventh in 1992. "In what has to be the most understated announcement in the nation's history, Secretary of State Thomas Jefferson informed governors of all the states on March 1,

---

[1] Richard Labunski, *James Madison and the Struggle for The Bill of Rights* (New York: Oxford Press, 2006).
[2] Labunski, 199; six had one, but North Carolina and Rhode Island had not yet joined the new United States.
[3] Labunski, 217.

[4] Labunski, 207.
[5] Labunski, 217. The House was convened as a committee of the whole, so the public was not admitted and full parliamentary procedure was not required.
[6] Labunski, 206.

1792, that [ten of] the amendments had been approved." They were the third matter listed, following notification of a new fishing law and the establishment of the post office.[7] What a humble entrance onto the American political stage for a document that was to become one of the pillars of the U.S. political culture.

DEFINITION AND NATURE OF CIVIL LIBERTIES

What do we mean by Civil Liberties? In our discussion of the shared values attached to U.S. democracy, we defined personal liberty as the greatest freedom for individuals which is consistent with the freedom of others. *Civil Liberties are a range of personal freedoms that are created by restraining the power of government with respect to certain personal and group activities.* It must be emphasized that our Civil Liberties are *not* unlimited. To paraphrase one of the most quoted basic descriptions of those limits, the freedom to swing one's fist stops at somebody else's nose.

This chapter started with a summary of the development of the Bill of Rights because they are the legal source of civil liberties in the U.S. political system. Recall that they were added to the Constitution as written guarantees of individual liberties, and that protection is provided by specific restraints placed on what the new national government could do. That summary mentioned that Madison's original proposal included recommendations that the states, and not just the national government, be prohibited from infringing on certain rights. That idea was rejected by most political leaders of that time, who gave state sovereignty priority.

An important feature of Civil Liberties in the United States is the role that the courts have played in their evolution. One of the first examples of this dealt with the question of the Bill of Rights applying to the states. In *Barron v. Baltimore* (1833), the Supreme Court clearly established the legal position that they did not—under the original Constitution. That decision was based on both the history of that idea being rejected by the first Congress and on the language used in the amendments. At that time the Court was under the leadership of Chief Justice John Marshall, moreover, who, you will learn, was not shy about asserting national government power.

It was not until the Fourteenth Amendment was adopted, and particularly its "due process" and "equal protection of the laws" provisions, that the courts found the legal basis for applying the limits of the Bill of Rights to the states and, incidentally, all of the local governments under their jurisdiction. This process of applying the Bill's restraints to the lower levels of our Federal Republic is known as the doctrine of "incorporation," and was the basis for a series of Supreme Court decisions dealing with most of the protections. Constitutional scholars debate exactly when the "incorporation" doctrine was first proposed, but its first application is usually cited as *Gitlow v. New York* (1925), which one called "a truly remarkable judicial about face."[8] It is now a well-established legal precedent, and the latest example of its use was *District of Columbia v. Heller* (2008)[9] setting the stage for *McDonald v. Chicago* (2009),[10] which applied the Second Amendment to all

---

[7] Labunski, 255, with brackets added.

[8] Robert E. Cushman, *Leading Constitutional Decisions*, 7th ed. (New York: F. S. Crofts, 1941), 86.
[9] 554 U.S. 570.
[10] 561 U.S. 3025 (2010).

state and local governments across the United States. This decision alone will enshrine the conservative reputation of the Roberts Court in history, since it settled a long-standing and intricate Constitutional Law debate.

The Bill of Rights provides a wide range of civil liberties to "all persons," not just citizens, as many believe. Our introductory overview to the topic will present highlights about many of them, but will not be comprehensive. Those of you who continue your study of American government will find a multitude of sources available on the subject. We will begin with the five freedoms protected by the First Amendment, discussing a few of them a bit more extensively than the rest to provide some sense of the depth and complexity of Civil Liberties as part of the U.S. political culture.

FREEDOM OF RELIGION

"*Congress shall make no law respecting an establishment of religion or prohibiting the free exercise thereof*" is the final language approved by the first Congress and ratified by the states regarding freedom of religion. Legal scholars emphasize that this provides two distinct protections:

1. *The Establishment Clause*: There has been, and continues to be, great debate over the precise meaning of this clause. It is generally accepted that the primary aim of adding this protection to the Constitution was to preclude the national government from designating an "official" religion for the United States, which most of the states had at that time. Beyond that, several interpretations have been put forth and defended in legal briefs, scholarly analyses, and case law over the years. Many of them debate the meaning

of the oft-quoted phrase of Thomas Jefferson's that it was intended to create a "wall of separation of Church and State."

The establishment clause has been applied in a large number of cases dealing with legal conflicts about national, state, and local government actions regarding religion and religious institutions. Any interested reader should have no trouble finding a wealth of sources providing a range of perspectives on this extremely controversial subject. One of the Supreme Court's clearest elaborations of the clause can be found in *Everson v. Board of Education* (1947). The most straightforward summary description of what it means with respect to public policy that this author has ever encountered is that it mandates "that government can neither promote more discriminate against religious beliefs."[11] Issues dealt with in recent court cases that would be useful subjects for classroom discussion include school voucher programs and "moments of silence."

2. *The Free Exercise Clause*: Again, a range of interpretations have been offered for this clause over the years. Two key points regarding its application are worth noting. First, while beliefs cannot be regulated, religious activities can. Second, religious beliefs cannot be used as justification for violating valid laws. Therefore, while it was clearly intended "to protect a wide range of religious observance and practice from political interference,"[12] they *can* be limited if they

---

[11] Steffen W. Schmidt, Mark C. Shelley, and Barbara Bardes, *American Government and Politics Today*, 13th ed. (Mason, OH: Thomson Wadsworth, 2008), 112.

[12] Cal Jillson, *American Government: Political Development and Institutional Change* (New York: Routledge, 1999), 374.

violate an otherwise constitutional law. Examples of religious practices that have been banned by the courts include polygamy and illegal drug use. A number of court rulings have also protected the free exercise of religion. One that might be of particular interest to students is *Good News Club v. Milford Central School* (2001), which held that religious clubs must be treated the same as other clubs with respect to the use of public school property.

FREEDOM OF EXPRESSION (SPEECH AND PRESS)

It did not take long for the Anti-Federalists' concern about the new central government to manifest itself with respect to freedom of expression. In 1798 the Sedition Act was passed making it a crime to defame that government or its officials. Although the courts did not rule against it (in fact, they applied it vigorously in several cases), the people had their say at the ballot box, replacing many Congressmen in 1798 and making John Adams the first one-term president in the election of 1800. It should be noted that the Supreme Court had not yet formally asserted its power of judicial review over acts of Congress at that time.

As noted above, our freedoms are not unlimited, so the core issue is what justifies imposing legal limits. Civil liberties scholars usually trace their evolution by citing the series of different doctrines presented in Supreme Court rulings. The current "clear, present, and imminent danger test" regarding free speech set forth in *Brandenburg v. Ohio* (1969) clearly fits the pattern. Perceived danger as justification for limiting speech originated in a ruling 50 years earlier including the now classic analogy to shouting

"fire" in a theater, but followed a rather serpentine path. Supreme Court doctrines often reflect both the dialectical dance of ideology and response to changing political circumstances.

With a tremendous volume of opinions and scholarship available on the subject of free speech, we will limit ourselves to a few more illustrative points. You should be aware that "free speech" involves more than just expressing opinions with words. Court rulings have protected both symbolic (for example, wearing black armbands to protest the Vietnam War, and even burning the flag) and commercial speech (i.e., advertising). Political speech has always been at the heart of freedom of expression, and that has now been extended for corporations and interest group/associations through the *Citizens United* (2010) decision. The Supreme Court has also, however, consistently limited certain categories of speech, most notably sexually explicit material deemed obscene (the definition of which has its own serpentine history) and slander (false public statements that defame someone).

Freedom of the press has its own specific issues and applications. Libel is the printed version of slander, and is also not protected, so it subjects the publisher to civil suits by defamed parties. However, the Supreme Court has ruled that public figures must meet higher standards than ordinary people to win a libel suit, reinforcing the "watchdog" role that the media plays in our political system, along with supporting the personal right we all have to criticize public officials. One of the core judicial doctrines in this area places extreme limitations on "prior restraint" of expression. Any attempt by government to prevent publication of anything that is not otherwise restricted (for example, obscenity) is viewed by the courts "with a 'heavy presumption' against its constitutionality" (*Nebraska*

Press Association v. Stuart, 1976)[13] to prevent censorship.

Freedom of the press was extended beyond print media by the courts, but broadcast media (films, radio, and television) never received the same protection as print media. The telecommunications revolution has created a host of new issues related to free speech that must be dealt with. Several laws enacted by Congress attempting to protect children by controlling pornography on the Internet have been overturned by the Supreme Court because they restricted access to many other types of information. Computer animation now makes it possible to create an image of just about any idea, and the court has ruled that both virtual pornography and violent video games must be treated legally as other forms of free speech are. The twenty-first century is likely to feature an exciting and intricate debate over free speech, particularly as surveillance technology mushrooms in the same manner that data collection and analysis technology did.

THE RIGHT TO ASSEMBLE AND PETITION THE GOVERNMENT

Our early political leaders were very familiar with public demonstrations of disapproval of government actions and policies. More than a few British tax collectors were tarred and feathered by angry American mobs in the run-up to our Revolution. In the 1960s, civil rights and antiwar demonstrations went from being considered criminal or treasonous to being tolerated, and finally to being planned in advance with local government officials. The Supreme Court has ruled that state and local governments cannot

bar individuals from assembling, but can require permits so that order can be maintained, and can impose appropriate security measures (for example, restricting locations) to protect public safety.

RIGHTS OF THE ACCUSED

Our First Amendment rights, which were only highlighted above, all relate to what one group of political scientists labeled the "original dilemma" of government: freedom versus order.[14] Another set of rights that relate more directly to that dilemma are the protections that the Bill of Rights grants to individuals accused of crimes. They were added to the basic right of *habeus corpus* provided in Article 1, which requires the government to explain and defend any person's detention before a judge, and these rights have also evolved considerably and contentiously since then.

They have been a topic of particular controversy since 2001, due to the "War on Terror." Since then, some of the following key protections that have become accepted as applying to standard criminal defendants have been "reinterpreted" for application to individuals accused or suspected of terrorism or related activities:

- *No "Unreasonable Searches and Seizures" (Fourth Amendment)*: The Constitution clearly states that a warrant is required "particularly describing the place to be searched, and the persons or things to be seized." This protection led the courts to create the "exclusionary rule," which made illegally obtained evidence inadmissible at trial. Since the courts had routinely applied this protection

---

[13] 427 U.S. 539 (1976).

[14] Kenneth Janda, Jeffrey M. Berry, and Jerry Goldman, *The Challenge of Democracy: Government in America* (Boston: Houghton Mifflin, 1995), 15–19.

to telephone communications, the use of "roving wiretaps" to identify and track suspected terrorists has been challenged by civil liberties advocates.

- *Prohibition Against Self-incrimination (Fifth Amendment)*: Since "No person . . . shall be compelled in any criminal case to be a witness against himself," the recent use of "enhanced interrogation techniques" has also been challenged.

- *The Right to Counsel (Sixth Amendment)*: A major example of the "incorporation doctrine" is the *Gideon v. Wainwright* (1961) case, in which the Fourteenth Amendment was used to apply the requirement for adequate legal counsel to state courts. It established the responsibility of all governments in the United States to provide a lawyer for defendants who cannot afford one.

- *No "Cruel and Unusual Punishment" (Eighth Amendment)*: The death penalty has been unsuccessfully challenged as a violation of this protection, but the courts have recently imposed restrictions on its use against persons with developmental disabilities and minors. Recently, this protection has also been successfully used to challenge serious prison overcrowding.

OTHER IMPORTANT PROTECTIONS

- The Second Amendment protects the right to bear arms, which the Supreme Court, after long debate, clearly certified as an individual right in the *Heller*[15] and *McDonald*[16]

---

[15] 554 U.S. 570 (2008).
[16] 561 U.S. 3025 (2010).

cases, the latest "incorporation" rulings. Gun control is another example of a policy issue that clearly represents the original dilemma of government—freedom versus order.

- The Fifth Amendment prohibits the government from taking "life, liberty or property, without due process of law," and allows taking property "for public use" only with "just compensation." The recent Supreme Court decision in *Kelo v. City of New London* (2005) allowing economic development activities authorized by local officials to be considered a public use generated nationwide controversy. A very large supermajority of state legislatures took up the issue of "public use" in some form; in some, legislation is being held over due to the continued revenue squeeze and/or successful lobbying by real estate developers at that level.

THE RIGHT TO PRIVACY

We will close out our overview of Civil Liberties by discussing the right to privacy. Many Americans are not aware that the Constitution does not explicitly include a right to privacy; in fact, the word "privacy" does not appear in it anywhere. That right was first recognized by the Supreme Court in *Griswold v. Connecticut* (1965) based on the First, Third, Fourth, Fifth, Ninth, and Tenth Amendments,[17] and it should

---

[17] The story of how the Supreme Court recognized the right to privacy in the case is nicely summarized in Alex McBride, "*Griswold v. Connecticut*," at http://www.pbs.org/wnet/supremecourt/rights/landmark_griswold.html. The written "opinions" (as they are called) of the Supreme Court justices fully explain their rationales for asserting or denying that a constitutional right to privacy exists can be read at http://caselaw.lp.findlaw.com/scripts/getcase.pl?court=US&vol=381&invol=479.

be clearly noted that most Americans supported the Court's decision. Various public opinion surveys over the years document that support, and show that we consider it one of the most important rights we have:[18]

- In a 1965 Harris survey, 92 percent of the respondents said they felt "personally satisfied" that they had a right to privacy.
- In a 1978 Harris survey, 76 percent of the respondents said that the right to privacy should be added to the rights of life, liberty, and the pursuit of happiness as "fundamental for both the individual and a just society."
- In a 1986 Gallup survey, 77 percent responded "Yes" to the question, "Do you think the Constitution guarantees the right to privacy?"
- In a 1997 survey done by the University of Connecticut, 78 percent of respondents said the right to privacy was "essential" and another 21 percent said it was "important."

Like the rights of the accused, the right to privacy became a public issue in relation to the "War on Terror," due to policies such as surveillance of telephone conversations by the National Security Agency and reported government "data mining" operations. In a 2005 *CBS News/New York Times* survey, 30 percent of respondents said that the right to privacy had "already been lost," another 52 percent saw it "under serious threat,"

and only 16 percent thought it "was basically safe." Concern grew to the point that a major study was conducted by the National Academy of Science, which recommended that "Congress should reexamine existing law to consider how privacy should be protected in the context of information-based programs (e.g., data mining) for counterterrorism."[19]

We will conclude with three points about the right to privacy. First, this issue epitomizes the "informal" method of changing the Constitution by judicial interpretation. The justification of "emanations" from the other civil liberties specified in the Bill of Rights reignited the tug-of-war between judicial activism and judicial restraint, and helped fuel the New Federalism movement and the resurgence of the Jeffersonians toward the end of the twentieth century. Second, this asserted right to privacy impacted a number of other Supreme Court cases involving important issues, including a woman's right to have an abortion and the right to die. Third, with very real threats like terrorism to consider, the right to privacy clearly illustrates the complexity of the original dilemma and authoritative decision making. Which value, freedom or order, should have priority? Is a balance of the two possible?

DEFINITION AND SOURCE OF CIVIL RIGHTS

The political scientists who formulated the "original dilemma" of government called it that to contrast it with the "modern dilemma" of

---

[18] October 1965 survey by Louis Harris & Associates, as reported in the *Washington Post, November–December 1978 survey by Sentry Insurance and Louis Harris & Associates; July 1986 survey by Newsweek* and the Gallup Organization; July–August, 1997 survey by Freedom Forum and the Center for Survey Research and Analysis. All data retrieved July 30, 2007 from the iPOLL Databank, The Roper Center for Public Opinion Research, University of Connecticut http://www.ropercenter.uconn.edu/ipoll.html.

[19] National Research Council, *Protecting Individual Privacy in the Struggle Against Terrorists: A Framework for Program Assessment*, 2011, available at http://www.nap.edu/openbook.php?record_id=12452.

government: freedom versus equality.[20] That dilemma is at the very center of Civil Rights, and recall from our discussion of democratic values that equality is also a very complex concept. Most constitutional scholars agree that the three "Civil War Amendments" significantly changed the U.S. political system. Abolishing slavery with the Thirteenth Amendment was a giant step toward a more democratic political culture, and the Fifteenth Amendment also made the United States more democratic by expanding voting rights.

The most far-reaching, however, was the Fourteenth Amendment, for two reasons. That amendment spelled out the legal criteria for U.S. citizenship for the first time, and also created the legal basis for what became known as "Civil Rights." While they are connected to Civil Liberties both legally and historically, Civil Rights are a distinctive value in the U.S. political culture. We will first cover the contrast between the two, and then discuss the connections.

Civil Rights refers to a constitutional mandate on every government in the United States to provide "due process of law" and "the equal protection of the laws" to "any person within its jurisdiction." The Fourteenth Amendment is the core legal source of Civil Rights in the U.S. political system, and it has been interpreted by the courts as requiring the government to act to ensure that citizens are treated "equally." The difficulty in achieving that ideal principle was noted in earlier discussions. The main point to be understood here is how this contrasts with Civil Liberties, which are based on restraints placed on all U.S. governments. The implementation of Civil Rights requires the opposite—action.

There are two clear connections between Civil Liberties and Civil Rights. The legal one

was noted above, the doctrine of "incorporation." The legal source of Civil Rights also made the Bill of Rights applicable throughout the U.S. Federal Republic, enhancing individual freedom for everyone. The second connection is historical. Civil Liberties (particularly our freedoms of speech, press, assembly, and petition) have been, and continue to be, the primary tools used to fight for Civil Rights. Anyone with any knowledge of U.S. history is aware that ratification of the Civil War Amendments, while a great formal leap forward, in actuality was merely a baby step toward making Civil Rights a reality for African Americans (and others). As with Civil Liberties, we can only present a few illustrative highlights of that struggle in this brief introductory overview.

It is important to note that many are still fighting to equalize opportunity and minimize discrimination based on age, ethnicity, gender, mental or physical capacity, race, religion, and sexual orientation. This quest reaches far back in our history. The colonies attracted a diversity of settlers, including a few who preached tolerance. Many of the delegates to the Constitutional Convention wanted to abolish slavery, but the desire to maintain one union of states overrode all other concerns. The importance of organized action in democratic politics was noted in our definition of that term (and will be discussed again), so the founding of the American Anti-Slavery Society in 1833, the First Women's Rights Convention in 1848, and the founding of the National Women's Suffrage Association in 1870 are noteworthy examples of early "Civil Rights" efforts.

We will end this overview with some highlights of the most prominent historical example of the struggle for Civil Rights, the fight to end legal segregation of African Americans. They

---

[20] Janda et al. (see Note 14).

were selected to illustrate the tugs-of-war be-tween the national and state levels and the three branches that characterize the workings of the U.S. Federal Republic. It is assumed by many Americans today that the Supreme Court has always been a champion for Civil Rights, for ex-ample. The exact opposite was true in the early stages of the struggle. In *Dred Scott v. Sanford* (1857),[21] the Supreme Court ruled that Blacks were not citizens and had "no rights which the white man was bound to respect," while declar-ing the Missouri Compromise (which banned slavery in certain territories) unconstitutional, making the Civil War basically inevitable.

Congress enacted several Civil Rights acts after the Civil War, but the Supreme Court de-clared some unconstitutional, and interpreted the Civil War Amendments very narrowly, ren-dering the laws ineffective. It also applied a strict view of federalism that favored state sovereignty, which the Southern states used to employ a variety of tactics designed to prevent former slaves from voting. These included party primary elections restricted to whites, limiting voting to those whose grandfathers had voted before 1867, literacy tests, and "poll taxes" (taxes some-one had to pay in order to vote), which were not effectively banned until the mid-1960s. Since it involved the core concurrent power of taxation, ending them required a Constitutional Amend-ment and subsequent survival of a Supreme Court challenge, making it a notable part of the "dialectical dance."

The Southern states used federalism stra-tegically and tactically. Some used their "states' rights" to pass laws mandating (*requiring*) the segregation of the races in public places, which became known as "Jim Crow" laws, referring to

a popular minstrel show character from that era. They were challenged, but in *Plessy v. Ferguson* (1896),[22] the Supreme Court ruled that "sepa-rate but equal" public facilities did not violate the Fourteenth Amendment, making most seg-regation legal throughout the United States. It remained legal for more than another half century. Not until *Brown v. Board of Education* (1954)[23] did the Court overturn *Plessy*, ruling unanimously that "separate was inherently un-equal," leading to the eventual end of all legal segregation. *Brown* is also notable for being the first application of "social science" research in a Supreme Court decision.

Brown was also a key example of the "checks and balances" in the U.S. Federal Re-public, because the judiciary acted when the other branches could not. Preventing African Americans from voting kept political power in the hands of segregationists. The Southern states reelected the same people over and over, and then took full advantage of seniority rules and other procedures in Congress to prevent Civil Rights legislation from being considered, and to block judicial nominees suspected of being unfriendly to states' rights. No president during the first half of the twentieth century showed any interest in pursuing Civil Rights, in part be-cause they needed to work with Congresses in which the Southern states were very powerful. So, the Supreme Court took the lead. Some call this an abuse of their power. From the perspec-tive of federalism, it was "retaliation" on the part of the national level against a version of "state-shirking"[24] that violated our national political

---

[21] 60 U.S. 393 (1857).

[22] 163 U.S. 537 (1896).
[23] 347 U.S. 483 (1954).
[24] Jenna Bednar, *The Robust Federation: Principles of Design* (New York: Cambridge University Press, 2009), 68.

parameters. These concepts will be elaborated later in our journey.

Many political scientists consider the long battle over basic Civil Rights for African Americans the greatest failure of U.S. Federalism in our history, this author included. States' rights were used to create and continue segregation for more than 100 years after the Civil War Amendments, a struggle that this overview has merely touched on. This was partly a structural problem, but also reflected the U.S. political culture during those times. The reality was that the majority of Americans, who were white, were either indifferent to the plight of African Americans or sympathetic toward segregation. Madison's fear of the "tyranny of the majority" proved to be true in this case. We are still struggling with racism and other forms of discrimination that impair our authoritative decision making. The United States is, after all, a human (i.e., imperfect) community.

U.S. federalism was also the mechanism that eventually led to the end of legal segregation, however, when the national government took positive action in response to the post—World War II Civil Rights Movement. As we will see in the Conclusion, that was a major step in the evolution of U.S. federalism. Organized political action, leadership, and our ingrained Civil Liberties were key factors in the success of that movement. One clearly circumstantial factor in the Movement's success was the role of television news in bearing witness to the abuses of peaceful demonstrators. Video coverage of "Freedom Rides," sit-ins, marches, and boycotts under strong leaders epitomized by the Rev. Dr. Martin Luther King of the Southern Christian Leadership Conference transmuted the dominance of indifference into support for change. The transformative role of the newest mass media at that time—broadcast television news—must be acknowledged. Broadcasts of brutal suppression of peaceful protests made many people realize how un-American discrimination of all types is. The Civil Rights Movement changed our political culture, not just some policies, and paved the way for even further change.

CHAPTER 4

*Political Socialization
and Political Ideology*

WHAT IS POLITICAL SOCIALIZATION?

In the opening comments for this section, a political culture was defined as the set of shared values regarding politics and government that predominates across a political community. It is an important concept in political science, particularly in the subfield of comparative politics, because these shared values "define the situation in which political action takes place."[1] Recall the power continuum presented in Chapter 1. One thing that clearly distinguishes a democratic political system from an authoritarian or totalitarian system is its political culture. The "ideal principles of U.S. democracy" presented in Chapter 1 represent our shared core political values—our political culture.

From a systems perspective, political socialization is how the political culture of a community is transmitted to new members (children and immigrants),[2] and it is critical for system maintenance:[3]

> *[A]ll Societies, from the meanest tribal village to the most advanced nation state, view it as one of their principle tasks to convey to new members a clear awareness of the proper and accepted procedures for reaching common decisions.*

A community's political culture shapes the political behavior that most community members expect, and will tolerate, from themselves and other members, particularly public officials. These expected patterns of behavior have been labeled "political roles." Where do they come from? "Roles and role behavior are clearly not established from the time of birth, but are taught and learned

---

[1] Sydney Verba, "Comparative Political Culture," in Lucien Pye and Sydney Verba, eds., *Political Culture and Political Development* (Princeton, NJ: Princeton University Press, 1965), 513.

[2] Cal Jillson, *American Government: Political Development and Institutional Change*, 5th ed. (New York: Routledge, 2011), 79–80.

[3] Edward S. Greenberg, "Consensus and Dissent: Trends in Political Socialization Research," the Preface to *Political Socialization*, which he edited (New York: Atherton, 1970), 5.

phenomena. As such, they are a part of the content of political socialization."[4] In its most basic sense, political socialization is the process by which individuals learn about politics and government.

More specifically, *political socialization is the process by which individuals learn about and develop beliefs and attitudes about politics and government.* Believing in the shared core values of U.S. democracy is what "being American" means with respect to politics, and acquiring one's sense of national identity will shape an individual's actions. Some individuals are taught or learn only some of the values, and others simply reject them. They acquire a different "political identity," and will act differently. This can occur when they are children, or later in life. If they develop extreme views, they may turn to violence. Timothy McVeigh, the Oklahoma City Bomber, was an example of this.

Some of the other dimensions of political culture were noted in the section introduction. They are the attitudes that would be reflected by the answers most of us would give to questions like these:

- What should we expect from our government(s)?
- What should be the average citizen's role in politics and government?
- How should our legislators make their decisions?
- How much power should the president have?
- What kinds of decisions should judges make?
- How involved should political organizations be in policymaking?

- Who should be able to run for public office?
- What should be the role of money in politics?

Although only the last question contains the specific word, each of them deals with political roles. The answer to the first question is at the center of political ideology, which will be discussed below. In the United States we expect, even urge, everyone to participate in authoritative decision making in some way. It could be by voting, joining a political organization, donating to a candidate, or simply expressing one's opinion on public issues, but the United States prides itself on having a "participant" political culture.[5] The remaining questions will be revisited as we proceed along our journey.

The study of political socialization was nicely summarized by one of the first political scientists in that subfield as: research into "(1) who (2) learns what (3) from whom (4) under what circumstances (5) with what effects."[6] As with all of our topics, we cannot cover political socialization extensively. We will highlight key aspects within a discussion of what are generally labeled "agents" of political socialization:[7] persons, institutions, and settings "from which political attitudes and behaviors are acquired."[8] Our discussion will begin with a focus on children, but it is important to remember

---

[4] Gregory S. Mahler, *Comparative Politics: An Institutional and Cross-National Approach* (Upper Saddle River, NJ: Prentice Hall, 2008), 174.

[5] Gabriel A. Almond and Sydney Verba, *The Civic Culture* (Princeton, NJ: Princeton University Press, 1963), 440.
[6] Fred I. Greenstein, *Children and Politics*. Rev. ed. (New Haven: Yale University Press, 1969), 12. The origin of the subfield is usually credited to Herbert Hyman, *Political Socialization* (New York: The Free Press, 1959).
[7] Jillson (see Note 2) offers an excellent summary outline of agent categories and some notable effects, 79–80.
[8] Robert D. Hess and Judith V. Torney, "The Development of Political Attitudes in Children," in Edward S. Greenberg, ed., *Political Socialization* (New York: Atherton, 1970), 71.

that individuals continue to learn about politics and government throughout their lives. As we proceed, keep in the back of your mind the importance of communication in the socialization process.

AGENTS OF POLITICAL SOCIALIZATION

This political scientist has found it useful to distinguish three categories of agents of political socialization: personal, demographic, and environmental. While demographic characteristics are certainly personal, they tend to be treated distinctively in the arena of social science and are primarily used to compare behavior among different social groups. Personal factors are those that generate more individual impacts.

Personal Factors

Family

Most young people do not yet fully appreciate the impact that their family upbringing has had on them. Parents and other adult family members serve as a child's primary role models for a wide range of behaviors, including those related to politics. A few things that leave imprints that eventually impact one's political perspective are:

- *Basic patriotism:* Most parents promote positive views of U.S. democracy.
- *Attitude toward authority:* Households are run differently, some being more "democratic" and others more "authoritarian"; this impacts one's worldview.
- *Attitude toward politics:* Most U.S. households encourage participation; some urge the opposite, however, condemning politics as a corrupt activity.

- *Personal values:* Some families promote competition and winning; others support helping others and sharing. Religion is emphasized more in some households than in others, which influences how individuals will view the world.

In terms of behavioral impacts, from the earliest research down to the present, one outcome that has been consistently and markedly significant has been the transmission of political party identification. About two-thirds of young people from families with both parents identifying with the same party (Democrat or Republican) or as independents self-identify themselves as the same. Those from families with divided identification scatter uniformly among the three basic options.[9] Subcategories are also studied, and some yield interesting findings. For example, "first generation" Americans, mentioned in the opening comments to this section referring to children of immigrants, often find themselves performing what has been labeled "reverse socialization." That is, they educate their parents about how things are done in America, including politics. Another interesting new finding involves children influencing their parents' and other adults' attitudes and behavior by sharing ideas using new, Internet-based media.[10]

---

[9] M. Kent Jennings, Laura Stoker, and Jake Bowers, "Politics Across Generations: Family Transmission Reexamined," *Journal of Politics*, 71 (3) (July 2009), 782–799, a follow-up to M. Kent Jennings and Richard G. Niemi, *Generations and Politics: A Panel Study of Young Adults and Their Parents* (Princeton, NJ: Princeton University Press, 1981).

[10] Michael McDevitt and Stephen H. Chaffee, "Second Chance Political Socialization: 'Trickle-up' Effects of Children on Parents," in Thomas J. Johnson et al., eds., *Engaging the Public: How Government and the Media Can Reinvigorate American Democracy* (Lanham, MD: Rowman & Littlefield, 1998), 57–66.

Education

"The school apparently plays the largest part in teaching . . . about the operation of the political system," but "stresses ideal norms and ignores the tougher, less pleasant facts of political life in the United States."[11] The "participant" political culture is promoted, but the social setting of a school can have a major impact. Schools with diverse student bodies that segregate themselves tend to isolate minority children, particularly those who were born elsewhere, from the mainstream culture. As a result, these children do not acquire the same attitudes toward political participation.[12] Some value imprints that most children receive are:

- *Advanced patriotism and national history:* "The Pledge of Allegiance," celebration of national holidays, and national achievements are taught to build pride.
- *Attitude toward "outside" authority:* Teachers/other titleholders must be obeyed.
- *How to behave in group settings:* Rules of conduct must be followed.

A rather clear pattern has also been found regarding how children learn about "government" as they progress through the elementary grades. They start by identifying it with individuals (police officers, the president, their mayor), move to seeing it in less personal terms and become aware of its "group character" and major institutions, and piece together how representative democracy works.[13] As individuals progress in their political education, they gain more sophisticated knowledge about the operation of their own political system and more comparative information about others. One of the historically documented impacts of additional education has been enhanced participation skills, usually leading to greater involvement in politics. That may be changing, however, since the proportion of citizens voting has hovered between approximately 50 percent and 60 percent while the share of citizens completing their high school education grew to approximately 95 percent during the second half of the twentieth century.[14]

Peers

As children grow up and seek to develop their own personal identities, most will question the values promoted by older generations, including their families and educators, and pay increasingly greater attention to what their peers deem important. This includes political values. Some youths "rebel" against the "political establishment," a few will embrace it, but most seem to develop an attitude of indifference toward politics as they focus on personal matters. Recent research supports that thesis,[15] and my fifteen years of experience teaching introductory political science to college students would reinforce that perception.

The telecommunications revolution appears to be permanently changing both politics and the socialization process, however. One of the leading contemporary scholars in this subfield has argued that the "Internet Generation"

---

[11] Hess and Torney (see Note 7), 71–72.

[12] Ingrid G. Ellen, Katherine O'Regan, Amy E. Schwartz, and Leanna Stiefel, "Immigrant Children and New York City Schools: Segregation and Its Consequences," *Brookings-Wharton Papers on Urban Affairs,* 2002.

[13] Davis Easton and Jack Dennis, "A Child's Image of Government," in Greenberg (see Note 3), 42.

[14] Kenneth Janda, Jeffrey M. Berry, and Jerry Goldman, *The Challenge of Democracy: Government in America* (Boston: Houghton Mifflin, 2008), 218.

[15] Jane Eisner, *Taking Back the Vote: Getting American Youth Involved in Our Democracy* (Boston: Beacon Press, 2004).

is different from any other in history: "There is some evidence that young people are developing their political identities online, and that these identities are consistent with the norms of engaged citizenship."[16] These "digital natives"[17] are not unique simply because they grew up immersed in technology, but due to a change in the very nature of their peer interaction. This will be discussed further shortly, but some highlights of peer impact studies are:

- *"Transformative events"*[18] Their impact is very real. Certain events leave an indelible imprint on the political attitudes of those whose early socialization is centered on them. Some call this the "generational effect." The Great Depression and World War II certainly shaped the political attitudes of those who grew up experiencing them. For this author, the Vietnam War was the defining event of his political socialization, as discussed in the Preface.
- *Career choice(s):* This influences everyone. Whichever profession(s) one trains for and spends any length of time pursuing creates key political peer group(s) that influence individual political judgments. With

many people now having serial careers and ongoing economic uncertainty, we must anticipate shifts in political perspectives as this unfolds. The basic intersection of economics and politics is indisputable, moreover. People will vote "their wallets" over their hearts and/or minds. Our discussion of political ideology below will touch on these topics.

Physiological

In the Introduction, political science was described as an observational science like astronomy. Both fields are constantly seeking better ways of "observing" political phenomena, including using new technology as it becomes available. One of the most interesting new directions that political science research is venturing into is physiological data. This research seeks links correlating political attitudes and behavior to identify patterns. This author would like to propose that some credit be given to our space program for the breakthroughs in collecting and processing physiological data. The United States made a commitment to human flight with safe return, spawning the need for a new generation of medical monitoring equipment. Two interesting examples of this new research direction are:

- *DNA?* "Political opinions spring from DNA, research asserts," was the headline for a newspaper article reporting on a 2008 study suggesting that "Die-hard liberals and conservatives aren't made, they're born. It's literally in their DNA."[19] The article goes

---

[16] Diana Owen, "Political Socialization in the Twenty-first Century: Recommendations for Researchers," paper presented for presentation at "The Future of Civic Education in the 21st Century" conference cosponsored by the Center for Civic Education and the Bundeszentrale fur politische Bildung, James Madison's Montpelier, September 21–26, 2008. Downloaded from http://www.civiced.org/pdfs/GermanAmericanConf2009/DianaOwen_2009.pdf, 7/23/11. She cites W. Lance Bennett, "Civic Learning Online: Responding to the Generational Shift in Citizen Identity," *Around the CIRCLE*, vol. 5 (2008), 1–2.

[17] Marc Prensky, "Digital Natives, Digital Immigrants," *On the Horizon*, 9(5) (October 2001).

[18] Jillson (see Note 2), 82–83, also discusses transformative personalities.

[19] Denise Gellene, "Political opinions spring from DNA, research asserts," *The Star-Ledger*, 9/19/08, 4, reporting on Douglas R. Oxley and Kevin B. Smith et al., "Political Attitudes Vary With Physiological Trait," *Science*, 321 (2008), 1667–1670.

on to explain that the hypothesized link is the level of fear people feel, and also mentions other studies showing that identical twins think more alike than nonidentical siblings, and that "the brains of conservatives and liberals process information differently."

- *Brain chemistry?* "Red Brain, Blue Brain?" reported on a study that "put self-identified Democratic and Republican partisans in brain scanners and asked them to evaluate negative information about various candidates."[20] The new finding was that when these people holding strong political attitudes rejected such information about those they supported, the "reward centers" in their brains were activated in the same way that drug addicts "reward themselves for wronged headed behavior."

Please note the question marks used with both of the above entries. These are examples representing the current frontiers of political science research, and the cited reports go on to note that each theory has those who dispute it. But there is one clear physiological reality that becomes very relevant to all of us:[21]

> *Generally, older Americans tend to be somewhat more conservative than younger Americans, particularly on social issues and, to some extent, on economic issues. This effect is known as the lifestyle effect. It probably occurs because older adults are concerned about*

their own economic situations and are likely to retain the social values that they learned at a younger age.

This "lifestyle effect" implies that as you age and progress through life, your political attitudes/values will change. With the limitations of generalization in mind,[22] that does appear to be true. Keep in mind that political socialization is a lifelong process.

Demographic Factors

Socioeconomic Status

Americans are hesitant to talk about "class" (although the Occupy Wall Street movement has nudged it onto the public policy agenda), so instead social scientists created a parallel concept, "Socioeconomic Status":[23]

> *An individual's or group's position within a hierarchical social structure. Socioeconomic status depends on a combination of variables, including occupation, education, income, wealth, and place of residence. Sociologists often use socioeconomic status as a means of predicting behavior.*

You will often see the abbreviation SES used for socioeconomic status, and some of the early studies uncovered notable disparities in the imprints created by "child-rearing practices" in households with clear differences in SES. Compared to those from "upper-status" households,

---

[20] Shankar Vedantam, "Red Brain, Blue Brain?" *The Washington Post National Weekly Edition*, 2/6–12/06, 35, reporting on research by Drew Westen, *The Political Brain* (Jackson, TN: Public Affairs, 2007).

[21] Steffen W. Schmidt, Mark C. Shelley, and Barbara Bardes, *American Government and Politics Today*, 13th ed. (Mason, OH: Thomson Wadsworth, 2008), 196.

[22] This is an issue every social scientist must deal with, and an excellent summary discussion can be found in Mahler (see Note 4), 9–12.

[23] *The American Heritage® New Dictionary of Cultural Literacy, Third Edition* (Houghton Mifflin Company, 2005). July 24, 2011. <Dictionary.com http://dictionary.reference.com/browse/socioeconomic status>.

"lower-status" children "acquire less political information and fewer incentives to participate in politics," and they "are less likely to develop the sorts of skills that facilitate political action and communication." Lower-status households also "foster compliance to authority."[24]

Race and Ethnicity

Individuals of different races and ethnicities do experience the world in different ways in different places. When this author was growing up in the Bronx in the late 1950s and early 1960s, one's ethnicity was a serious matter. Race was an even more serious matter, leading eventually to a series of devastating urban riots. If you think our country was divided over Vietnam or about sending the National Guard to Iraq and Afghanistan, those arguments pale in comparison to the one over what to do when the cities started to burn. Seeing U.S. Army tanks rolling through the streets of Detroit live on television was one of the scariest sights of this author's youth.

Individuals raised in households that experience discrimination and many of the other problems related with minority status (see SES above) undoubtedly develop "other than average" personal histories. This means their political socialization will be different. This is a good point to introduce the notion of "subcultures," segments of a community that share most of the political culture, but have some distinctive positions or behavioral traits. Subcultures give a community greater diversity, and therefore bring a system strength, but can also be the source of extra division and conflict.

Religion

We noted the role of religion under family, but here we are more concerned about group impacts. Just as with race, individuals raised in households in which religion and its related philosophies are emphasized are living "other than average" lives, and will therefore have different political socialization experiences.

A straightforward look at history shows that religious intensity can spell political trouble. It should also be noted that churches have always been avenues of upward mobility for low status individuals. The role of churches in the African-American community is in many ways a model of community development networking. It has the unifying umbrella of the Christian faith, but is decentralized down to the neighborhood, and it is embedded within its community like no other help network ever witnessed by this political scientist. Racial, ethnic, and religious groupings do have a tendency to reinforce each other, moreover.

Gender

The earliest studies detected a carryover effect from general socialization:[25]

> *From an early age girls showed less political interest and awareness than do boys, even though girls are better able to manipulate language than are boys and are, by many psychosocial standards, more "grown-up" than boys. Here the crucial factor evidently is the early sex-typing of interests, especially nonpolitical interests.*

---

[24] Fred Greenstein, "Children and Politics," in Greenberg (see Note 3), 58–59.

[25] Greenstein, "Children and Politics," in Greenberg (see Note 3), 59.

This has changed markedly in the United States since the women's movement of the late twentieth century, and women are now surpassing men in some basic areas of political participation, most notably voter turnout. We are clearly trending toward having a woman president within the next decade or two. Women may also be the underlying factor for the interesting growth of most educated voters (Master's degree recipients) favoring the liberal faction and the Democratic Party recently.

Environmental Factors

Geographic Factors

The concept of "subcultures" was introduced above under race and ethnicity, but this clearly manifests itself with respect to geography in the United States. Two variables that impact political perspective and behavior are type of community and region:

- Individuals who are raised in urban environments experience a completely different relationship with their neighbors than those raised in rural or suburban communities. The more urban an area, the greater the interdependence among people sharing that living space, and recognizing the need for additional order over freedom. This shows up in voting patterns, with urban voters favoring Democratic presidential candidates by approximately 60 percent to 40 percent and rural voters supporting Republicans also by approximately 60 percent to 40 percent fairly consistently.
- We sometimes joke about the differences among different sections of our country, but they are real. New England clearly has a recognized subculture, as does the Northeast,

the South, the Southwest, the Midwest, the Northwest, and the West Coast. One observer of American development patterns has argued that all of North America is actually divided into nine different "nations":[26]

> *Some are clearly divided topographically by mountains, deserts, and rivers. Others are separated by architecture, music, language, and ways of making a living. Each nation has its own list of desires. Each nation knows how it plans to get what it needs from whoever's got it. Most important, each nation has a distinct prism through which it views the world.*

Regional and community differences based on population density have been tracked by social scientists for years. A recent study "analyzed billions of anonymized cell phone records to show how calling and texting patterns shape communities." It showed that "cell phone patterns follow state lines to a surprising degree," but several states had split communities, while "some states appear to merge seamlessly with neighboring states."[27] The key point here is that political subcultures are a factor in political socialization. Shared specific values and views get continuous reinforcement, giving them some extra worth to us when compared to the broader political culture. Federalism supports diverse subcultures by providing a decision-making structure much more amenable to different perspectives.

Opinion Leaders

Although the mass media has homogenized many aspects of our culture, the distinctive

---

[26] Joel Garreau, *The Nine Nations of North America* (New York: Avon, 1981), 1–2.
[27] Leslie Kwoh, "Sprinkles or jimmies? Cell phone usage calls out north-south divide," *The Star-Ledger*, 7/19/11, 22.

communities noted above also impact their residents by highlighting different opinion leaders. These tend to fall into three categories:

- *Formal:* elected and appointed officials; religious and social leaders
- *Informal:* friends, teachers, coworkers, fellow professionals, etc.
- *Semiformal:* celebrity activists who become associated with certain political causes (e.g., Willie Nelson and family farmers, Bono and international debt relief for poor countries)

Mass Media

While the impact of newspapers, magazines, television, and radio were not ignored, political scientists "relegated the mass media to secondary status among the agencies of socialization, assigning them a minor, primarily reinforcing role in the politicization process." If that was true for the twentieth century, it no longer is:[28]

> *The most significant development warranting the attention of scholars may be the influence of technology on twenty-first century political socialization. If we view socialization as primarily a communications process, technology has fundamentally altered the core mechanisms that sustain the enterprise. The means by which people receive and process information has been essentially altered. Communication takes place more through technological intermediaries than via face-to-face contact.*

Research specifically designed to compare the impacts of different agents will be needed to definitively determine this, but it appears that the mass media may now be overtaking the family as the primary agent of political socialization in the United States—at least for new generations. It would be difficult for anyone to deny that children and youth spend the bulk of their time submerged in technological media today; this must be having an impact. Two other recognized media influences illustrate the range of mass media's impact. In addition to the direct influence that political news reporting and political commentary can have on audience perceptions, the indirect influence of subtle messages that are transmitted must also be considered.

First, thinking back about how minorities and women were portrayed in movies and television shows through the middle of the twentieth century, one can see images of subordination clearly being reinforced. That has now changed; the U.S. president has been cast as a minority or a woman several times. Second, television and radio news reporting also changed as we moved into the new century. The proliferation of media outlets seems to have spurred a movement toward "niche" programming, with networks and stations seeking to lock in their news audiences by aligning themselves with particular political, social, or style (for example, the spread of "infotainment") subcultures. Thus, we seem to have returned to blatant media partisanship being acceptable, as it was during the early decades of our national history.

With media conglomeration continuing, the impact of these technological and style changes could be compounding. The Internet has succeeded in mating with every other form of communication, creating both completely new forms of interaction (e.g., Twitter® and Facebook®) and new forums for conventional political debate (e.g., the "blogosphere" supplementing and intertwining with major newspapers and magazines). The overall role of technology-based

---

[28] Owen (see Note 16).

mass media in our political system seems to be growing, and this topic will pop up throughout our journey.

Readers should have realized by this point that political socialization is one of the most interdisciplinary topics in political science, clearly intersecting with aspects of anthropology, psychology, and sociology. Some highlights have been presented in three categories here regarding how it occurs. The range of activities discussed above should make the conclusion that political socialization is a complex process obvious. Its functional importance for political systems was noted above, but how does it impact individuals? It is how each of us acquires, and tailors, his or her own political ideology.

WHAT IS POLITICAL IDEOLOGY?

Like political culture, political ideology deals with beliefs and attitudes about politics, government, and how the political process should work. Ideology, however, pertains to individuals rather than communities. Different political theorists have stressed different characteristics of ideology:

- Some stress intellectual consistency, defining it as "an organized and coherent set of ideas that forms a perspective on the political world and how it works."[29]
- Some stress ideology's importance as guidance for political action, as "a practical attitude to the world"[30] or reference point for making authoritative decisions.
- Some stress ideology's focus on "attitudes toward political change,"[31] making it a

gauge of the desirability of change and the pace at which it should be pursued.

Each of these characteristics tells us something about ideology and how it can help us understand how a political system operates. Incorporating all the ideas presented above into a single definition, tells us that *ideology refers to an individual's set of beliefs and attitudes about politics and government with a key focus on the desirability and pace of change that often serves as a guide to political behavior.* Previous discussions about federalism and the Constitution introduced the idea that politics in the U.S. Federal Republic is a "dialectical dance" centered on the basic role of government. The two core ideologies in the U.S. political system are "liberalism" and "conservatism," and research consistently shows that our two major political parties reflect them. Table 4-1 contrasts the two using a few basic generalizations.

A third group was mentioned in our discussion of party identification above, Independents. These are individuals who pay attention to politics but prefer to focus on issues and circumstances rather than political organizations or principles for ways to address public issues. While some of them lean toward one of the two basic ideologies (and parties), many use pragmatism as their guiding political principle. *Pragmatism* is the belief that public policymaking should be based on projected consequences rather than ideological principles. This promotes bargaining and compromise with a focus on dealing with issues to maximize community benefit. A clear streak of pragmatism permeates the American political culture, planted there by the Founders

---

[29] Jillson (see Note 2), 107.
[30] Howard Williams, *Concepts of Ideology* (New York: St. Martin's Press, 1988), 122.

[31] Mahler (see Note 4), 34–36. He stresses that this is "very much a relative scale."

LIBERALISM	CONSERVATISM
Generally *favors* government action	Generally *against* government action
Promotes government regulation	Promotes deregulation
Promotes government help for the needy and increasing opportunity	Favors private charity caring for the needy and promotes competition
Favors national policymaking	Favors state and local government control
Democratic Party (Obama, Kennedys)	Republican Party (Bush/Cheney, Reagan)

TABLE 4-1: Simplified Contrast of Liberalism and Conservatism

at the Constitutional Convention. Other major political ideologies, with very brief descriptions drawn from various political science sources and classic dictionary definitions[32] include:

- *Libertarianism:* A political philosophy that favors minimal government involvement in the social and economic lives of individuals, so ongoing government operations should be limited to public safety and security.
- *Populism:* A political philosophy that favors government involvement in the economy, but opposes government protection of individual liberties that seems then to threaten traditional or historical social values.
- *Socialism:* Various economic and political theories advocating promotion of economic equality and collective or governmental ownership and/or control or administration of key industries that people rely on (e.g., energy, water).
- *Capitalism:* An economic system characterized by private ownership of capital goods, and by investments determined by private decision rather than by government control, with prices, production, and distribution

mainly determined in a free market. There is a range of capitalistic systems.
- *Anarchism:* A political theory holding all forms of governmental authority to be unnecessary and undesirable and advocating a society based on a voluntary cooperation and free association of individuals and groups.
- *Fascism:* A political philosophy exalting nation and race and marked by centralized autocratic government, a dictatorial leader; and severe economic social regimentation, including forcible suppression of opposition.

While some of these ideologies focus primarily on economics, all have political applications and promote certain political values. Some political scientists include the "Green Movement," which argues that environmental concerns must take priority over everything else, in their list of ideologies, but it does seem a bit too narrowly focused to be so classified. The four ideologies most frequently associated with the U.S. political system have been usefully compared by applying the three values that clash to create the two "dilemmas of government"[33] we have occasionally referred to on our journey.

---

[32] *Webster's Seventh New Collegiate Dictionary* (Springfield, MA: G. & C. Merriam, 1972).

[33] Kenneth Janda, Jeffrey M. Berry, and Jerry Goldman, *Study Guide for The Challenge of Democracy: Government in America* (Boston: Houghton Mifflin, 1995), 10.

With respect to the now triangular tug-of-war among order, freedom, and equality:

- Liberals favor freedom over order but equality over freedom.
- Conservatives favor freedom over equality but order over freedom.
- Libertarians favor freedom over both order and equality.
- Populists favor both order and equality over freedom

One can see that ideology is an important concept in political science. It is useful for comparing the political values promoted by individuals, groups and organizations, and can be helpful in explaining why certain decisions were made. While ideology is not the determinative factor in the U.S. political system that it is in some others, one cannot fully understand how authoritative decisions are made here without taking it into account. With value judgments at the core of politics, and individuals and organizations the primary actors in our political process, ideology reveals the important link between the two. This very brief look at political socialization and ideology completes our discussion of the U.S. political culture. Having introduced the intellectual foundations of our political system, we can now examine its framework for action.

SECTION TWO
Our Political Configuration

The next leg of our journey will be an examination of the "Political Configuration" of the United States. In the Introduction, this was presented as the second component of a community's political system and defined as the operational framework within which authoritative decision making takes place. Almost all of the formal structures that make up our national (usually referred to as "federal") government are illustrated in the official organization chart from *The United States Government Manual 2009/2010*, reproduced here as Figure S2-1. Take a minute to look it over and try to appreciate its scope. The range of activities that the national government (the U.S. bureaucracy and the decision-making bodies that direct it) have come to be involved in is quite extensive. In most cases, this is been the result of demands placed on the political system by members of the community, more and more often through lobbying by their interest groups/associations.

Before proceeding to examine specific elements of our Political Configuration, let's revisit our basic approach. Recall from the Introduction that the political "system" was chosen as our focus "to keep us attuned to the broad implications of political acts and institutions, and to the interrelatedness of events." The very first model applying the system concept to politics was:[1]

primarily concerned with portraying the relationships between a system and the

---

[1] Stephen Wasby, *Political Science-The Discipline and its Dimensions* (New York: Charles Scribner's Sons, 1970), 109; brackets added.

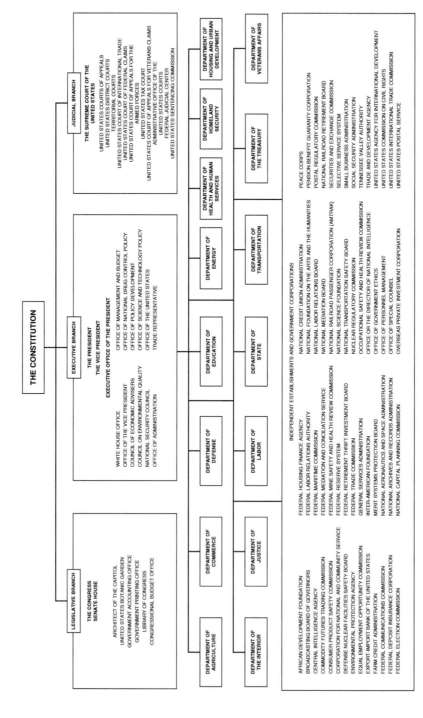

FIGURE S2-1: Organization Chart of the United States Government

environment in which it was located . . . [and] . . . directed attention to the boundary between politics and other aspects of social life and postulated the existence of a close relationship between system and environment.

We also noted that this applies to subsystems as well, with the larger system being the environment for its subsystems, using the metaphor of a Russian matryoshka, or babushka, "nesting" doll as the best way to visualize this phenomenon. The original, basic "model" (diagram) presented by David Easton[2] identified "demands" and "supports" as "inputs," and "decisions or policies" as "outputs" generating "feedback" as subsequent "inputs." It unleashed a surge of theoretical analysis because it provided "an opportunity for the political scientist to relate the more specific work he is doing to the larger political world":[3]

Until the systems approach was developed, political scientists studying one area of politics or government had no way in which to place in context the phenomena they were studying or to relate institutions to each other systematically.

Others offered several refinements, and Easton himself developed much more elaborate portrayals.[4] Keeping the systems model in mind through our journey will serve as a reminder of the interrelatedness of the configuration elements. Another operational concept that can help provide a broader analytical context is the public policymaking process. This has been studied

extensively by political scientists, and a number of "models" of it exist. Most portray the process as a series of overlapping, intertwining stages. The more detailed the description, the greater the number of stages included. Some key points that help to justify a focus on decision making as a useful approach to explaining politics should be recalled and clarified before presenting our basic model.

First, we described politics as a social process of exercising power rooted in authority by making deliberate choices for communities regarding public issues that arise. Deliberately making choices was characterized as decision making, including "nondecision making," a concept intentionally constructed to describe the exercise of political power by preventing decisions from being made. This characterization is in keeping with the basic operational definition used in Decision Theory research that "a decision at a minimum is a choice of one from two or more alternative future courses of action, which includes the alternative of doing nothing."[5]

Next, it was noted that public officials spend considerable time performing nondecision making while formulating specific proposals to act upon. This includes intentionally postponing action for strategic or tactical purposes, and the recent broadened use of the filibuster in the Senate is an extreme example of this tactic. Adopted policies are most often the product of negotiations and bargaining among all interested actors able to participate directly or indirectly. Having control of the decision-making process provides the greatest degree of power, and the extent of

---

[2] David Easton, "An Approach to the Analysis of Political Systems," *World Politics*, 9 (1957), 384.
[3] Wasby (see Note 1), 109.
[4] David Easton, *A Systems Analysis of Political Life* (New York: John Wiley & Sons, 1965).

[5] JoAnn Poparad Paine, "Decision Theory," in Stephen Wasby, *Political Science-The Discipline and its Dimensions* (New York: Charles Scribner's Sons, 1970), 135.

an actor's ability to influence the process is an excellent measure of that actor's relative power.

For purposes of our compact overview, the following five-stage model of public policymaking will suffice:[6]

1. *Agenda Setting*: Public officials must become aware that an issue requires action, and choose to act. The media play a critical role in this stage, along with interest groups/associations, political parties, and candidates for public office.
2. *Policy Decision or Nondecision*: Various proposals are offered and debated among government officials and the public, with interest groups/associations and the media playing key roles (often called the *policy formulation*), leading to a specific proposal being chosen in compliance with authoritative procedures from among those that have been considered (called *policy adoption*).
3. *Implementation*: Government officials act to carry out the adopted policy; a new public program is created or an existing public program is modified or terminated, a very rare occurrence in the U.S. political system.
4. *Evaluation*: Both systematic, *formal* examinations (periodic reports, committee hearings or investigations) and *informal* reactions by citizens, the media, interest groups/associations, candidates or potential candidates for office, and political parties to activities undertaken by governments are generated and circulated.
5. *Feedback*: Evaluative information, often involving unexpected consequences from decisions, and changed circumstances

renew interest in policy issues or create new agenda items for subsequent decisions.

As we examine the Political Configuration of the United States, we will at times refer to these stages and their components. The core element of this operational framework is the government, a community's formal and related informal social structures through which public policies are made. Recall that "social structures" does not refer to physical things, but rather to the "patterned, but not necessarily formalized regular behavior"[7] of people. The other major elements of the operational framework are organizations created for political purposes.

The U.S. Federal Republic was designed to allow, even generate, channeled political competition according to the "Madisonian Model of Government."[8] We summarized that model as *separation of powers* (three competing, counterbalancing independent branches) plus specific *checks and balances* (competing roles and rules) plus *federalism* (competing levels of government) producing a government capable of controlling its people and itself. These are the three core processes that shape how our political system operates, and the summary portrayals provided in parentheses tell you what key function they bring to our political system—competition. More on this below.

These were labeled as "Fundamental Principles" of governance embedded in the Constitution of 1787, along with limited, representative government, in Chapter 2. These principles were "brought to life" in the Constitution by the

---

[6] This is a fairly standard model adapted primarily from Shatfritz et. al., *Introducing Public Administration* (New York: Pearson Longman, 2007), 48–60.

[7] Wasby (see Note) 1, 98.

[8] It should be noted that historians and political scientists include and/or emphasize different components. Many of Madison's writings discuss these ideas; the key sources usually cited are *Federalist Papers #51* and *#10*.

authorization of actual institutions to create a system in which the people choose representatives to make authoritative decisions for them with ongoing direct and indirect input from them. The people's direct input mechanisms (voting, elections, and public opinion) will be discussed in Section Three, since those are the activities that most directly shape and reflect changing political circumstances.

The people's indirect input mechanisms are political organizations that compete to influence (interest groups/associations) or actually direct (political parties) public policymaking. These are presented at the end of this section, following overviews of how U.S. federalism has evolved since it was invented via our Constitution, and how Congress, the Presidency, the Bureaucracy, and the Judiciary are organized and operate. Although concise, these descriptions will reveal the separation of powers, checks and balances, and federalism in action.

Recall the link between modern democracy and competition discussed in Chapter 1: "[T]he people are powerless if the political enterprise is not competitive." In modern democracies, moreover, "it is the competition of political organizations that provides the people with the opportunity to make a choice."[9] Most readers probably are aware that the primary political organizations in the United States are political parties and "interest groups." Many of you know that political parties compete in elections, but are likely not aware of the underlying system function they perform. Some of you have heard or read that "special interests" have "taken over

Washington, DC," corrupting our democracy. The reality is more complex than that, and you will learn how the ongoing competition among these organizations performs key complementary system functions, and in so doing contributes directly to the robustness of the U.S. Federal Republic.

In the Introduction it was also noted that political configuration primarily shapes political "rules" while impacting political "roles" (expected and allowable behaviors for positions of authority). Political rules were defined as the basic operational parameters for authoritative community decision making, both formal (legal or otherwise "official") and informal (adopted as customary). In the U.S. political system, the ultimate set of formal rules is the amended U.S. Constitution of 1787, and some very significant informal procedures (legislative filibusters, executive budgets, and judicial rejection of "political questions" are examples) have also become accepted as the norm after repetitive usage during the last two and a quarter centuries.

Again, since our goal is a compact overview, only major aspects of how the three branches, political parties and interest groups/associations operate will be discussed. Basic functions and roles will be emphasized, with linkages to overall system operation noted, in keeping with this monograph's focus on fundamentals. Each of the elements behave to various degrees as self-contained subsystems, but they do so always within the context of the overall system, which is why we reintroduced it above. They can neither escape the parameters imposed by the U.S. political culture nor the reality that they are intertwined, at least not for long. Let's resume our journey by looking at the evolution of U.S. federalism.

---

[9] E. E. Schattschneider, *The Semi-Sovereign People: A Realist's View of Democracy in America* (Hinesdale, IL: Dryden, 1975), 135–138.

CHAPTER **5**

U.S. Federalism in Operation

TYPES OF POWER

Back in Chapter 1, federalism was introduced as a theoretical concept. Recall that in federal systems power is shared among the various levels of government, with the specific structures and functions of each set out in that system's "constitution," be it written or unwritten. A logical place to start our discussion of how U.S. federalism actually works would be to look at how political power has actually been shared over the course of our history. A tremendous amount has been written about the evolution of U.S. Federalism, and one basic fact underlies it all:[1]

> *The American federal system has never been static. It has changed radically over the years, as tides of centralization and decentralization have altered the balance of power and the allocation of functions among the different levels of government.*

Most political scientists today discuss that historical development as a contest between "nation-centered" and "state-centered" federalism.[2] We begin our examination of that tug-of-war by distinguishing *six basic types of power* recognized by most political scientists related to the U.S. Constitution:

- *Concurrent Powers* are those that may be exercised by all levels of government. The most basic examples are the powers to tax and borrow money.
- *Denied Powers* are those that all levels, or specific levels, are prohibited from exercising. For example, the Constitution denies both Congress and the States the power to pass "ex post facto laws" (ones that would punish an act that was not illegal when committed) and to grant titles of nobility. It also specifically prohibits Congress from taxing exports and the States from coining money.
- *Enumerated Powers* refers to those directly granted to the national government in the Constitution. This was one of the mechanisms

---

[1] Samuel Beer, "The Future of the States in the Federal System," in Peter Woll, ed., *American Government: Readings and Cases* (Boston: Little Brown, 1982), 92.

[2] Bruce Ackerman, *We the People: Foundations* (Cambridge, MA: Harvard University Press, 1991), 40

used by the Founders to control the power of the new central government. Some key examples are the power to regulate interstate commerce, to coin and regulate the value of money, to declare war, to establish lower courts, and to create the District of Columbia.

- *Implied Powers* have been the most controversial, since they allow the national government to make authoritative decisions that fall outside the expressed powers (concurrent or enumerated ones). The constitutional basis for implied powers is the "necessary and proper clause," supported by two early Supreme Court decisions that are discussed below:

To make all laws which shall be necessary and proper for carrying into execution the foregoing powers, and all other powers vested by this Constitution in the government of the United States, or in any department or officer thereof.

- *Inherent Powers* are powers recognized internationally as authorized to all nation states. They will be discussed under the Presidency.
- *Reserved Powers* have also been controversial, often as the counter argument to claims of implied power for the national government. According to the Tenth Amendment:

The powers not delegated to the United States by the Constitution, nor prohibited by it to the States, are reserved to the States, respectively, or to the people.

THE "TUGOF- WAR" OVER IMPLIED POWERS

Twice so far during our journey the Hamilton—Jefferson dialectic has been used to portray the basic dynamic of American politics. This deals

with dueling visions of U. S. federalism, and gets to the heart of the power question. How much power did the Constitution allocate to the new central government? One of the reasons Hamilton is often cited as a leader of the pro-national faction is his early support for the concept of implied powers. "It is not denied that there are *implied* as well as *express* powers and that the former are as effectually delegated as the latter," he wrote.[3]

McCullough v. Maryland (1819) was actually not the first Supreme Court decision to acknowledge the existence of implied powers, but it is the one usually recognized as having validated the concept because of the "important political issues" involved.[4] Acknowledged as the chief justice who established the Supreme Court as a true check and balance in our system, John Marshall's declaration goes straight to the point:

We admit, as all must admit, that the powers of the governments are limited, and that its limits are not to be transcended. But we think the sound construction of the Constitution must allow to the national legislature that discretion, with respect to the means by which the powers that confers are to be carried into execution, which will enable that body to perform the high duties assigned to it, in a matter most beneficial to the people. Let the end be legitimate, let it be within

---

[3] *The Papers of Alexander Hamilton*, v8, 99, "Final Version of an Opinion on the Constitutionality of a Bank." Biographer Ron Chernow openly states, "He was crafting a rationale for the future exercise of numerous forms of federal power," in *Alexander Hamilton* (New York: Penguin, 2004), 354.

[4] Robert E. Cushman, *Leading Constitutional Decisions* (New York: F. S. Crofts, 1941), 10. He cites *U.S. v. Fisher* (1805) as the first case "in which Marshall himself had given expression to the doctrine" of implied powers.

the scope of the Constitution, and all means which are appropriate, which are plainly adapted to that end, which are not prohibited, but consistent with the letter and spirit of the Constitution, are constitutional.

This "expansive reading of the 'necessary and proper' clause, holding that Congress's Article 1, Section 8 enumerated powers imply unspecified but appropriate powers to carry them out"[5] launched a tug-of-war that continues today. Recall that the first U.S. Congress specifically rejected including the word "expressly" to what became the Tenth Amendment during the debate over the Bill of Rights. Marshall included that fact in the *McCullough* opinion, noting the contrast with the language in the Articles of Confederation. The second case usually acknowledged as solidifying the concept of implied powers actually dealt with interpreting the interstate commerce clause. In *Gibbons v. Ogden* (1824), the Supreme Court again applied an expansive approach to interpreting the Constitution:[6]

It was perhaps the only genuinely popular decision which Marshall ever handed down. It was received with widespread expressions of approval, for it was, as one writer has put it, 'the first great anti-trust decision.' The economic consequences of it in freeing a developing commerce from the shackles of state monopoly can hardly be overestimated; and it established for all time the supremacy of the national government in all matters affecting interstate and foreign commerce.

This tug-of-war over implied powers has taken many twists and turns over the last two and a quarter centuries. The Supreme Court's eventual acquiescence to the New Deal and aggressive exercise of judicial power to break the Civil Rights deadlock and make Civil Liberties meaningful after World War II clearly reflected a nation-centered view of U.S. federalism. Chief Justice Warren Burger (1969–1986) began to move the Court toward the state-centered view, and under Chief Justice William Rehnquist (1986–2005), the Court "clearly and undeniably positioned itself on the side of the states in most conflicts with the national government."[7] This included several decisions that "substantially narrowed Congress' authority to legislate in the name of regulating interstate commerce."[8]

Three examples clearly illustrate the Court's embrace of states' rights. *U.S. v. Lopez* (1995)[9] dealt with Congress's attempt to establish "Gun Free School Zones," which the Supreme Court overturned, ruling that it cannot stretch the interstate commerce clause to mean anything it wants it to mean. The *Lopez* case represents the end of an arc of expansive readings of the clause that began with the *Gibbons*[10] case about 170 years earlier. In *Printz v. U.S.* (1997),[11] the issue was whether Congress could order local law enforcement officials to conduct checks on prospective gun purchasers. The decision was that state or local officials cannot be ordered to act by the national government on its behalf,

---

[5] Cal Jillson, *American Government: Political Development and Institutional Change*, 5th ed. (New York: Routledge, 1999), 59.
[6] Cushman (see Note 2), 275.

[7] Ann O'M. Bowman and Richard C. Kearny, *State and Local Government*, 7th ed. (Boston: Houghton Mifflin, 2008), 36
[8] "The Rehnquist Court, 1986-2005," The Supreme Court Historical Society, http://www.supremecourthistory.org/history-of-the-court.
[9] 514 U.S. 549.
[10] 22 U.S. 1 (1824).
[11] 521 U.S. 898 (1997).

establishing a clear limit to implied powers. The *Kelo v. City of New London* (2005)[12] decision in essence authorized municipal officials to override basic property rights subject only to state government restrictions.

Under Chief Justice John Roberts's leadership, the Court has continued this trend, earning the label "Most Conservative in Decades."[13] Of course, the evolution of U.S. federalism has involved much more than court decisions. The nation versus state-centered federalism tug-of-war involved all operational aspects of the U.S. political system over the last 225 years, as will be illustrated by highlights presented throughout the remainder of our journey. Different political scientists and historians have offered a variety of "eras" or "stages" in the history of the U.S. Federal Republic. The following list of basic stages was culled from a range of sources encountered over the years, and attempts to represent the general consensus of the field (although some scholars will certainly disagree).

BASIC STAGES IN THE EVOLUTION OF U.S. FEDERALISM

Dual Federalism I (1787–1860): The national and state governments were envisioned as having separate and distinct functions, and Morton Grodzin's "layer cake" metaphor[14] has often been used to describe it. The tug-of-war began

almost immediately, however, over economic issues such as whether there should be a national bank and which level of government should fund "internal improvements" (public works). As new national and international issues (notably the Mexican War) arose that the national government had to deal with, its power slowly expanded in piecemeal fashion. Slavery was, of course, the great challenge that the U.S. Federal Republic tried very hard to finesse through a series of political compromises during its early existence, but in the end it could not. This failure led to the operational breakdown of U.S. federalism.

Civil War (1860–1865): While the policy issue was clearly slavery, the underlying legal issue of our Civil War was federalism. Can states choose to ignore constitutionally adopted national policies? The champion of the South, John C. Calhoun, forcefully argued that they could since the Constitution was a "compact" negotiated among the states. Although the Civil War did validate the basic supremacy of the national government, this state-centered view of federalism significantly impacted the evolution of the U.S. Federal Republic, and continues to do so today.

Dual Federalism II (1865–1932): The involvement of the national government in public issues continued to expand, often in response to international and economic crises, but the nature of the relationship between citizens and government was clearly distinct with respect to the national and state/local levels. Our rise as an international power, most notably our entry into and victory in World War I, solidified the power of the national government. States' rights still held powerful sway in legal and political circles,

---

[12] 545 U.S. 469 (2005).
[13] Adam Liptak, "Roberts' Court Most Conservative In Decades," http://www.nytimes.com/2010/07/25/us/25roberts.html?pagewanted=all.
[14] Originally presented, I believe, in *The Federal System* (1960).

however, and "Congress did little to regulate state and local affairs until the Great Depression seemed to demand change in the broad character and basic structure of American federalism."[15]

Cooperative Federalism (1933–1964): President Franklin Roosevelt's "New Deal" policies for dealing with the Great Depression involved creating partnerships among national, state and local governments to fend off economic (and political?) collapse. The use of national grant programs to implement public policies became the norm. As more and more connections developed among different governments across all levels, the system became like a "marble cake." Distinctive levels of authority became blurred.

Creative Federalism (1964–1968): President Lyndon Johnson initiated a national "War on Poverty" to attack the most serious social problems facing the nation. It included the creation of over 200 new grant programs, and several involved funding local projects directly from Washington, DC, which reignited the "nation versus state-centered" federalism debate. This also generated a backlash when local community projects would be approved without the knowledge of state or county officials. A built-in review process was established[16] that mitigated some of that resentment. As the western states grew, federal constraints based on the national government's control of much of the land became perceived as more stifling. The Southern states also began their Civil Rights transition, which would reshape their political landscapes.

New Federalism (1968–2000): President Richard Nixon began the process of returning power in the form of decision-making authority regarding the use of federal grant funds to the states through a general revenue sharing program and the use of block grants (more on this later). Under Presidents Gerald Ford, Jimmy Carter, Ronald Reagan, George H.W. Bush, and Bill Clinton, this reversal of the flow of power continued, and was reinforced by the series of Supreme Court decisions noted above. The election of a Republican majority to the House of Representatives in 1994 launched the peak of New Federalism, "The Devolution Revolution,"[17] which was also marked by a surge of deregulation of business and industry.

Twenty-first Century Federalism: President George W. Bush was elected in 2000 on a platform of continuing New Federalism, but he directed a major expansion of national government involvement in state government operations and citizens' lives due to "homeland security" concerns ignited by the 9/11 terrorist attack, including initiating a national incursion into K-12 education. He also accelerated the deregulation of business and industry begun under New Federalism, contributing to the "Great Recession" of 2008. The first analyses of President Barack Obama's approach to federalism portray him using a "hybrid model" of "nuanced federalism"

---

[15] Jillson (see Note 5), 60.
[16] This author recalls scrambling to get timely "A-95" (OMB Circular) clearances for various HUD projects.

[17] See, for example, Chung-Lae Cho and Deil S. Wright, "The Devolution Revolution in Intergovernmental Relations in the 1990s: Changes in Cooperative and Coercive State–National Relations as Perceived by State Administrators," *Journal of Public Administration Research and Theory*, 14 (4) (2004), 447–468.

characterized by "a very unique mixture of collaborative and coercive strategies in dealing with states and localities."[18]

Undoubtedly, some more descriptive label will supersede "Twenty-first Century Federalism" in the future, after the "smoke" of the new century clears a bit and analysts can evaluate what occurred. A jump in the national debt caused by President Obama's economic stimulus program and health care reform initiative sparked an upwelling of Jeffersonian, "small government" sentiment, embodied by the populist "Tea Party Movement," that led to the recapture of the House of Representatives by Republicans in 2010. An alternative political movement ("Occupy Wall Street") emerged in 2011 promoting aggressive reregulation of business, particularly the finance industry, and more national government action to help those suffering from the recession's effects.

Both of these movements were able to get their issues onto the national policy agenda through organized action and skillful use of the mass media. These successes illustrate the vitality of American democracy, and represent the latest steps in our "dialectical dance" over the role of the national government in our political system. The historical record tells us that crises of this magnitude usually provide the national level with greater leverage to apply in the federalism tug-of-war. While the economy will most likely be the decisive factor in the 2012 election, federalism will be an underlying issue.

INTERGOVERNMENTAL RELATIONS

Very eloquently defined as *the "complex web of relationships that is constantly being respun"*[19] among *the approximately 88,000 government units in the U.S. Federal Republic* by two prominent scholars who specialize in the subject, intergovernmental relations are the operational side of U.S. federalism. That metaphor seems very appropriate, since it captures both the intricacy and the dynamic nature of the process so well. When most people think of federalism, they tend to think in terms of national, state, county, and municipal government. That is, they think "vertically." Even most political scientists are referring to relations between the national and state levels of government when they discuss federalism.

However, one of the major aspects of U.S. federalism is the continuous interaction among governments at the same level. For example, neighboring states, counties, and municipalities are coordinating some operations every day. This is called "Horizontal Federalism," and is an important part of overall intergovernmental relations. One recent work included a discussion of "the international dimension of federalism."[20] Economic competition is no longer merely interstate, but is now global. Environmental and immigration issues invoke both cries for more national action and pleas for state freedom to address special circumstances.

A second point of interest regarding U.S. federalism is the special nature of Native

---

[18] Peter A. Harkness, "What Brand of Federalism Is Next," *Governing* (January 2012), 16–17, quoting Timothy J. Conlan and Paul L. Posner, "Inflection Point? Federalism and the Obama Administration," *Publius*, 41 (3) (2011), 421–446.

[19] Bowman and Kearny, *State and Local Government: In Brief*, 5th ed. (New York: Pearson, 2005), 38.

[20] Larry N. Gerston provides excellent discussions of Horizontal Federalism (Chapter 7) and the international dimension (Chapter 8) in *American Federalism: A Concise Introduction* (Armonk, NY: M. E. Sharpe, 2007).

American tribes as government entities in the United States. Tribes are "semisovereign nations exercising self-government on their reservations . . . under the general authority and supervision of Congress. . . and subject to the federal courts and the U.S. Bill of Rights."[21] Their relationships with state governments are particularly complex, and in some states, this is a serious issue. While this particularly impacts those out West, New York State has recently been battling Native American tribes over cigarette taxes.

The U.S. Constitution includes several provisions that specifically deal with intergovernmental relations and provide the basic legal framework within which they occur. The first three *basic formal methods of intergovernmental relations* come from Article 4; the last from Article 1, Section 10:

- States must recognize the legal actions of other states.
- States must treat visitors basically the same as they treat their own citizens.
- The U.S. Constitution provides for extradition of fugitives between states.
- The interstate compact mechanism is provided for states to work together.

The last is the "most formal" method of horizontal federalism, the interstate compact. These are specifically authorized in the Constitution, but in an indirect manner. States are denied the power to sign agreements with other states—unless Congress approves. Therefore, they are allowed to do so with congressional approval. This serves as an interesting illustration of how formal rulemaking operates at times. Often, specifically identifying prohibited behavior serves as indirect authorization of what

is not prohibited. Some interstate compacts are legal agreements resolving minor disputes, while others represent some of the most ambitious examples of intergovernmental cooperation ever attempted. Originally created to manage their harbor, for example, the Port Authority of New York and New Jersey now manages all major transportation facilities (including all airports, bridges and tunnels) for the entire New York City metropolitan region.

Informal intergovernmental relations can be something as simple as officials from neighboring municipalities talking to each other on the phone about some common concern. This *sharing of information* also takes place in more organized ways through professional associations (e.g., League of Municipalities, County Engineers Association, Patrolman's Benevolent Associations). In New Jersey, most emergency response services are provided by primarily volunteer local rescue squads or fire companies. This is possible because a *"mutual aid"* network evolved. Depending on the particular legal framework in each state, mutual aid arrangements may sometimes be formalized, but do not necessarily have to be. Two amazing examples of mutual aid were the responses to the World Trade Center attacks and the Hurricane Katrina aftermath.

Other informal methods used include *joint legal action* (e.g., the national tobacco settlement and the lawsuit by 26 state attorneys-general against "Obamacare"), and *shared service contracts between and among governments*. These contracts can become quite formal, but from the national system perspective they model the interstate compact. Finally, there is *joint political action*, both regular lobbying in Washington by the National Association of Counties, the National

---

[21] Bowman and Kearny (see Note 7), 40.

Governors Association, and others, and special actions like the Streamlined Sales Tax Project, a multistate effort to forge an agreement to share Internet sales tax revenue. This brings us to the most practical aspect of U.S. federalism—money.

GRANTS: THE "LIFEBLOOD" OF U.S. INTERGOVERNMENTAL RELATIONS

Intergovernmental transfers are an important source of revenue for state and local governments. These *intergovernmental transfers, usually money but sometimes involving other assets like land or equipment, are commonly called grants.* There are different types of grants, and the type of grants being used tells us something very important about intergovernmental relations. Two "variables" used to distinguish types of grants are "recipient discretion" and the "allocation method."[22]

Recall our discussion about politics and public policy. The distribution of grants is clearly an example of "who gets what, when, and how." Authorizing and implementing grant programs are important decision-making processes. Choosing what to fund is the first decision. What policy areas (security, health care, education) should get priority? These are the basic value judgments that public officials must make. Next, what specific activities should be funded? For example, should preventative health care services be emphasized? Mass transit over roads? Decision making permeates the grant process, and who gets to make the final decision about exactly what gets funded is what "discretion" is all about.

When the government providing a grant *narrowly restricts what recipient governments can use the funds for* (i.e., limits their discretion), it is called a *categorical grant program.* When the grant provider *only requires that the funds be used within a broad, functional area* (e.g., community development, K-12 education), and allows recipient governments to choose exactly how to use the funds, it is called a *block grant program.* Block grants were "the principal tool for devolving federal financial and programmatic authority,"[23] and the use and expansion of block grants (often created by consolidating several categorical grant programs) was one of the main features of New Federalism. Recall that the goal of that approach to intergovernmental relations was to reverse the flow of political power back down to the states.

It was precipitated by the explosion of new categorical grant programs under President Johnson, along with the burst of national action on civil rights, the end of a war perceived by many as a failure, and economic turbulence. Richard Nixon was the first president to actively promote block grants and call the approach New Federalism, which is why 1968, the year he was elected, is used herein as the beginning of that stage. During the heart of the "Reagan Revolution," one study of U.S. federalism described it as "far more complex than the founders of our Republic could have foreseen," marked by "tangled fiscal relationships," "extensive administrative and regulatory ties," and "dynamic political interdependencies among elected and appointed officials at all levels of government."[24] The New

---

[22] Bowman and Kearny (see Note 7), 43.

[23] Bowman and Kearny (see Note 7), 39.

[24] Arnold M. Howitt, *Managing Federalism: Studies in Intergovernmental Relations* (Washington, DC: CQ Press, 1984), 1.

Federalism approach eventually succeeded in turning the tide of federal regulation, peaking during the early George W. Bush years.

The second variable used to compare grant systems is the allocation method, the mechanism by which funds are distributed. Two basic approaches are contrasted. *Formula grants allocate funds based on certain conditions*, which are usually measured *using data* that are specified in the authorizing legislation. A simple example would be grants to fund reading improvement programs for first graders being allocated using the latest Census data on how many 5-year-old children each state has. Although this may sound very objective, even scientific, note that the key decisions then become what formula, measures, and data to use. There is usually significant debate surrounding such decisions, with different states, cities, and regional coalitions pushing particular criteria that favor them as legislation and regulations are finalized.

In contrast, the other basic approach is to have *state and local governments (or nonprofit organizations that provide government services)* apply on an individual basis and *compete for grant funds based on the quality of their proposals for using the funds.* These are called *project grants*, because they are awarded based on the strength of the specific, individual projects proposed. From the perspective of federalism, in project grant programs the decision-making authority is retained at the higher level. President Lyndon Johnson favored project grants because national government officials decided what was funded. The "Devolution Revolution" sought to reverse that trend, and succeeded.

So, one very useful way to trace the flow of power between national and state governments is by looking at the grant mechanisms used. This is one of the reasons grants were labeled "the lifeblood" of intergovernmental relations. The basic reason is that the flow of grants among the levels of government (most states provide substantial funding to their local governments) clearly indicates how dynamic the system is. More grants mean more interaction. The prioritization of (i.e., value judgments made about) policy areas can also be traced by looking at grant flows. Budgeting, including grants, is the ultimate policymaking process. Anyone can declare support for "better schools," "better roads," or "better crime control." Until resources are provided in the form of funding authorized and allocated for personnel, equipment, etc., it is all just talk.

KEY ISSUES IN AMERICAN FEDERALISM TODAY

In the ongoing tug-of-war between nation-centered and state-centered federalism, certain key issues stand out. The two that invoke the most debate are *unfunded mandates* and *preemption*. A *mandate* is a requirement imposed by a higher level government that a lower-level of government undertake a specific activity or provide a particular service. Federal mandates tend to draw the most complaints, but state governments often impose mandates on counties, municipalities, school districts, and special districts. Both mandates and *preemption*, when the national government seizes all authority for a given function (like bankruptcy rules in 2006) or sets minimum national standards (called partial preemption), directly remove decision-making authority from the lower level involved. It is understandable, then, why state and local officials dislike them, since no one likes to have political power taken from them.

Mandates are particularly irritating to public officials when no or insufficient funding is provided to carry out imposed requirements. Why? Requiring a state, county, town, or school district to spend money on one activity means it must either raise taxes or reduce other services. A major example of an unfunded mandate was the REAL ID Act of 2005, which imposed national standards for drivers' licenses that cost states billions to meet and is still being contested. Congress actually attempted to address the unfunded mandates issue back in 1995, but the effort has proven to be toothless. The National Conference of State Legislatures maintains a website that tracks unfunded mandates on state governments during the previous five fiscal years;[25] their recent figures have been in the hundreds of billions, but it should be noted that they use a broad definition of unfunded mandate.

The use of unfunded mandates and preemption by the national government in recent years has expanded. The expansion of national government involvement in health insurance management will be one of the major areas of contention as twenty-first-century U.S. federalism evolves. The states will continue to resist national intrusion into their decision-making authority, while many of them, ironically, expand unfunded mandates and preemption with respect to their local governments. These are ongoing tugs-of-war that will never end.

Probably the most underestimated problem in the U.S. political system today is the *complexity of our decision-making structure*. While most Americans are aware of the fact that we live under multiple layers of government, they do not realize how complex that web of governments has become. Figure 5-1 illustrates that some of us live under as many as *ten* levels! Many condominium owners do not think of their property owners' associations as "governments," but they are the authoritative decision-making structures that set and spend our fees and deal with our common issues.[26]

The United States is grappling with the cost of government like it never has before, and this complexity will need to be addressed. With changing technology, consolidation of government services will become technically easier as the twenty-first century unfolds, but will Americans be ready to relinquish decision-making authority to larger entities? Sound familiar? That is the issue that Americans have been dealing with since they chose "self-government" two and a quarter centuries ago. Those battles will be fought primarily at the state and local levels, and along with the impacts of globalization, will help to shape the evolution U.S. federalism in the twenty-first century. Will it survive?

WHAT MAKES U.S. FEDERALISM WORK?

The secret to the success of U.S. federalism has been its dynamic nature, its ability to adapt to changing circumstances, its resilience.[27] In the far future one of the key things the United States will be remembered for is the invention and development of modern federalism as a form of government. A wide-ranging and extremely thorough theoretical

---

[25] http://www.ncsl.org/standcomm/scbudg/manmon.htm.

[26] Bowman and Kearny (see Note 7), 325–326.
[27] Jenna Bednar, *The Robust Federation: Principles of Design* (New York: Cambridge University Press, 2009).

work on federalism recently identified eight characteristics of successful federations. To design a "robust" federation, one must include as many built-in safeguards as possible that are arrayed to achieve three design goals: redundancy, complementarity, and coverage. The U.S. Federal Republic rebounded from its breakdown in the early 1860s, and over the last 150 years developed five types of effective safeguards:

- Intergovernmental Competition/Retaliation (U.S. federalism as it evolved)
- Structural (The Madisonian Model: Separation of Powers plus Checks and Balances)

- Popular (competitive elections, public opinion, and interest articulation)
- Political (especially interest aggregation through an integrated party system)
- Legal (effective judicial review supported by popular and structural safeguards)

We will return to this concept of the "robust" federation in our Conclusion, using it as a framework to highlight some key points about the U.S. political system. Each type of safeguard and the three goals will be discussed individually, along with how they work together to make a political system adaptive and resilient.

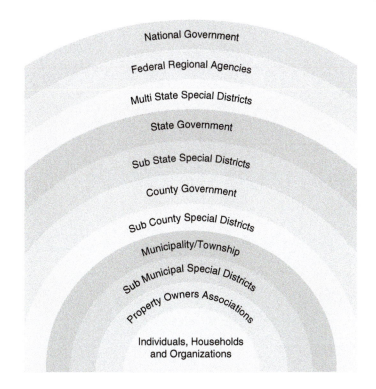

FIGURE 5-1: The Multiple Layers of Government in the U.S.

CHAPTER **6**

The U.S. Congress

KEY FACTS AND FUNCTIONS

We begin looking at how the U.S. Congress operates by considering two key facts. First, Congress was clearly *intended to be the most powerful branch* by the Founders. It is no coincidence that the first article of the Constitution deals with the legislative branch and makes up about half of the original document. Legislatures were the only government bodies that had presumptive legitimacy to most Americans at that time. Congress was given many enumerated powers, the "necessary and proper clause," and the neglected but important "all other powers" clause. To this political scientist, the three together provide Congress a basis for claiming the authority to draw upon *all* power vested anywhere in the national government by the Constitution. The scope of its decision-making authority is extremely broad, but every application of that power is subject, of course, to the executive veto, judicial review, and other safeguards.

The second key fact is *bicameralism*, the division of our national legislature into two distinct chambers. Its specific composition embodies "The Great Compromise" on representation that was the cornerstone of the Constitution of 1787. The large states benefited from the population-based House, while the distinctive nature of our union as an aggregation of states was maintained in the Senate, satisfying the smaller states. Bicameralism also serves as a marvelous built-in "check" by providing a mandatory "second look" at every legislative decision. By providing an additional forum for elected representatives of the people, the bicameral nature of Congress provides a redundant safeguard for the democratic quality of our republic. In addition to reflecting the new "federal" approach, Congress was designed to serve different constituencies:

- The U.S. House of Representatives has always been directly elected by the people of specific districts so that their local community views would be represented. After the official census is completed every ten years, the 435 "seats" are reapportioned among the states to reflect population shifts, maintaining a relative balance of power among local communities within states and across the U.S. population as a whole. The official organization chart of the House is presented in Figure 6-1.

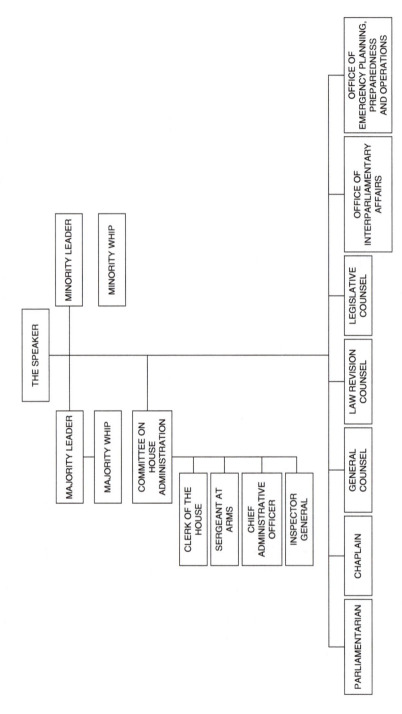

FIGURE 6-1: U.S. House of Representatives Organization Chart

The United States Government Manual 2009/2010 (Washington, DC: U.S. Government Printing Office, 2009), 27.

- The Senate was originally selected by the state legislatures to represent states' elites; not until the Seventeenth Amendment was ratified in the early twentieth century (one of the goals of the Progressive Movement) did U.S. Senators face direct election involving statewide races. Today, U.S. Senators are expected to represent statewide interests, which can be very wide-ranging. The official organization chart of the Senate is presented in Figure 6-2.

FOUR BASIC FUNCTIONS

Congress performs four basic functions: policymaking, representation, oversight, and constituent service. Each of these functions will be discussed individually:

- *Policymaking:* There are two key aspects to public policy making, *lawmaking and allocating a community's limited public resources,* most directly manifested in the various aspects of the budgeting process. These cover the very core of politics, being authoritative decision making over who gets and pays for what, when, and how.

Most lawmaking is actually amending existing laws (tax codes, criminal codes) and involves an array of formal procedures.[1] The formal process of lawmaking involves a series of steps that unfold at times in parallel fashion, but other times in sequential fashion or some combination of the two. The basic steps outlined in Figure 6-3 must be completed in each chamber, except that only the House uses a Rules Committee to set the parameters for floor debate. The importance of committees will be elaborated below, and the House Rules Committee is one of the most important of them. As the larger chamber that must deal with a much longer and more detailed menu of potential and actual demands from the public, the House requires this extra control mechanism.

Recall that the first stage in the policymaking process was agenda setting. The quickest way onto the congressional agenda is to get the attention of one of the leaders of Congress. One of the notable informal changes that came about in twentieth century U.S. politics was the shift to chief executives proposing annual legislative agendas. Issue networks compete for a mere mention in a president's State of the Union Address, which is another path to the congressional agenda. A third basic approach is to gain the attention of a fairly large number of members. For a proposal to receive meaningful consideration, some kind of majority coalition supporting it needs to take shape among the various interests and issue networks. At the very least, the proposal must not draw active opposition from any issue network.

It is not unusual for a Representative or Senator to draft and introduce a bill knowing that it will never get beyond the early steps of the legislative process in order to fulfill a campaign promise or respond to requests from constituents or lobbyists representing interests important in their district or state. This is called "symbolic politics," and it serves a purpose. At a minimum, the people feel they have the right to have their "petitions" heard, and even symbolic acknowledgment

---

[1] Both the House and Senate have formal sets of operating rules that they set and amend themselves; see "How Our Laws Are Made," House of Representatives Document 110–49 Revised and Updated July 24, 2007, U.S. Government Printing Office. "Parliamentary procedure" must also be followed; see, for example, Darwin Patnode, *Robert's Rules of Order: The Modern Edition* (New York: Berkley, 1989).

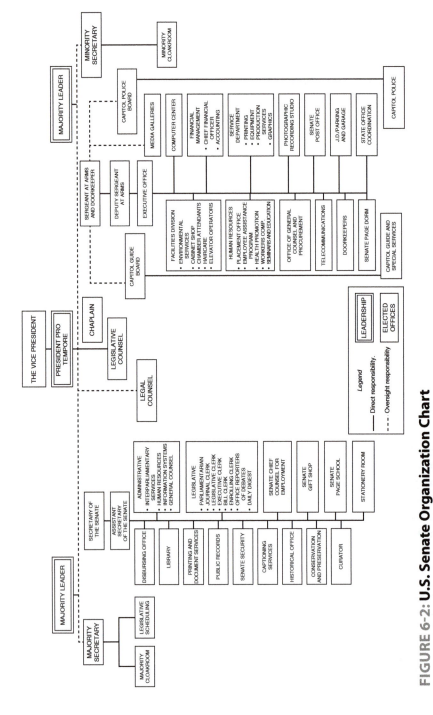

FIGURE 6-2: U.S. Senate Organization Chart

The United States Government Manual 2009/2010 (Washington, DC: U.S. Government Printing Office, 2009), 26.

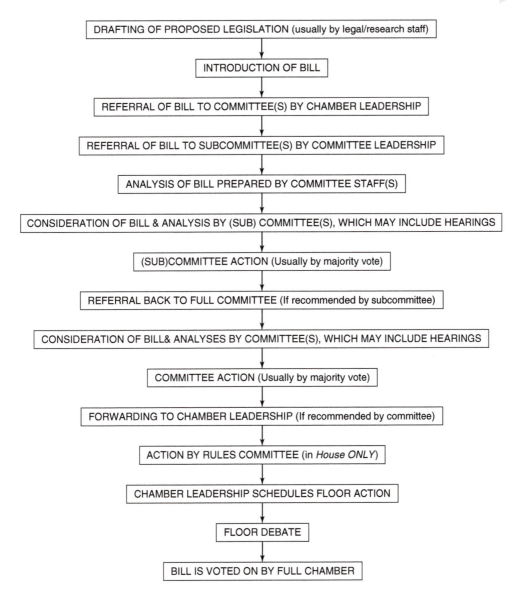

FIGURE 6-3: Basic Steps in the Lawmaking Process

has representational value and can provide entrée into the authoritative decision-making process for an issue or interest group.

To really understand how Congress works, particularly the recent frequent gridlock, one must learn about at least some of the *special tactics* involved in law making. These can be considered semiformal rules in the U.S. political system. One grew out of the basic tradition in the U.S. Senate of unlimited debate. That tradition spawned the *filibuster*, a parliamentary tactic used to control floor debate as a means of preventing a vote on a proposal. It had traditionally been used sparingly as an important mechanism for protecting minority rights in the legislative process, but has been more frequently used in recent Congresses. It should be noted that both political parties have recently increased their use of the filibuster, but the Republicans have clearly adopted it as a regular tactic.

The formal aspect is the procedure for ending debate, which is established by Senate rules. The *cloture* process, which ends floor debate, requires 60 votes, reduced from the original requirement for 67. It also is worth noting the now-accepted custom of triggering a filibuster merely by filing your intention, as opposed to actually conducting unlimited debate. This has certainly facilitated its use. This also illustrates the potential impact of "how" decisions within the overall political process. As you review Figure 6-3, keep in mind our focus on decision making. Consider what choices are being made:

- What words shall be used to express legislative intent?
- Should the bill be introduced in both chambers? If not, which first?
- To which committees will it be referred?
- To which subcommittees will it be referred?

- What kind of staff analysis will be conducted?
- Will hearings be conducted?
- What level of priority will the bill receive?

Among the primary *keys to success* in lawmaking is *coalition building*, as noted earlier. A workable amalgamation of *party support through legislative leaders*, including committee chairs; *executive branch support*, especially from the White House or other top officials, and *support from interest groups/associations* is needed. The study of American politics has long recognized the existence and importance of this core triad structure in public policymaking; they will be discussed in some detail below. The most basic requirement for legislative success is, of course, enough votes at each stage (subcommittee, committee, floor) to keep a bill moving forward. Budgeting, or resource allocation, is a special form of lawmaking that extensively involves elements of the Executive branch.

We will close this overview of the lawmaking function with some final points about Congress's fundamental operations. All bills must be introduced in each chamber by a member; the president cannot introduce a bill directly. In a typical session less than ~5 percent of proposed legislation actually gets signed into law; the other ~95 percent "dies" in committee. The destiny of a bill can easily rest in the committee path chosen for it by a chamber leader. Finally, the House and Senate must reconcile different versions into one final bill to be sent to the president. Both of these topics will be discussed below.

- *Representation*: The second basic function of Congress is voting, speaking and facilitating on behalf of constituents. One of the classic studies of political roles examined representation.[2] Legislators from several states were studied using survey and other data, and this *typology of three legislative roles* (how they thought they should behave, particularly with respect to voting decisions, to best represent their constituents) was developed:

- *Trustee*: A legislator who uses his or her best judgment in making authoritative decisions
- *Delegate*: A legislator who actively reflects his constituents' opinions
- *Politico*: A legislator who acts partly as a delegate and partly as a trustee, depending on the issue being decided, the nature of his or her district, and circumstances. This takes true political skill. Success requires learning to play both roles well and when to play each. One key is distinguishing the issues that are most relevant to your constituents and community.
- *Constituent Service*: This is acting as liaison with government agencies for those directly represented. It often takes the form of casework, in which legislative staff members help constituents solve problems or gain access to programs. Constituent service reinforces both Representation and Oversight.
- *Oversight*: This is monitoring the actions of the other branches, including formal checks and balances (such as overriding presidential vetoes, approving judicial appointments), the basic competition among them, and informal contacts. One of the core functions of Congress is to check whether the policies it has adopted are being implemented as intended. Besides casework, several other

methods are used to evaluate how effectively and efficiently public programs are working. These include annual budget reviews, confirmation of appointments by the Senate, proposed changes to enabling legislation, conducting hearings and investigations (including impeachment in the most extreme cases), and informal coordination among legislative and executive staff members.

KEY OPERATIONAL ASPECTS

Two informal aspects of congressional operations, *party-based leadership* and *committees*, shape how it works. Both play critical roles. Leaders of both chambers are chosen by majority vote from candidates selected through party-based "caucus" (face-to-face) elections. This is why political parties focus on gaining legislative majorities. The top leaders of the Congress of the United States are the Speaker of the House of Representatives and the Senate Majority Leader. They direct the flow of legislation by choosing policy priorities, assigning bills to committees, setting schedules, and brokering compromises. The "leadership" also includes the Minority Leaders of both chambers, committee and subcommittee chairs, and "Whips" (who assist the leaders).

Committees have been called "a defining characteristic of the Congress,"[3] "little legislatures," and "the workhorse of the legislature."[4] There are permanent ones tied to major public policy areas (e.g., agriculture, banking), which

---

[2] John Wahlke et al., *The Legislative System* (New York: John Wiley & Sons, 1962).

[3] Cal Jillson, *American Government: Political Development and Institutional Change*, 6th ed. (New York: Routledge, 2005), 270.
[4] Ann O'M. Bowman and Richard C. Kearny, *State and Local Government: In Brief*, 5th ed. (New York: Pearson, 2012), 129.

leads to specialization by members in particular policy subjects. Congressional committees also anchor the informal structures linking committees and subcommittees, interest groups/associations and executive agencies that attempt to control routine policymaking within specific areas. "Each group of specialists is one of the fabled *iron triangles*—powerful, decentralized, policy-making networks that, in effect, govern federal action in their delimited spheres of influence."[5] They are, however, now more appropriately described as "cozy" since their control has been diminished by their expansion into "issue networks" involving

more interests, along with the opening up of the policy formulation stage by the new technological mass media. Figure 6-4 portrays one of the basic "cozy triangles." This triangle represents mutual support among the three elements. The associations get policies that will benefit their members, the agency gets programs it can proudly administer, and the legislators get support for their reelection. The role of interest groups/associations will be covered in some detail in Chapter 9.

In addition to the permanent, or *Standing*, committees there are three other basic types. *Select* committees are temporary committees

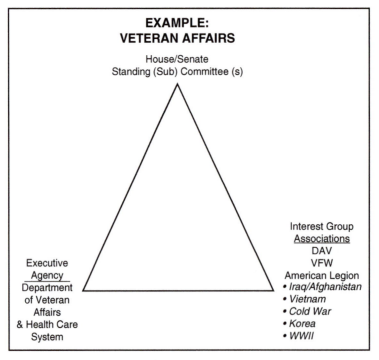

FIGURE 6-4: A Typical "Cozy" Triangle

---

[5] Arnold M. Howitt, *Managing Federalism: Studies in Intergovernmental Relations* (Washington, DC: CQ Press, 1984), 19.

created to review specific policy issues or conduct investigations. *Joint* committees include members of both chambers. Differences between House and Senate versions of a bill must be reconciled before it can be sent to the president; most of the time this is coordinated informally by the leaders. But for a small percentage of bills, a *Conference* committee is appointed. Members of each chamber selected by the leaders work out a compromise version, which is then approved by both chambers.

There are also some specific committees that deserve particular attention. These include all the committees that deal directly with money. *Appropriations* and *Budget* committees allocate specific annual funding levels to each government program in both chambers. The

House Ways and Means Committee originates all tax legislation. The *House Rules* Committee is very powerful, since it sets the specific rules under which bills can be debated and amended on the floor of the House. One of the key differences between the House and the Senate is the need for more rules and controls in the larger chamber that represents a much wider diversity of interests. Tables 6-1 and 6-2 show the committee structure of the 112th Congress.

It was noted above that 95 percent of bills "die in committee." Leaders, including committee chairs, can determine the fate of bills by simply deciding which subcommittee to refer them to. The final intersection is in the reconciliation process. Whether by informal coordination or by appointing the conference committee, the

STANDING:	SPECIAL, SELECT, AND OTHER:
Agriculture, Nutrition, and Forestry	Indian Affairs
Appropriations	Select Committee on Ethics
Armed Services	Select Committee on Intelligence
Banking, Housing, and Urban Affairs	Special Committee on Aging
Budget	
Commerce, Science, and Transportation	
Energy and Natural Resources	
Environment and Public Works	
Finance	
Foreign Relations	
Health, Education, Labor, and Pensions	*Joint*:
Homeland Security and Governmental Affairs	Joint Committee on Printing
Judiciary	Joint Committee on Taxation
Rules and Administration	Joint Committee on the Library
Small Business and Entrepreneurship	Joint Economic Committee
Veterans' Affairs	

TABLE 6-1: U.S. Senate and Joint Committees of the 112th Congress

Agriculture	Intelligence
Appropriations	Judiciary
Armed Services	Natural Resources
Budget	Oversight and Government Reform
Education and the Workforce	Rules
Energy and Commerce	Science, Space, and Technology
Ethics	Small Business
Financial Services	Transportation and Infrastructure
Foreign Affairs	Veterans' Affairs
Homeland Security	Ways and Means
House Administration	

TABLE 6-2: U.S. House Committees of the 112th Congress

leadership controls the finalization of bills for presentation to the president. The combined impact of the committee structure and party-based leadership in Congress clearly illustrates the power of informal adaptation through custom building in the U.S. political system.

FACTORS IN CONGRESSIONAL DECISION MAKING

Given our focus on decision making, it is logical to conclude our overview of congressional operations with a look at factors that influence the policy choices individual representatives make. Among the most common ones are:

- Constituent opinion and personal beliefs (Recall the Representation typology)
- Party and (sub)committee leader recommendations
- Regional and personal colleague recommendations
- Party loyalty and three other "norms" of behavior (discussed below)
- Interest group/association lobbying (examined in Chapter 9)

- Executive agency input/expertise (through the "triangles" and informally)
- Staff input (research, analysis and recommendations) from both committees and specialized congressional staff agencies, most notably the Congressional Research Service and the Congressional Budget Office, usually recognized as providing the best financial projections (see Figure 6-5).

We noted in the introductory remarks to this section that "configuration" significantly impacts political roles, and this is clearly the case with Congress. The stark differences between the House and the Senate with respect to size (435 vs. 100), terms of office (2 years vs. 6 years), and representational focus (local vs. statewide) create very different operating environments. The committee structure and political realities have shaped several congressional "norms," sets of behaviors that Representatives and Senators are expected to follow. They are:

- *Specialization:* All members are expected to specialize and develop expertise in policy areas covered by their assigned committees.

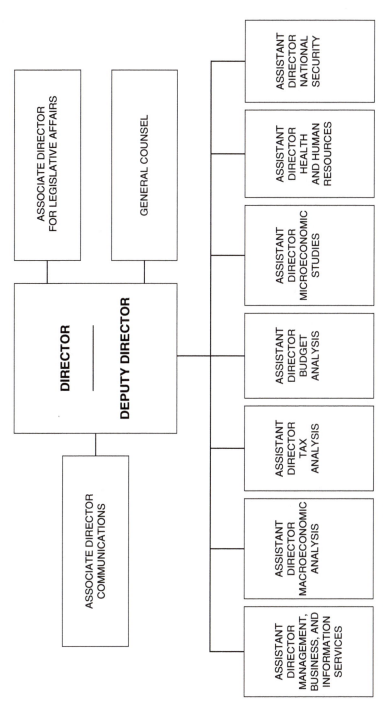

FIGURE 6-5: Congressional Budget Office

The United States Government Manual 2009/2010 (Washington, DC: U.S. Government Printing Office, 2009), 61.

- *Reciprocity:* Members of one committee defer to other committees and the expertise of their members (which reinforces specialization).
- *Seniority:* Usually determines committee chair assignments, but now no longer the exclusive factor; leaders have key input.
- *Honor:* A legislator's word must be his or her personal bond.
- *Consensus-building:* Agreement is the basic goal; policy issues must be addressed.
- *Compromise:* Willingness to negotiate details has been called "the backbone of the legislative process."[6]

So, to truly understand how Congress operates one must know the formal rules, but also take into account the informal adaptations and norms that have shaped, and continue to shape, its authoritative decision-making process.

KEY ASPECTS OF CONGRESSIONAL ELECTIONS

We will conclude our look at Congress by noting several important keys to understanding how they get elected. Until the 1920 Census, Congress kept adding seats to the House of Representatives. Having concluded that 435 members was about the maximum that could work together effectively, the House of Representatives then capped its size at that number. Ever since then, those same 435 seats have been reallocated among the states after each Census.

This is called *reapportionment.* The boundaries of the congressional districts within each state must then be redrawn to reflect any internal population shifts. This is called *redistricting.*

One of the growing issues regarding the U.S. Federal Republic relates directly to these two processes. It did not take long for political party leaders to realize they could benefit from creative redistricting. *Gerrymandering*, the drawing of legislative district boundary lines for the purpose of gaining partisan or factional advantage, is named after Elbridge Gerry, a delegate to the Constitutional Convention and Anti-Federalist who was later elected governor of Massachusetts and vice president. He was one of the first to apply this strategy to promote his party's reelection chances in the early 1800s, and the political cartoon lampooning his efforts became a classic.

This is one specific example of the power of incumbency, moreover. Those who currently hold an office have distinct advantages over challengers in our current electoral system. These include name recognition from ongoing media coverage, a clear fundraising advantage, paid staff, (including local district offices to facilitate constituent casework and public relations), and free postage for official business. The result has been that congressional incumbents get reelected at extremely high rates, which raises questions about the competitiveness of the elections for these important offices. We will return to the topic of competitiveness when we discuss campaigns and elections toward the end of our journey.

---

[6] Bowman and Kearny (see Note 4), 122.

CHAPTER **7**

The Presidency and the Bureaucracy

PRESIDENTIAL ELECTIONS

One of the truly unique aspects of the U.S. Federal Republic is our method of electing our president. Fearing direct election as an invitation to mob rule, and determined to maintain the independence of the three branches, the Founders created the Electoral College. In essence, the United States does not conduct *a* presidential election, but rather a collection of state and district elections. The Electoral College is a mechanism for translating the "Great Compromise" on representation into an election process. Each state is recognized as a distinct political entity, while the realities of population and its shifts are accounted for.

It was noted during our discussion of federalism that it can be undemocratic at times with respect to majority rule. There have been four instances in our history when an individual who did not receive the most popular votes did receive the most electoral votes, most recently in 2000. Some consider this a serious flaw in our democratic process that should be abolished by adopting direct election. This political scientist fears that change could undermine the federal nature of our political system. Converting to direct election by popular vote would severely impact the relationship between the states and the national government.

This does not mean that the Electoral College system cannot be improved. Maine and Nebraska currently allocate their electoral votes based on congressional district results, with the candidate winning the statewide race being awarded the final two. Adopting that system nationwide would better reflect the popular vote, but maintain the integrity of the states as political entities, which are the core of our political system. Changing to direct election would likely hurt the state political parties and political cultures. Small states would become less important as nationwide, media-based campaigns would focus more and more on the large ones. Choosing electors by district certainly seems worth considering, and will be under Elections.

THE PRESIDENCY AS AN INSTITUTION

The Presidency is *NOT* just one person, but an institution, a network of ~7,500 people, including:

- The Executive Office of the President: The White House Office consists of the direct staff whose job it is to coordinate the president's activities and get the information needed to facilitate authoritative decision making to the president in a timely fashion.
- Office of Management and Budget (OMB): The OMB assembles and monitors the annual budget, conducts policy analysis including legislative clearance, and provides in-house management evaluation and assistance. (See Figure 7-1.)
- National Security Council (NSC): The NSC coordinates the development and implementation of national security policy.
- The Cabinet: Fifteen (15) department Secretaries plus the OMB, NSC, and Environmental Protection Agency directors, their deputies, assistants, deputy assistants, and staff provide advice in their particular policy areas.
- Office of the Vice President: The vice president has very little formal power, but recent ones have wielded informal power based on roles assigned to them by the president. The basic role of the office and the staff is supporting the president. The vice president can serve as "Acting President" under the Twenty-fifth Amendment, and succeeds the president, if that becomes necessary.

THE ROLES OF THE PRESIDENT

The president fills a variety of roles in the U.S. political system. In contrast to most other democratic systems at present, the United States has an individual officeholder fulfill *both the governing and ceremonial functions of the Executive branch*. Many others have a "dual executive" with separate offices and individuals performing these basic functions. The specific roles that a U.S. president is expected to perform include:[1]

1. *Chief Executive/Head of Government*: The president is the chief executive officer of a complex, nationwide organizational network with about two million employees.
2. *Commander-in-Chief of the U.S. military* with the power to make war, but the expectation that peace will be preserved if it all possible.
3. *Head of State*: As the symbolic leader of our nation, the president represents the United States to the rest of the world and is expected to perform certain ceremonial duties, including "chief comforter" in times of national tragedy.
4. *Chief Diplomat*: The president is expected to direct, and personally lead when necessary, our nation's international relations efforts. This places him or her in the role of world leader at times. It should be noted that presidents have the authority to conclude executive agreements with other nations and international organizations that do not require Senate ratification, but these expire at the end of his or her term.

---

[1] This list is derived from the classic work by Clinton Rossiter, *The American Presidency* (New York: Mentor, 1960), reissued by John Hopkins University Press in 1987.

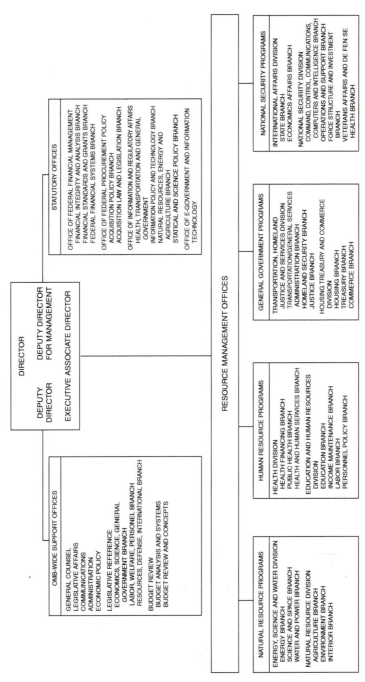

FIGURE 7-1 OFFICE OF MANAGEMENT AND BUDGET

The United States Government Manual 2009/2010 (Washington, DC: U. S. Government Printing Office, 2009), 93.

5. *Chief Policymaker:* The president is expected to direct the domestic policy agenda using a range of activities. The president:
   - Presents a policy agenda in the annual State of the Union message
   - Prepares and submits an annual budget (through OMB)
   - Appoints key personnel to pursue his or her agenda
   - Proposes and promotes legislation; uses or threatens to use the veto power
   - Issues Executive Orders and regulations covering all Executive branch units
   - Sets the regulatory tone and proposes changes to regulations

6. *Chief of National Political Party:* The president is expected to assist his or her party in winning elections by fundraising and personally supporting candidates, and to maintain and build the party through patronage appointments. Patronage is an important part of representative democracy also. It is how a newly elected public executive gets to take control of the bureaucracy and "reset" the direction and tone of public policymaking.

PRESIDENTIAL POWERS

How does the president accomplish all of this? The skillful use of a combination of formal and informal powers is needed. Three types of *formal powers* are usually identified with the Presidency:

1. *Constitutional Powers:* The Constitution specifically authorizes the president to perform the first four roles listed above, along with giving the office the power to veto congressional bills and issue pardons and reprieves.

2. *Statutory:* Almost every law enacted by Congress creates additional responsibilities for the Executive branch or modifies existing responsibilities, which usually involves granting additional authority to the president.

3. *Inherent:* Constitutional and statutory powers are often called "expressed" powers. A third type of power is acknowledged internationally. Rooted in the traditional rights of monarchs, certain powers inherent in the position of being the "sovereign" of a nation are recognized. These include the power to deploy the military resources of that nation, especially in times of emergency, and they are defined through practice rather than through law. This is the basis for "war powers" and "emergency powers" for the president.

To be truly successful, however, an individual must develop and skillfully use a number of *informal powers*:

1. *Leadership Skills:* Applied intelligence, personal charm, and outstanding communication skills are among the basic requirements for a successful leader. "The power to lead is the power to persuade" is the classic statement about presidential leadership, and that remains true today.[2]

2. *Political Skills:* Understanding the structure and operation of the political system, knowing the key people involved, plus good planning and timing are needed to get things done.

---

[2] Richard Neustadt, *Presidential Power and the Modern Presidents* (New York: Free Press, 1990), Chapter 3. The original version was written for President Kennedy and published in 1960.

3. *Public Support*: Molding public opinion to support his or her policies and programs is critical today, requiring excellent use of the mass media.

4. *Party Support*: The president does not control even his or her own party in the Congress, so this is needed to get legislation passed, appointments approved, and to assist with gaining public support.

The truly successful president must adeptly maneuver through the domestic and international political landscape using his or her personal skills and formal powers in just the right combinations at just the right times. We seem to expect consistent perfection. This is one reason why, at any point in time in today's world, a sizable portion of the people will not think the president is doing a good job. No one can match our hopes.

THE U.S. BUREAUCRACY

The first role for the president noted above is "Head of Government." Whatever policies a president promotes, the public does expect its government to be well run. Americans tend to express a rather low opinion of government bureaucracies, due in large measure to their basic antipathy toward government in general. Why do we even need bureaucracies? Why were they created? Recall that governments were originally created by force and families, and the authoritative decision-making process was heavily impacted by personal politics and favoritism. At one point in history, bureaucracy was actually considered the height of reform.

As people began to expect more and more from their governments, bureaucracy flourished. Bureaucracies were created to provide and manage the growing array of services demanded by growing populations. To most people, bureaucracy is at best

a necessary evil. The goal of an ideal bureaucracy is to provide continuous (24/7), impartial, efficient (using economies of scale and coordination), and clearly documented (for accountability purposes) implementation of public policy. The bureaucratic regulations that so many of us hate were created to provide a basic level of fairness. While the realities of human and political relationships make "equal" treatment unachievable, having everyone at least technically subject to the same procedures provides an evenhanded approach to governing.

What is a bureaucracy? In general terms, a bureaucracy is an organization marked by hierarchy, centralized decision making, and task specialization. Modern government bureaucracies also emphasize appointment, retention, and promotion of employees based on preset qualifications and procedures, and record-keeping. These are often referred to as "civil service" or "merit" systems. As with all aspects of life, the telecommunications revolution is seriously impacting organizational structure. Traditional bureaucracies are changing into less hierarchical structures and e-government is changing service delivery, but bureaucracy remains an important characteristic of public administration in the U.S. Federal Republic.

The U.S. bureaucracy is the set of all national administrative agencies and their workers, and it is important to note the federal nature of the overall government workforce in the United States. In our intertwined political system, ~60 percent of the total 20-plus million are local government employees, and over 20 percent are state employees. Another characteristic worth noting is the *five (5) different types of organizations* that have been created for our national government. The different types reflect the particular political circumstances surrounding their establishment and role. Examples of organization charts for each type have been provided as Figures 7-2 thru 7-6:

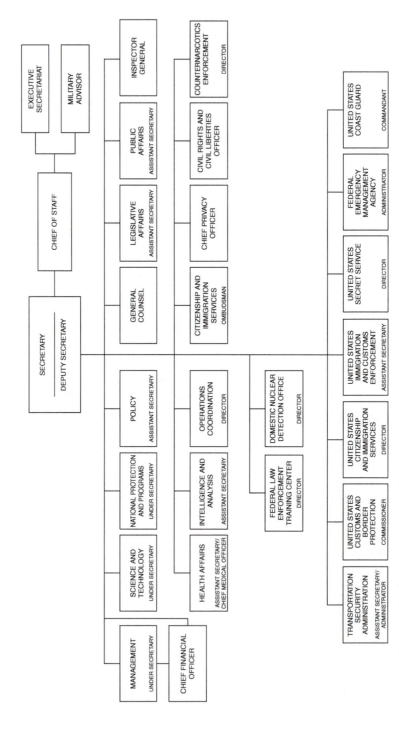

FIGURES 7-2 The Department of Homeland Security

The United States Government Manual 2009/2010 (Washington, DC: U. S. Government Printing Office, 2009), 227.

- *15 Cabinet Departments* (see Table 7-1) *carry out basic public policy functions and report directly to the president* through their appointed Secretaries. Figure 7-2 illustrates the organization of the Department of Homeland Security, the newest and largest one.
- *Independent Executive Agencies* were created as separate agencies to *carry out specific functions.* "The mission of the National Aeronautics and Space Administration," for example (Figure 7-3), "is to pioneer the future in space exploration, scientific discovery, and aeronautics research."[3] These specific tasks are reflected in its organization chart and limited locations.

| Department of Agriculture |
| Department of Commerce |
| Department of Defense |
| Department of Education |
| Department of Energy |
| Department of Health and Human Services |
| Department of Homeland Security |
| Department of Housing and Urban Development |
| Department of Interior |
| Department of Justice |
| Department of Labor |
| Department of State |
| Department of Transportation |
| Department of Treasury |
| Department of Veterans Affairs |

TABLE 7-1: The Cabinet Departments of the U.S. National Bureaucracy

---

[3] *The United States Government Manual 2009/2010* (Washington, DC: U. S. Government Printing Office, 2009), 426.

- *Government Corporations* were created since they primarily generate their own revenue, and could therefore be administered more like business corporations. The U.S. Postal Service (Figure 7-4) was converted from a cabinet department into a government corporation in 1970 after its workforce unionized following a bruising strike. It was succeeding in becoming a self-sustaining operation until the Internet revolutionized the mass communication process.
- *Independent Regulatory Agencies* are represented by the Securities and Exchange Commission (Figure 7-5), which "administers Federal securities laws." The extent of the authority they are given is discussed below, along with their peculiar structural composition. Note how the agency has regional offices in key cities covering the entire country.
- A range of *advisory boards, committees, and commissions* that provide policy recommendations. These range from major ones, like the National Transportation Safety Board (Figure 7-6) which investigates accidents, to minor ones like the Citizens' Stamp Advisory Committee, which chooses images for postage stamps.

Our independent regulatory agencies most clearly illustrate how politics is reflected in the formal structuring of government organizations. Basically they are bipartisan boards with members appointed to terms that overlap those of the president to prevent one from quickly packing them with supporters. This reflects the sensitivity of Congress to the impact that these agencies can have, since they are given rulemaking, rule application, and administrative adjudication authority over significant aspects of our society.

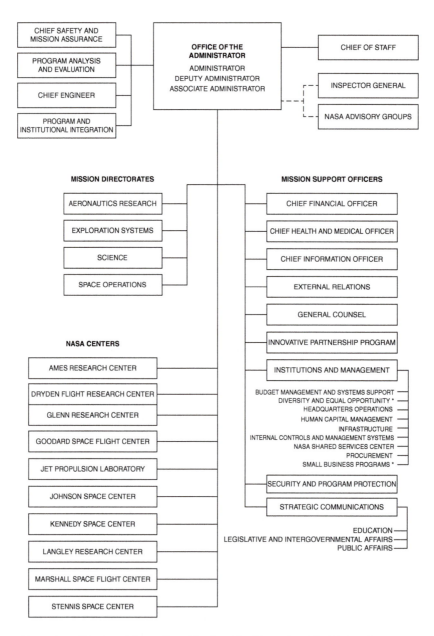

FIGURES 7-3: **National Aeronautics and Space Administration**

The United States Government Manual 2009/2010 (Washington, DC: U. S. Government Printing Office, 2009), 427.

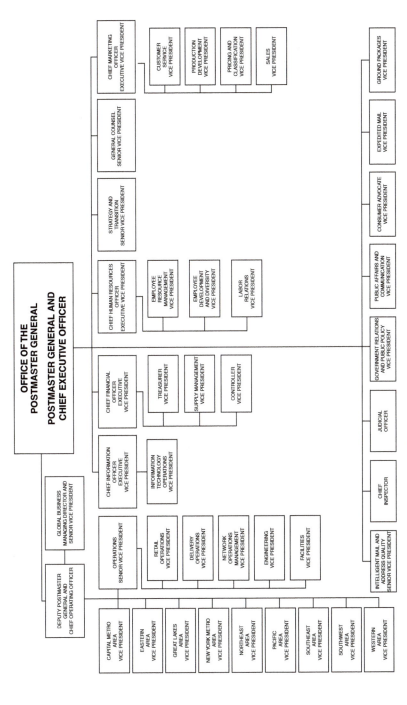

FIGURES 7-4: United States Postal Service

The United States Government Manual 2009/2010 (Washington, DC: U. S. Government Printing Office, 2009), 537.

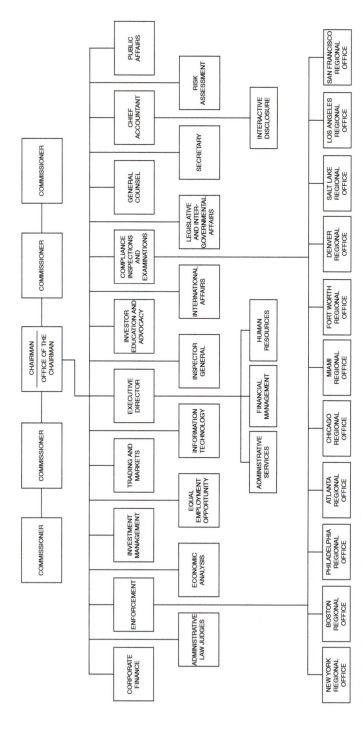

FIGURES 7-5: **Securities and Exchange Commission**

The United States Government Manual 2009/2010 (Washington, DC: U. S. Government Printing Office, 2009), 498.

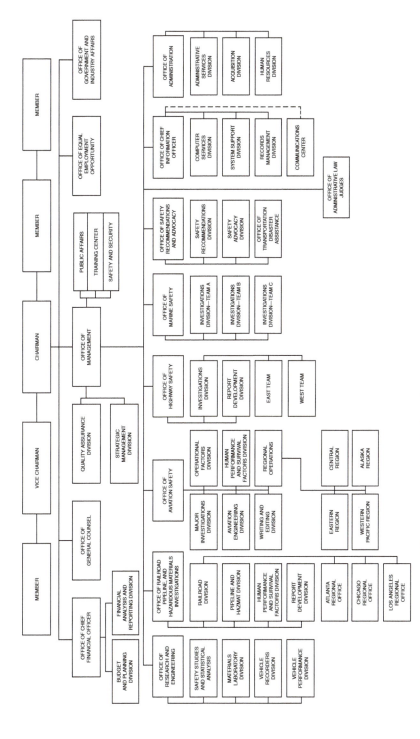

FIGURES 7-6: National Transportation Safety Board

The United States Government Manual 2009/2010 (Washington, DC: U.S. Government Printing Office, 2009), 467.

While the ~1,200 advisory bodies do not have the same impact, they do provide direct access to policymakers, and are very important to interest groups/associations.

The Executive branch consists of ~2.5 million civilians and ~1.5 uniformed military personnel. Employee hiring, advancement, and pay are based on preset Civil Service rules that emphasize "merit criteria," particularly specialized knowledge, skills, and experience. While patronage (rewarding party or campaign supporters) plays a direct role in higher-level appointments, its primary impact at lower levels takes the form of assistance provided in dealing with the Civil Service system by congressional staff. Under this system, the U.S. bureaucracy has become progressively more representative of the U.S. population with respect to race/ethnicity and gender.

BUREAUCRATIC POWER

Do bureaucrats make public policy? The standard view is that government workers should merely implement the policies established by elected officials. That is an oversimplification of reality, however. Policy implementation includes formulating regulations, applying them, and some kind of review and appeal process. These all involve authoritative decision making, rendering them all forms of public policymaking within our conceptual framework. Most analysts view this as a reflection of the complexity of modern public issues, but one author labeled it the "latitude problem."[4] Laws formulated in general terms effectively increase the range of

authority granted to bureaucrats. But specification is needed to maintain a fair, evenhanded approach in implementing public policies. For example, it is likely that many readers are receiving some federal financial aid. Some specific regulations had to be created to make these programs work. How many credits qualify someone as a full-time student? When do you include or exclude parents' income to determine eligibility?

This is the realm of "rulemaking," and the 1946 Administrative Procedures Act (APA) established mandatory processes and standards for rationality and fairness in bureaucratic rulemaking and administrative adjudication. A "rule means the whole or part of an agency statement of general or particular applicability and future affect designed to implement, interpret, or prescribe law or policy." The rulemaking task is given to the bureaucracy for several reasons. Legislators do not usually have sufficient specific expertise or understand the varied conditions that the rules will need to work in. If Congress tried to prepare specific regulations, it would have no time left for major policy decisions. An additional reality is that political bargaining among legislators and lobbyists often results in vague lawmaking.

In addition to "administrative discretion" (the range of authority to make, interpret and adjudicate regulations) and political alliances linking interest group/association and congressional support (recall the "iron/cozy triangles"), expertise based on specialized and experiential knowledge is a source of bureaucratic power. "Operational knowledge" is a term this political scientist applies only to knowledge acquired by direct experience. It connotes having both the technical administrative skill (e.g., accounting) needed for a task, combined with particular knowledge of an organization, community, and

---

[4] Kenneth Walsh, "Bureaucrats: At the Cutting Edge of Power," *U.S. News & World Report*, 1/28/85, 51: "Loosely drawn laws have given administrators immense latitude in making decisions affecting millions of Americans."

political environment that facilitates accomplishment of that task. Bureaucrats with operational knowledge will, at times, be called upon to help formulate public policy in their area of expertise, stretching their policymaking role.

There are controls, however, on bureaucratic policymaking. First, there are legal controls on the bureaucracy. The APA requires that all proposed regulations must be published in advance and are subject to public comment and congressional scrutiny and veto. The other "checks and balances" on the U.S. bureaucracy are:

- *Presidential Oversight* via appointees, procedural authority (Executive Orders) and through the OMB and White House Office staffs
- *Congressional Oversight* by the standing committees and through the use of specialized staffs (General Accountability Office, Congressional Budget Office)
- *Judicial Oversight* via court tests that impose judicial review for due process (procedural fairness and rationality) and constitutionality

- *Public Oversight* via casework and interest group/association activities
- *Media Oversight* via ongoing scrutiny for news and scandal seeking

THE FUTURE OF THE EXECUTIVE BRANCH

The adaptability of the U.S. political system has been emphasized throughout our journey. This is clearly evident in the evolution of the Presidency, which one author described as the "office that never stops changing."[5] That flexibility has allowed some presidents (Lincoln, both Roosevelts, Reagan) to build up the institution and others (Nixon, Clinton) to damage it. It is only in retrospect that an individual president's success or failure can truly be judged, however. The U.S. bureaucracy is just beginning to adapt to the telecommunications revolution, which could change the very nature of citizen interaction with government. That is the development citizens should most carefully watch as the twenty-first century unfolds.

---

[5] Joseph P. Shapiro, *U.S. News & World Report,* 1/28/85, 40.

CHAPTER **8**

The Judiciary

THE ROLES OF THE COURTS

From the beginning of our journey we have discussed politics as competition among the various segments of any community. The reality of human nature is that competition will eventually generate conflict. This is why we need courts. Since government's most basic responsibility is maintaining order, this conflict must be contained. The general role of courts is "to serve as an arena in which controlled conflict can take place."[1] They evolved as such based on the commonsense notion that when two parties have a conflict that they cannot resolve, one clearly rational approach is to bring in an impartial third party to help or intervene.[2]

Most readers will recall from their American history studies that our Founders wanted to create "a government of laws, not men." Our preference for putting legal matters in writing reaches

back to the Mayflower Compact, and was epitomized by the insistence on a written constitution from the very creation of our nation. Add to this focus on written law the fact that U.S. courts have had to deal with the numerous issues that naturally arise from serving a large, culturally diverse community. This combination of conditions has shaped the U.S. court system into the most powerful one in the world. In fulfilling their general role, our courts play several *specific roles*:

- *To administer justice:* In addition to providing a means for individuals, businesses, and other organizations to resolve disputes, they also decide whether or not there have been violations of law or regulations and determine whether or not laws and regulations meet U.S. constitutional standards.[3]
- *To oversee the other two branches:* Recall that the essence of the separation of powers within government is to provide a built-in

---

[1] Gregory S. Mahler, *Comparative Politics: An Institutional and Cross-National Approach* (Upper Saddle River, NJ: Pearson, 2008), 139.
[2] Martin Shapiro, *Courts: A Comparative and Political Analysis* (Chicago: University of Chicago Press, 1981), 1.

[3] Barbara W. Prabhu, ed., *Spotlight on New Jersey Government*, 6th ed. (New Brunswick, NJ: Rutgers University Press, 1992), 285. This book was sponsored by the League of Women Voters of New Jersey Education Fund.

"check and balance" of the branches by having each oversee the other two. This was formalized in the U.S. political system by the *Marbury v. Madison* (1803)[4] ruling establishing judicial review (defined below), particularly with respect to constitutionality.

- *To make public policy:* Although some disagree that they should, judicial review thrusts the courts into the policy making arena. They are the "referees" in our political system, and while most cases simply apply the law, some of their rulings will inevitably modify legislative and executive decisions, especially when constitutional issues are involved.

PUBLIC POLICYMAKING AND THE COURTS

How the courts fit into the public policymaking process is one of the ongoing great debates in American political science. Within the conceptual framework being used for this analysis, the answer to the question of whether or not courts make public policy is clearly, "Yes." U.S. courts are certainly involved in authoritative decision making. Keeping in mind that a variety of alternative frameworks are also used in the field, those readers who continue their studies will encounter serious, even vehement, opposition to that answer. A few basic concepts are at the core of this debate.

"Judicial review" is the power courts have in the United States to hold either part or all of any law or other official government action to be unenforceable because it is in direct conflict with the Constitution or with another valid higher

level (e.g., national over state) law that meets all constitutional standards. There is also a hierarchy within the basic structure of American law. The U.S. Constitution is our fundamental law, the highest source of authority for community decisions in our political system. Legislative acts (statutes, ordinances, resolutions with the force of law) come next, followed by orders from chief executives and procedural directives from executive agencies. Although judicial review was not explicitly included in the Constitution, it was acknowledged during the ratification battle (see *Federalist Papers* #78) and then formalized in the *Marbury* decision, which invalidated an act of Congress for the first time.

Is it legal for the courts to define their own powers? Recall our discussion about political culture and how it is created by historical developments. The basic legal culture of the United States was established by our history as British colonies and their tradition of "common law."[5] As the British monarchs progressively extended their authority, the rulings of their appointed judges began to be applied throughout their realms, overriding local customs and traditions. The legal principle of *stare decisis* ("Let the decision stand.") took root, under which previous decisions in similar cases are used as the basis for deciding new cases. The inherent fairness and flexibility of this approach was embraced by the American colonists, and legal precedent remains a powerful force in our legal system to this day.

The debate about the court's role in public policymaking is usually framed as "judicial activism" versus "judicial restraint." Even if one

---

[4] 1 Cr. 137 (1803).

[5] "Common law" is usually contrasted with "code law," which is based on a comprehensive set of official declarations. Its origin is traced to the Justinian Code created by that emperor in the fourth-century Roman Empire.

accepts that our courts make policy at least sometimes, the extent of such activity can be questioned. How aggressive should the courts be in this regard? What type of referee should they be? Should they be like basketball referees, who run up and down the court with the players as part of the action of the game? Or should they be like tennis referees, who sit passively observing from the sideline and only occasionally issue technical rulings? To this political scientist, something in between seems most appropriate.

National Football League officials could be an appropriate model. Most of the time they are off to the side and focus their rulings on technical matters, using specialists for certain tasks. When circumstances call for it, however, they will become more aggressive to make sure that the action does not exceed acceptable boundaries of conduct. This reflects the importance of circumstance in shaping the "official response" to any given situation, which fits nicely with both the adaptive nature of the U.S. political system and the decision-making structure concept. It is incidental, but interesting, to note that football was the first sport to integrate review processes ("replays") into its decision-making scheme, mimicking a judicial appeals process.

This debate whether judges should be "active" (seize every opportunity or even seek them out) or "restrained" (committed to avoiding or minimizing such actions) with respect to public policymaking often takes an ideological tone. Some analysts tie one or both of these positions to the two basic ideological factions in our political community, but research does not seem to bear this out. "Judicial activism or restraint have no natural or logical identity with liberalism or conservatism, big government or small government, active government or passive

government."[6] Just as the overall system does, our judicial subsystem responds and adapts to political circumstance as it unfolds.

THE STRUCTURE OF U.S. COURTS

Recall that the Founders created only the Supreme Court in the Constitution, and authorized Congress to "ordain and establish" inferior courts as deemed appropriate. Congress did so in the Judiciary Act of 1789. There were originally only three districts (eastern, middle, and southern), and federal judges traveled around their assigned territories to conduct trials. Even Supreme Court justices had to "ride the circuit" to hear appeals for the first century of its existence. The first Supreme Court was smaller than today's, and did not begin having a major impact until John Marshall was appointed Chief Justice in 1801. During his 34-year term, he "established it as an equal and coordinate branch of the national government." With decisions like *Marbury, McCulloch,* and *Gibbons,* "the Marshall Court also gave content and weight to the supremacy clause."[7]

The basic organizing principles for court systems are hierarchy and jurisdiction. Jurisdiction is the formal authority to hear and decide different types of cases. There are two basic types and two basic levels of jurisdiction, and every court in the United States can be described using them:

- general (any type of case) vs. special (limited to particular types)
- original (for initial trial) vs. appellate (to review decisions of other courts)

---

[6] Cal Jillson, *American Government: Political Development and Institutional Change,* 6th ed.(New York: Routledge, 2011), 391.
[7] Jillson (see Note 6), 372. He cites Bernard Schwartz, *A History of the Supreme Court* (New York: Oxford University Press, 1993).

These organizing principles used throughout the United States create three-tier systems. At the lowest level are the general and special jurisdiction trial courts, the middle level consists of intermediate appellate courts, and there is usually a final appeals court, also often called the court of last resort. Figure 8-1 portrays this basic configuration:

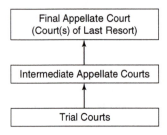

FIGURE 8-1: A Typical Court System in the United States

The specific structure of our national court system, portrayed in Figure 8-2:

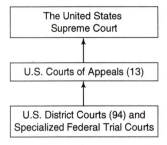

FIGURE 8-2: The U.S. National Court System

There are wide disparities in the sizes of the territories covered by the thirteen national court districts, primarily due to the basic reality that people, not land, file lawsuits. The smaller districts have higher population densities. Centers of commerce and government activity also generate higher levels of legal action, which is why the District of Columbia has its own national court district. The territories are referred to as "circuits" because originally federal judges traveled around them to hear cases. Among the specialized federal trial courts are the U.S. Tax Court, the Court of Federal Claims, the Court of Appeals for Veterans Claims, and the U.S. Court of International Trade.

BASIC OPERATION OF THE U.S. SUPREME COURT

The U.S. Supreme Court was given very limited original jurisdiction by the Founders in Article 3, Section 1 of the Constitution, but the cases it does hear usually have national, and sometimes international, significance. It is primarily known as our national court of last resort, the absolute final step in any appeal process under U.S. law. The Supreme Court consists of the Chief Justice of the United States and a number of Associate Justices set by Congress, which is currently eight. All federal judges are nominated by the president, and must be confirmed by the Senate. All federal judicial appointments are for life, subject to impeachment and removal for misconduct.

The Supreme Court chooses what appeals it will hear. Most cases get to the Supreme Court through the U.S. Courts of Appeals, but every year some decisions by state courts of last resort are appealed to it. In order to even be considered, such cases must involve a "federal question," a legal issue dealing with the U.S. Constitution, an act of Congress, an official Executive branch action, or an international treaty. A very important aspect of the U.S. judicial process is that an actual legal controversy must exist for a case to be heard. No U.S. court can deal with hypothetical legal questions or issue advisory rulings. Certain specific criteria (e.g., contesting parties from two different states) apply for some types of cases to qualify to be heard in a federal court.

One of the parties to a legal dispute can petition to have a case reviewed by the Supreme Court, which has established a "rule of four" for acceptance of cases. At least four of the justices must agree to hear a case, but that is reduced to three if only seven justices are participating. When a case is accepted, a "writ of certiorari" is issued ordering the lower court that last heard the case to send it up for review. Around 10,000 petitions for case review are filed with the Supreme Court each year, but only ~70 have been accepted during recent terms. In addition to full case reviews, approximately 1,200 applications for different legal actions have been submitted to individual justices in recent years. Petitions for a stay of execution are examples, which are often reported about by the mass media.

The Supreme Court convenes the first Monday of each October for its annual term, with most decisions usually announced during the spring or early summer. Both parties to a case submit written briefs to the Court, oral arguments are scheduled and heard, and then the justices deliberate. Third parties with an interest in the case can submit "*amicus curiae*" (friend of the court) briefs to present legal arguments on either side for the justices to consider. There is an explicit set of rules that must be followed for petitioning and presenting briefs to the Supreme Court.[8] In a few, rare instances an individual's personal petition has been accepted by the Court because a crucial legal issue is raised. A notable example was *Gideon v. Wainwright* (1963),[9] in which the Court ruled that governments must provide attorneys for defendants accused of felonies who cannot afford them,

based on a personal petition with an interesting history.[10]

The justices research the legal issues and relevant precedents assisted by law clerks, and meet in total privacy to discuss the cases and vote on them, with decisions made by majority rule. Since these are at times very critical authoritative decisions, it has always seemed ironic to this political scientist that the written rulings issued are called "opinions." That term reflects the fact that even when justices agree on a decision, they may not agree on the specific legal reasoning for it. In such cases, "concurring" opinions are issued along with the Court's "majority opinion." Justices who voted against the majority decision will often issue "dissenting" minority or individual opinions explaining why. These sometimes provide ideas for future decisions.

For cases being heard on appeal (all but about one per term), the Court either "affirms" the lower court's decision (most often the case), "reverses" all or part(s) of it, or "remands" (returns) it back to the lower court for further action. This last option usually involves cases in which a technical legal matter needed to be resolved before the lower court could proceed. All Supreme Court rulings are publicly announced and all opinions are published in the *United States Reports*, the official printed record of its decisions. Nowadays, they are published online as soon as they are announced.

WHAT CHECKS OUR COURTS?

Since all U.S. courts, and particularly the Supreme Court, get involved in public policy-making at times, how does our political system

---

[8] These can be reviewed at http://www.supremecourt.gov/ctrules/2010RulesoftheCourt.pdf.
[9] 372 US 335 (1963).

[10] Anthony Lewis, *Gideon's Trumpet* (New York: Random House, 1964).

"check and balance" them? In several formal and informal ways:

Executive Checks: Primarily, presidents use their power of appointment to influence the policy direction of the courts. Recent history shows that a president will fill between 35 percent and 60 percent of federal judgeships during his or her time in office.[11] Only the Executive branch has the means to actually implement or enforce judicial decisions, moreover. In rare cases a president has refused to do so (Jackson), and some presidents have only acted on key decisions grudgingly (Eisenhower). They also impact the judicial process by choosing what legal issues to pursue (or ignore) through Executive branch litigation.

Legislative Checks: In response to court decisions, Congress can amend laws, pass new laws, and propose amendments to the Constitution. The most prominent legislative check is the requirement that the Senate confirm all judicial appointments. Nominees are expected to be approved by the Senators from the state in which they would serve under the custom of "senatorial courtesy," and the confirmation process has become a partisan and ideological battlefield.[12] Congress also controls the resources available for court operations and must fund all implementation activities.

Public Opinion: The public can ignore rulings within local communities where challenges are unlikely (e.g., praying certainly still takes place in some public schools) and pressure state and local governments in response to an unwelcomed court ruling (e.g., new laws to limit eminent domain property seizures passed by legislatures after the *Kelo* decision). There is also some direct influence at times. "In truth, the Supreme Court has seldom, if ever, flatly and for very long resisted a really unmistakable wave of public sentiment."[13]

Judicial Traditions and Doctrines: Keep in mind the importance of precedent in our legal culture, and that courts can only deal with actual cases. Historically, U.S. courts have also tended to avoid "political questions," leaving them for Congress and the Executive branch to decide, although "fewer questions are deemed political questions by the Supreme Court today than in the past."[14] The historical record shows that our national courts are quite judicious; rejection of legislative acts is relatively rare.

Federalism: State courts will reinterpret opinions, read circumstances differently than federal courts did, or limit the application of decisions that run counter to state laws. State constitutions and laws address some issues not dealt with at the federal level.

This overview of the U.S. judicial subsystem provides only a basic description of its roles, structure, operation, and how it fits into the overall political system. There are many excellent resources in addition to the few cited here available

---

[11] Deborah Barrow, Gary Zuk, and Gerald Gryski, *The Federal Judiciary and Institutional Change* (Ann Arbor: University of Michigan Press, 1996), 12.

[12] Mark Silverstein, *Judicious Choices: The New Politics of Supreme Court Confirmations* (New York: Norton, 1994).

[13] Robert G. McCloskey and Sanford Levinson, *The American Supreme Court*, 4th ed. (Chicago: University of Chicago Press, 2005), 14.

[14] Steffen W. Schmidt, Mark C. Shelley, and Barbara Bardes, *American Government and Politics Today*, 13th ed. (Mason, OH: Thomson Wadsworth, 2008), 476.

for those readers interested in more details. The power that the courts have in the United States is one of the key ingredients of our success. They serve as a very strong check and balance on the other branches throughout the system, and are one of the key means by which we have adapted to changing circumstances for two and a quarter centuries. They have been, and will hopefully continue for a long time to be, one of the sources of our resilience.

CHAPTER 9

Political Organizations

In introducing this section on Political Configuration, we noted that the core elements of this operational framework for a political system are the government and private organizations created for political purposes. Our government structures were presented in the last few chapters; we now turn our attention to the private structures involved in our authoritative decision-making process. For these organizations to contribute to the success of our democratic Federal Republic, the primary political purposes they must support are the Ideal Principles extensively discussed in Chapter 1, most notably popular sovereignty, liberty, and fairness. Those are the criteria by which they should be judged.

   Recall that our consideration of how democracy can be achieved in today's modern, complex world in the early chapters led to the question, "How does popular sovereignty manifest itself today?" Applying our basic conceptual framework turned this into, "How are the people involved in authoritative decision-making today?" We explored and accepted E. E. Schattschneider's answers:[1]

Above everything, the people are powerless if the political enterprise is not competitive. It is the competition of political organizations that provides the people with the opportunity to make a choice. Without this opportunity popular sovereignty amounts to nothing….Democracy is a competitive political system in which competing leaders and organizations define the alternatives of public policy in such a way that the public can participate in the decision-making process.

The structure of the U.S. Federal Republic was designed to allow, and even encourage, channeled political competition according to the "Madisonian Model of Government,"[2] which we have discussed extensively. What private structures are involved in authoritative decision making, and what roles do they play? Most readers are likely aware that the two basic types of private organizations created for political purposes are *interest groups/associations* and *political parties*. Key comparative information about them is summarized in Table 9-1 and elaborated below.

---

[1] E. E. Schattschneider, *The Semi-Sovereign People: A Realist's View of Democracy in America* (Hinsdale, IL: Dryden, 1975), 135–138.

[2] It was previously noted that historians and political scientists include and/or emphasize different components. Many of Madison's writings discuss these ideas; the key sources usually cited are *Federalist Papers #51* and *#10*.

	POLITICAL PARTIES	INTEREST GROUPS & ASSOCIATIONS
DEFINITION:	Groups of political activists sharing basic political perspectives who organize to win elections so they can operate the government and direct the public policymaking process	Organized (most formal = associations) groups of individuals sharing common interests or objectives that actively attempt to influence public policies which directly or indirectly impact group members based on those shared interests or objectives
BASIC GOAL:	To win elections & make public policy	To shape public policies relevant to their members
PRIMARY SYSTEM FUNCTION:	*Interest Aggregation* = "filtering" the many interests into general-ized, workable public policy proposals	*Interest Articulation* = promoting public policies (What & When) and processes (How) that would benefit their members (Who) & opposing those that would hurt them.
BASIC STRUCTURE:	State = principle organization Local, County, District committees National Committees National Convention (every 4 years)	National organizations with State Chapters; many also have Local Chapters in counties and major cities.
BASIC FUNCTIONS:	Being responsible for governing Acting as the organized opposition Recruiting & training candidates Organizing & running campaigns Presenting alternative policies Political Socialization of activists	Lobbying elected and appointed public officials Campaign Assistance (e.g. $, ratings, endorsements) Building Alliances in relevant "issue networks" Generating public pressure & "climate control" Unconventional pressure (e.g. boycotts) Political Socialization of activists

TABLE 9-1: Basic Comparison of Private Political Organizations in the U.S.A.

INTEREST GROUPS/ ASSOCIATIONS

One of the standard complaints frequently heard about the U.S. political system is that it has been "captured by special interests." Many Americans have a vision of unscrupulous lobbyists skillfully manipulating the public policymaking process to cheat the public by gaining undeserved government benefits for their clients or by planting loopholes in the tax code so they avoid paying their fair share of taxes. There are, undoubtedly, some groups and some lobbyists who fit that image. For the most part, however, the "special interests" that actively and legitimately seek to influence the formulation and adoption of public policy, dear reader, are you and I and all of our neighbors.

Interest Groups are groups of individuals sharing common interests and objectives who actively attempt to influence public policy. A large and extremely diverse community such as ours has a very wide range of interests, and different types of interest groups are discussed below. These social structures vary considerably in their degree of organization, with the most formally structured ones usually labeled "associations." The function that they perform for the political system is called *interest articulation*. This means *promoting public policies (what and when) and processes (how) that would benefit their members (who), and opposing those that would hurt them.* This is one of the core input functions of all political systems.[3]

Recent editions of the *Encyclopedia of Associations and National Organizations* have listed over 24,000 "nonprofit membership organizations of national and international scope located in the U.S."[4] This represents an increase of over 300 percent during the last 50 years![5] While many of these organizations are not focused on politics, they will get involved when their interests are threatened or opportunities to benefit arise. The reality is that formal organizations are now the public's primary indirect input mechanisms into the public policymaking process. Any interest group that wants to compete today must organize.

These groups/associations form and operate for a variety of reasons. They are important from our perspective when they enter the political arena and pursue *their basic goal of seeking to shape public policies that are relevant to their members.* Different analysts break interest groups/associations into various categories to draw attention to different points. The following typology is intended to highlight their political perspective:

1: *Business and Occupational*: The vast majority (~75 percent) of private organizations that involve themselves in politics represent the economic interests of their members:
   • Business (farmers, manufacturers, etc.) and "Peak" Associations (national conglomerations of regional, state, and local organizations)
   • Professional Associations (doctors, lawyers, nurses, etc.)
   • Labor Unions (AFL-CIO, UAW, NJEA, Teamsters Union, etc.)

2: *Issue Groups*: Individuals who share common concerns about particular issues and/or issue areas have been organizing and lobbying for their preferred policies since the early days of our Republic. Some key examples of groups/associations that concentrate their political activities in certain policy areas are:
   • Environmental (Audubon, Sierra Club, etc.)
   • Veterans (DAV, VFW, American Legion, etc.)
   • Single Issue (Pro-Choice/Life, ACLU, NRA, etc.)

3: *Social Equity*: There is an identifiable set of interest groups/associations that focus their attention on preventing discrimination and exploitation and attempting to assist those who continue to be impacted by past discrimination:
   • Minorities (NAACP, LULAC, NARF)
   • Consumers (Better Business Bureau)
   • Women (NOW)

---

[3] Gabriel A. Almond, "Introduction: A Functional Approach to Comparative Politics," in *The Politics of Developing Areas* (Princeton, NJ: Princeton University Press, 1960).
[4] (Manassas, VA: impact, 2012) http://www.impactpublications.com/encyclopediaofassociationsnationalorganizationsoftheus.aspx.
[5] Frank L. Baumgartner, "The Growth and Diversity of U.S. Associations, 1956–2004," March 29, 2005. See http://www.personal.psu.edu/frb1/EA_Data_Source.pdf.

4: *Public Interest*: One of the great debates in political philosophy is whether a "public interest" truly exists and can be identified at any point in time. For our purpose here, we consider groups/associations that promote opening the political process to increase public participation and focus on community benefit as pursuing the "public interest." Some key examples are:

- League of Women Voters, which promotes voter registration and debates
- Common Cause, which promotes "good government" reforms such as transparency and citizen participation, along with campaign finance reform
- Public Citizen/Public Interest Research groups, which conduct research on various public policies and programs from a public benefit perspective

5: *Public Sector*: This category is intended to identify organizations that represent and promote the interests of various levels of government and various types of public sector employees. These are often lumped into the Business and Occupational category, but I believe they deserve their own. The intimate involvement that these organizations and their members have in the public policymaking process give them a unique standing that needs to be recognized and taken into consideration when analyzing their impact. Some key examples are:

- National Governors Association
- National Association of Counties
- National Urban League, which promotes municipal interests
- Various general (American Society for Public Administration) and specific (American Society of Government Accountants) professional associations

WHAT FACTORS GIVE AN INTEREST GROUP/ ASSOCIATION INFLUENCE?

In examining the impact that interest groups/ associations have in the public policymaking process, political scientists have discovered that a number of factors in addition to basic level of organization give some greater influence. These include:

a. *Size*, the number of actual members, and *"coverage,"* the number of individuals claimed to be represented by an organization and their distribution across the political system, will affect its influence. The National Student Association claims to speak for every college student across the United States, for example, although only a very small percentage actually join and pay dues.

b. The *Unity/Cohesion* of a group certainly impacts its success, along with the *Motivation/ Intensity* of its members. These factors can make a group extremely competitive by making them more active and productive.

c. *Expertise and Leadership* are critical variables. Despite the common image of the lobbyist as a wheeler-dealer, the primary tools they use are accurate information and skillful communication. Skills in research and organizational management are needed for success.

d. *Financial Resources* certainly make a difference. The ability to assist the campaigns of candidates who tend to favor your interests can certainly impact an association's success, along with the ability to fund research and communication activities. Size and skill in raising and managing money become involved here also.

e. *Alliance and Coalition* building is often the decisive factor in influencing public policymaking. As issues have become more intertwined (e.g., the impact of environmental policies on energy, health care, transportation, etc.), the number of interests affected by any authoritative decision has expanded. In a system designed to make it easy to stop the policymaking process, coordinating with other interest groups has become an essential ingredient in successful lobbying.

As shown on Table 9-1, *lobbying* is the top basic function performed by interest groups/associations. Although many people consider lobbying an "other than noble" activity, for the most part it involves *getting accurate, organized information presented effectively to the right people, in the right place, at the right time*.[6] In pursuing their goal of influencing public policy, interest groups/associations tend to primarily focus on either an "insider" strategy aimed directly at elected and appointed public officials or an "outsider" strategy directed toward the general public. The second approach involves actively maintaining a positive public image of the group (sometimes called "climate control"), along with having the means in place to generate telephone calls, e-mails, and so on, to public officials in a timely manner when necessary.

Lobbying is certainly made easier with public officials who are sympathetic to your cause. Interest groups/associations, therefore, provide *campaign assistance* (endorsements, ratings, and donations) to friendly candidates. One of their most questioned behaviors is their use of campaign contributions to gain access to public officials. Some consider the exchange of donations for support for specific policies a form of bribery. Others view this as reflecting the realities of modern democracy. Most members of a community must rely on specialists to represent their various interests as public issues are debated and decided, and money is the medium of exchange today. The relationships between elected officials and the interest groups that support them usually involve much more than donations, moreover. Campaign finance is an issue that does require our attention, and will be discussed in Section Three.

It was noted above that *building alliances and coalitions* can be the decisive factor in influencing public policymaking. Some political scientists apply the label "policy subsystem" to amalgamations of groups and individuals whose interests converge on a specific issue or issue area, including "experts, advocates, and officials."[7] Historically, "iron triangles" was the label "used to describe strong ties among the bureaucrats who administer programs, the legislators who authorize and fund them, and the constituents who benefit from them,"[8] which were illustrated in Figure 6-4. With the Internet making information much more widely available, however, the privacy surrounding these ongoing relationships has been diminished, and they are now often called "cozy triangles." Broad-based policy subsystems involving large numbers of groups and associations from various interest sectors are now referred to as "issue networks."[9]

An important basic function performed by interest groups/associations is to apply "unconventional pressure" at times regarding an issue.

---

[6] Robert J. Samuelson, "Lobbying Is Democracy in Action," *Newsweek*, December 22, 2008, 29.

[7] Robert A. Cropf, *American Public Administration: Public Service for the 21st Century* (New York: Pearson, 2008), 264.

[8] Cal Jillson, *American Government: Political Development and Institutional Change*, 6th ed. (New York: Routledge, 2011), 318.

[9] Cropf, 141–142, citing Hugh Heclo, "Issue Networks and the Executive Establishment," in Anthony King, ed., *The New American Political System*, ed., 87–124 (Washington, DC: American Enterprise Institute, 1978).

This usually involves a strategy in which the public is mobilized to communicate their displeasure to the government and the target interest using the mass media, including press releases and paid advertising, combined with boycotts, demonstrations, and even civil disobedience to generate public attention. Another term sometimes applied to these activities is "direct action," but that is often reserved for the grimmest example of petitioning the government for redress of grievances, which is taking to the streets to commit violence.

The final basic function we will take note of, which both types of political organizations perform, is *political socialization to recruit, motivate, and prepare future activists* to carry on their work. This is often studied as a second, distinct stage of the political socialization process described in Chapter 4, one intended to identify and groom individuals for specialized roles.[10] One classic study, for example, identified three categories of participants ranging from "spectators" to "transitionals" to "gladiators," those most actively involved in the political arena.[11]

At this point it should be reiterated that the "chief instrument of influence" for lobbyists is useful, timely, accurate information that helps officials make the decisions facing them. A longtime observer who does not hesitate to be critical of the process has clearly asserted that, "Lobbyists primarily woo lawmakers with facts."[12] It is also worth noting that lobbying targets all three branches of government. Lobbyists certainly focus on enabling legislation and funding decisions, but also direct their efforts through those "cozy triangles" toward executive branch agencies to influence "rulemaking" and related decisions that implement all laws. Interest groups/associations will also prepare and submit *amicus curiae* briefs to try to influence judicial decisions.

There is a long history of Congress trying to control lobbying through regulation that will not be discussed here,[13] but we will note that lobbyists must register and report their activities every six months. Exactly who should register and what they should report has long been a point of contention, but there has clearly been efforts to expand disclosure recently. Along with information that must be filed regarding donations to political campaigns, this at least allows "public interest" groups to track the affiliations and involvement of public officials with the various interest groups/associations.

We will close out this overview of interest groups/associations by asking the question, "What keeps the multitude of 'special interests' from totally fragmenting our political system?" The reality is that we are all subject to "cross-pressures." These are the "conflicting pulls on an individual from more than one source, e.g., groups to which he belongs or whose views he tends to follow."[14] This phenomenon of most

[10] See, for example, Joel Silbey, ed., *The Congress of the United States: Patterns of Recruitment, Leadership, and Internal Structure, 1789–1989* (Los Alamitos, CA: Carson Publishing, 1991), and Robert Putnam, *The Comparative Study of Political Elites* (New York: Prentice Hall, 1976).
[11] Lester Milbrath, *Political Participation* (Chicago: Rand McNally, 1965).

[12] Jeffrey Birnbaum, quoted and described in Samuelson (see Note 6) as "a veteran lobbying reporter" for the *Washington Post*.
[13] Steffen W. Schmidt, Mark C. Shelley, and Barbara Bardes, *American Government and Politics Today*, 13th ed. (Mason, OH: Thomson Wadsworth, 2008), 242–243, provides an excellent brief summary.

citizens having a multitude of interests, preventing them from focusing exclusively on just one, fosters the recognition of the need for compromise in public policymaking in order to balance various interests.

POLITICAL PARTIES

The other "intermediary organizations"[11] or "mediating structures"[15] with primarily political functions in the U.S. political system are *political parties, groups of political activists sharing basic political perspectives, who organize to win elections so they can operate the government and direct the public policymaking process.* Note how their basic goal differs from why interest groups organize for political action (more on this below). Political parties exist to win elections so they can make public policy for their community. In the U.S. political system, political parties must appeal to "the Swing Vote,"[16] which tends to be attracted to moderate, centrist, pragmatic public policies.

Cross-pressures, a popular safeguard in that they promote compromise among people and groups, are insufficient by themselves for channeling competition in an open democracy

as large and diverse as the United States. There needs to be a more reliable, preferably structural, safeguard. Although our Founders did not build political parties into the formal structure of the new Federal Republic (and some actually feared and tried to prevent their development), they emerged. They are a prime example of the importance of the informal aspects of both the evolution and operation of the U.S. political system.

The parties' need to attract the moderate swing vote shapes the process by which they perform the critical system function of *interest aggregation*. This refers to *filtering of the many interests of their members into generalized, workable public policy proposals.* A visual metaphor that may help explain this process is that of a giant colander. All the various perspectives these interests have on different issues are pushed through it and strained into specific proposals acceptable to them all, or at least not objectionable to any. The metaphor of sausage making has often been applied to the legislative process. Interest aggregation is packaging of the various ground meats into an appealing casing fashioned by legislative leaders.

While parties clearly do articulate the various interests of their members, their primary system function is to balance and combine them into a workable plan for governing. Ideally, the desires and demands of the various elements and "wings" (ideological factions) of the party can be meshed into proposals that can be supported by all of them, or at least not generate significant internal opposition. Just as parties perform some interest articulation, interest groups/associations accomplish some aggregation through their internal deliberations and debates. Each type of political organization does make its distinctive contribution as an indirect input mechanism for the people, however.

---

[14] Stephen Wasby, *Political Science–The Discipline and It's Dimensions: An Introduction* (New York: Charles Scribner's Sons, 1970), 54, based on Seymour Martin Lipset, "Some Social Requisites of Democracy: Economic Development and Political Legitimacy," *American Political Science Review*, 53 (1959), 69–105.

[15] Theodore M. Kerrine and Richard J. Neuhaus, "Mediating Structures: A Paradigm for Democratic Pluralism," *The ANNALS of the American Academy of Political and Social Science*, 446:1 (1979), 10–18.

[16] See, for example, Daniel M. Shea and Michael John Burton, *Campaign Craft: The Strategies, Tactics, and Art of Political Campaign Management* (Westport, CT: Praeger, 2000), 75–98.

At the national level, interest aggregation sometimes occurs publicly during the process of selecting candidates through primary elections, caucuses, and conventions. Every four years at their national conventions, a set of positions and proposals on various issues (called "planks") are formally adopted and assembled into the "party platform" that the party presents to the public. Most of this filtering process takes place through negotiations among representatives of affiliated interest groups/associations and the acknowledged leaders of the parties' different "wings" conducted out of the public eye.

While interest groups/associations focus all their activities on the particular needs and preferences of their members and affiliates, those who are active in political parties want to run the government. This is a very important distinction for which political parties and their members are not given sufficient credit. These individuals are willing to take responsibility for making decisions that will affect the lives of all their neighbors, and in so doing subject themselves to wide open personal scrutiny and attack. *Being responsible for governing* (when they are successful) and *acting as the organized opposition* (when they are not) are the two most visible basic functions performed by political parties.

Other significant basic functions include *recruiting and training candidates* and *organizing and running campaigns*. Political parties seek to identify qualified, capable individuals to run for office, and provide both formal training and informal coaching in the art of political campaigning. They also do many of the basic tasks required to get on the ballot (obtaining the required signatures on petitions, filing all required reports, etc.), increase the party's voter base (recruit and register new voters, represent the party at public events, etc.), and *get out the vote* (distributing yard signs and bumper stickers, arranging rides to the polls for voters, etc.).

The last two basic functions political parties perform are *negotiating policy alternatives* and *political socialization of future activists*. Recall from our discussion of the policymaking stages in the introduction to this section, that the policy decision stage is often studied as two somewhat distinctive substages, formulation and adoption. Moving from one to the other is most often a process of negotiation, and particularly in the legislative process, the leaders of both the majority and minority parties are the key authoritative decision makers. Parties target youth, and college students in particular, in their membership development activities, and are an important element in the entire political socialization process, as discussed in Chapter 4.

Of course, all the functions that political parties perform intertwine and blend together at times as parties pursue their basic goal of winning elections. As with interest groups/associations pursuing influence, organization is one of the important factors in the pursuit of electoral success. U.S. political parties are more "democratic" than most people realize. One of the contributions that federalism makes to the democratic nature of our Republic is the multiplicity of authoritative decision-making positions it requires. These provide increased opportunities for both direct (voting) and indirect popular input into the process.

A basic characteristic that political parties and interest groups/associations in the U.S. political system share is their hierarchical structure that parallels the federal nature of the Republic. The National Committees of our two major parties have strengthened themselves recently, but the core structure of the U.S. party system consists of the 50 state party organizations.

These, in turn, are comprised of county, local (municipal), and district (submunicipal) committees, often elected directly by registered party members during primary elections. An interesting note in this regard is that these committees often require male and female representatives, which provided a historical role for women in authoritative decision making that is perhaps worthy of research.

One additional aspect of their structure that should be noted is the existence of specialized party organizations. Many readers have likely heard of "Young Republican" or "Young Democrats" clubs; there are also recognized organizations for minorities and women and other subgroups. One of the ways a new group is publicly "accepted" into the authoritative decision-making process is recognition by political parties and other social organizations. We have been discussing the formal structure of party offices, often called the *party organization*, one of three recognized standard components of political parties.

The other two are the *party in the electorate* and the *party in government*,[17] which simply refers to *all the elected and appointed officials who are affiliated with a* particular *party*. The party in the electorate refers to the *individuals associated with the party*. Different analysts use various definitions, but three frequently used subcategories are activists, "identifiers" (usually measured by self-identification), and "leaners" (usually based on voting patterns). For members of minor parties (more below), identification is often more of an emotional rather than an intellectual commitment.

---

[17] Marjorie R. Hershey, *Party Politics in America*, 12th ed. (New York: Pearson Longman, 2007), 8–10.

THE TWO-PLUS PARTY SYSTEM

The political party subsystem of the U.S. political system is most often described as "Two Party," but a more accurate description would be "Two-Plus." Our history includes a rich array of third-party movements that have left a range of legacies, including proposing policies later adopted by the major parties and influencing some national election results. Among the contributions that minor parties make to U.S. democracy, the principal one is bringing attention to issues that the major parties choose to ignore. They also offer different ideas/perspectives (with good ones often absorbed by the major parties), represent groups and issues that are often otherwise neglected, serve as a "safety valve" (a peaceful outlet for nontraditional political beliefs), and provide voters with more choices, increasing political competition.

Keeping in mind that political parties exist primarily to win elections so that they can govern, it is understandable why minor parties remain minor in the U.S. political system. First, our "winner take all" election system prevents minor parties from gaining any traction by building on initial victories. Political activism thrives on either success or challenge. With little chance of victory, minor parties in the United States tend to be cause-driven. The two major parties also basically control election procedures through their operation of state and local governments, and usually do not make it easy for challengers. We also, of course, have the long two-party tradition that began with the Federalists and the Anti-Federalists battling over ratification of the Constitution. Finally, party identification has traditionally been strongly reinforced by the political socialization process, although there is evidence this may be changing in the twenty-first century.

WHO DO THE TWO MAJOR PARTIES REPRESENT?

As noted in our definition, members of political parties share basic political perspectives that they apply when they govern. Research consistently shows that the two major U.S. parties have consistently differed along the two basic, contrasting ideological viewpoints of "liberalism" and "conservatism," with degrees of intensity represented by different "wings" within each party. The basic contrast of key values reflected by these viewpoints summarized in Chapter 4 is reproduced as Table 9-2 below.

Political Sociology, a subfield of both Political Science and Sociology, has been studying political parties for centuries, and there is a rich literature available for those interested in details. For our purposes, identifying the key demographic groups that each party attracts, as we have done in Table 9-3, helps to explain their ideological contrast. The moralistic subcultures of the Midwest, South, and Southwest reinforce the agricultural and business preference for lack of regulation and independence. The interdependence of people living in urban areas, grown-out older suburbs, and the new "edge cities,"[18] however, reinforces the perceived need for public sector support.

The traditional view has been that youth tend to be more liberal and vote Democratic, and that choosing a career, starting a business, and beginning a family lead people to become more conservative. As individuals become "stakeholders" in their communities, therefore, they tend to vote Republican more. Education has always been associated with higher earnings, which also tends to generate more conservative

LIBERALISM	CONSERVATISM
Generally favors government action	Generally against government action
Promotes government regulation	Promotes deregulation
Promotes government help for the needy and increasing opportunity	Favors private charity caring for the needy and promotes competition
Favors national policymaking	Favors state and local government control

TABLE 9-2: Basic Ideological Divide between U.S. Political Parties

REPUBLICAN:	VS.	DEMOCRATS:
• Conservative	*vs.*	Liberal
• Business/Agriculture/rural and suburbs	*vs.*	Labor/urban/"edge cities"
• College/training	*vs.*	Least and Most Educated
• Midwest, South, and Southwest	*vs.*	Northeast and West

TABLE 9-3: Basic Demographics of U.S. Political Parties

---

[18] Joel Garreau, *Edge City: Life on the New Frontier* (New York: Random House, 1991); an excellent summary of the concept is available at http://geography.about.com/od/urbaneconomicgeography/a/edgecity.htm.

leanings. Interestingly, however, there is recent evidence that individuals earning postgraduate degrees are increasingly identifying and voting as Democrats.[19]

IS THIS DEMOCRACY?

At the beginning of this chapter we recalled that modern democracy is rooted in competition among political organizations and leaders. Does the U.S. subsystem of interest groups/associations battling it out to resolve policy questions in issue networks and our "Two-Plus" political party subsystem add up to "democracy?" Structurally, it appears they do. Theoretically, at least, *interest articulation and interest aggregation complement each other rather nicely as indirect input mechanisms for the people* into authoritative decision making. Each interest's policy preferences are sorted internally, then reconciled with those of related interests through the "issue networks," and finally input as specific proposals through their associated parties and public officials. The parties then aggregate these proposals into formal legislative or regulatory initiatives, and negotiate the final result.

Interest articulation is certainly flourishing, as evidenced by the proliferation of interest groups/associations in recent decades and their willingness to expend resources promoting their policy preferences. The Internet has certainly revolutionized the world of interest articulation, moreover, providing an almost unlimited forum for political debate and an amazing tool for political organization. We will return to those themes in Section Three. Political parties in the United States, perceived to be threatened by the rise of candidate-centered campaigns relying on telecommunications, seem to have regained their footing. Even in the many communities were one party tends to dominate, political competition among "factions" and "wings" keeps our democracy alive.

Is the competition among interest groups/ associations and political parties in the United States today strong enough to enable us to truly claim the label "democratic?" This harkens back to the classic "pluralism" versus "elitism" debate conducted by American political science during the twentieth century, which concluded that "multiple, competing elites (including interest groups) determine public policy through bargaining and compromise."[20] One analyst labeled this "pluralistic democratic elitism" that "can be roughly described in terms of three characteristics: social pluralism, diverse, competing, and accessible elites; and a basic consensus on the rules of democratic competition."[21]

Elites? Yes. Schattschneider noted the critical role of leadership in modern democracy; Thomas Dye and Harmon Ziegler later explained it:[22]

> *Democratic values have survived because elites, not masses, govern. Elites in America–leaders in government, industry, education, and civic affairs; the well-educated, prestigiously employed, and politically active–give greater support to basic democratic values and*

---

[19] Steffen W. Schmidt, Mark C. Shelley, and Barbara Bardes, *American Government and Politics Today*, 13th ed. (Mason, OH: Thomson Wadsworth, 2008), 198.

[20] Harmon Ziegler, *Pluralism, Corporatism, and Confucianism: Political Association and Conflict Regulation in the United States, Europe, and Taiwan* (Philadelphia: Temple University Press, 1988), 3.

[21] Grover Starling, *The Politics and Economics of Public Policy* (Homewood, IL: Dorsey, 1979), 126.

[22] Thomas R. Dye and Harmon Ziegler, *The Irony of Democracy*, 2nd. ed. (Belmont, CA: Wadsworth, 1972), 20.

"rules of the game" than do the masses. And it is because masses in America respond to the ideas and actions of democratically minded elites that liberal values are preserved.

So, elite support preserves our democratic political culture, but does structural pluralism provide sufficient competition? It appears to be the best we can achieve: "Workable democracy is the inclusive representation of interests in the interaction process among strategic organization centers,"[23] according to one prominent theorist of democratic pluralism. The most complete set of criteria for a "polyarchal democracy" was set out by Robert Dahl more than half a century ago, who recognized the growing role of formal organizations in pluralistic political systems at that time: [24]

Thus the making of governmental decisions is not a majestic march of great majorities united upon certain matters of basic policy. It is the steady appeasement of relatively small groups....In time, all these manifold specialized groups become vested interests with leaders and non-leaders dependent upon the permanence, the income, the prestige, and the legitimacy of their organizations. They become part of the fundamental warp and woof of the society.

Organizational competition is the key, and what they compete for is access to the public policy-making process:[25]

A central guiding thread of American constitutional development has been the evolution of a political system in which all the active and legitimate groups in the population can make themselves heard at some crucial stage of the process of decision.

Does the U.S. political system still meet that criterion? Is our authoritative decision-making process open and competitive? Some relevant questions are:

- Are political resources diffuse and shared or concentrated in the hands of a few?
- Are decisions made by the same people/groups all the time?
- How difficult is it to become an authoritative decision maker?

We will explore these questions and the issue of political competition in general in Section Three. The combination of interest articulation and interest aggregation performed by our primary political organizations is only half the story. Working together, this formidable pair of complementary indirect input mechanisms also complement the direct input mechanisms of public opinion and voting, which are the topics of the next two chapters. The last stop on our journey will be a look at political campaigns. First, however, the concept of Political Circumstance will be explored and explained.

---

[23] Emmette Redford, *Democracy in the Administrative State* (New York: Oxford University Press, 1969), 197.
[24] Robert Dahl, *A Preface To Democratic Theory* (Chicago: University of Chicago Press, 1963), 136–7.
[25] Dahl, 146.

SECTION THREE
Political Circumstance

B ack in the Introduction, the concept of "political circumstance" was presented as the third component of a political system's authoritative decision-making structure and concisely described as "the sum of determining factors beyond willful control."[1] This concept is offered as a tool for discussing the most variable, changeable aspects of the political process. While that basic dictionary definition of "circumstance" does capture the randomness of events that everyone and everything is subject to, it does not help us understand politics. It must be related to our basic conceptual framework, authoritative decision making. Let's explore how they are connected.

It seems appropriate to return to where we began: Paul Deising's observation that "all decisions have to be made in an actual context of actions and commitments resulting from previous decisions." Political circumstance is the accumulated consequences of "the commitments already accepted by a [community] and the courses of action in which it is already engaged, i.e., the cumulative outcomes and effects of all previous public policymaking."[2] Like it or not, all public policymakers must deal with the realities resulting from all the related (whether intentionally or not) preceding authoritative decisions that led to the situation for which they are now formulating

---

[1] *The American Heritage Dictionary*, 2nd College Edition (New York: Houghton-Mifflin, 1982), 275.

[2] Paul Deising, *Reason in Society: Five Types of Decisions and Their Social Conditions* (Urbana: University of Illinois Press, 1962 [rpt. Greenwood, 1973]), 171–172, with modification by this author in brackets.

policy. Deising reminds us that no one can change the past, so anyone making a decision today must cope with the specific consequences of all previous decisions that impacted the current state of affairs and the specific matter being handled. Certainly, President Obama would have preferred to begin his term in office without having had to face our nation's most serious financial crisis since the Great Depression, but he had no choice.

This conceptualization fits into the "stream" model of public policymaking, which portrays the process as a flow of events converging to produce adopted policies in various forms (laws, executive orders and regulations, court rulings, etc.).[3] Within our conceptual framework, these events are chains of linked (whether intentionally or not) authoritative decisions. "Concatenation" is the complicated word used to describe this complicated process through which distinct subprocesses intersect and intertwine to produce outcomes. Seemingly minor incidents and apparently unrelated decisions can converge to generate significant impacts. Two implications of this for policymaking are notable. First, authoritative decision makers should attempt to identify any unintended consequences of proposed actions when projecting outcomes. Second, they should not assume that similar conditions will always produce similar results. The complexity of the modern world precludes simple assumptions about system behavior like homeostasis. Few human systems operate like thermostats; deviance is not always counteracted.[4]

One of the great debates in the public policy subfield of political science has been about the basic nature of the policymaking process. Two distinctive schools of thought portrayed the process as either "incremental" (i.e., proceeding in small steps) or "rational," proceeding in an "orderly, intentional, purposeful, deliberate, consistent, responsible, accountable, explainable" manner.[5] In keeping with the dialectical nature of inquiry, a third school emerged which combines elements of both. "Mixed-scanning" portrays policymaking as a blend of "incremental" decision making shaped by periodic "fundamental" decisions. One of the reasons for distinguishing the two types is to recognize when it would be worthwhile to expend the time and resources attempting "rational" policymaking, which requires considerable research and analysis for success. The importance, or "fundamentalness,"[6] of the culminating decision in the policymaking process increases as more interests (and, therefore, more issue networks) perceive potential impact, and as the projected scope (from narrow to wide-reaching) and duration (from short to long term) of its potential impact increases.

Note that it is the perceptions of the consequences of past policies and projected impacts of proposed policies on the part of the public and other decision makers that shape their actions, which makes things even more complicated. Humans create "prism(s) through which we interpret the world" and "ignore information inconsistent with our own core values . . .

[3] John W. Kingdon, *Agendas, Alternatives, and Public Policies* (New York: HarperCollins, 1995).
[4] Magoroh Maruyama, "The Second Cybernetics: Deviance-Amplifying Mutual Causal Processes," *American Scientist,* 51 (1963), 164–179.

[5] Graham Allison, *The Essence of Decision: Explaining the Cuban Missile Crisis* (Boston: Little, Brown, 1971), 129.
[6] Amitai Etzioni, "Mixed-Scanning Revisited," *Public Administration Review,* 46 (1986), 8–13.

(cognitive dissonance).[7] While this might be obvious on the international level, since the differences in political cultures are very distinctive, it is also important in a large, diverse community with multiple subcultures like the United States. A recent example of cognitive dissonance is how about 10 percent of the American people still refused to accept President Obama's Hawaiian birth certificate as genuine even after it was prominently published.

An analogy may help readers better understand this concept of circumstance. Envision in your mind a route you frequently drive, perhaps your usual commute to work or campus. Its "formal structure," the road itself and the traffic control system (road and lane configuration, signals, signs) installed on it, is basically the same each time you use it. More than likely, at least one "informal structure" for its use, meaning patterns of behavior that you anticipate and probably participate in, has evolved. For example, rush-hour commutes often involve dealing with bottlenecks, and for every one this author has encountered, some pattern of accommodation that had developed quickly became evident. A classic bottleneck is a "Stop" sign at a "T" where two continuous streams of cars intersect. What usually keeps traffic flowing is that a pattern of one car from each stream alternately moving through the intersection becomes the norm. Failing to comply with the pattern draws swift expressions of displeasure in various forms.

Every time you actually travel that route, however, the specific circumstances you face are

different. Some days, traffic flows very smoothly and you "make every light." On other days, you get stuck behind a school bus that stops frequently or a large truck that slows you down. The behavior of others, both immediate (i.e., current actions, like slamming on the brakes in response to a squirrel running across the road) and consequential (circumstances created by past decisions, like a car breaking down due to failure to perform routine maintenance), is part of the reality you must face. More seriously, you are exposed to the random misperceptions and mistakes of all the other users of that route, as well as such extremely low probability events as being struck by a falling tree. One variable that everyone must deal with directly or indirectly every day is the weather, which epitomizes how circumstance shapes situations. Traveling even an extremely familiar route quickly becomes an adventure when wind, rain, snow, or ice is present, with each presenting different specific conditions that must be handled.

One of the most memorable lessons regarding circumstance and decision making that this author ever learned involved weather. The key to the most successful use of artillery is "registering" your weapons, test-firing the specific weapons you will be using in their actual fire locations under the specific firing conditions you will face. Registration provides the sight adjustments that will account for wind and weather. It may have been just a legend, but the story was told of a young lieutenant who, per protocol, registered his battery as soon as possible during a drill, which happened to be during a severe thunderstorm. When the live-fire exercise resumed, the weather had cleared, but the young lieutenant refused to re-register the howitzers for fear he would be accused of wasting ammunition.

---

[7] W. Raymond Duncan, Barbara Jancar-Webster, and Bob Switky, *World Politics in the 21st Century* (New York: Houghton Mifflin Harcourt, 2009), 253. This is an excellent short summary of the application of this core premise of the "constructivist" approach to social science to international politics.

The legend continued that his experienced sergeant urged him to at least fire with standard settings, rather than use the registration data acquired during the thunderstorm. That data reflected the turbulence of the storm, making it useless under more normal conditions; firing with no adjustments would be more accurate than using bad data. But the young lieutenant chose to stand his ground, and the sad conclusion of the legend was that several animals were killed when training rounds fired using that registration data destroyed their barn, which was adjacent to the firing range. No people were hurt, fortunately. That story clearly illustrates how the relationship between any system and its environment is another *variable* that must continuously be taken into account when making decisions. Learning to distinguish between "normal" and extreme environmental conditions is a critical decision-making skill which is particularly relevant in political systems that consider themselves responsive to the public.

Circumstance has been used previously as a factor in studying political behavior, most notably for historical comparisons. Why are some presidents considered great, while others of apparently equal talent and skill are not? Research on presidential success "suggests that greatness requires a great challenge—revolution, civil war, depression and world war—for a president to meet and overcome. Presidential failure comes from facing great challenges ineffectually."[8] Political circumstance seems worthy of broader study, however. Meaningful insights might be gained from closer scrutiny of unexpected events that lead to significant unforeseen consequences.

Two recent examples are Senator Jim Jeffords' deliberate decision to switch parties in 2001 and Senator Ted Kennedy's untimely and unplanned for death, both of which led to change in the control of the Senate, with major consequences.

One of the most variable elements of the U.S. political process has always been "Citizen Participation," which does not, of course, require formal citizenship. This is the standard political science term applied to the complete range of popular inputs, from apathy to activism, from completely ignoring political information to direct action. Our overview of citizen participation will include a specific examination of "Public Opinion." As methods for measuring public opinion have become more and more sophisticated, this aspect of political circumstance has become more of a factor in authoritative decision making. Recall the typology of representational roles used by legislators that was presented back in Chapter 6. I expect that even the most ardent "trustee" legislator has a pollster on his or her staff who is consulted on a regular basis.

Citizen participation and public opinion really cannot be discussed today separately from the "Mass Media", since the two are becoming increasingly intertwined. Although the mass media's primary social function is clearly entertainment, our focus will be on the political roles that it plays in our communities. Those political scientists who first emphasized the importance of communications noted its connection to systems theory ("it is through communications that inputs are received and acted upon and outputs are generated by a system") and system maintenance: "Putting it another way, it is through communications that a political system relates to and copes with its environment."[9] The major

---

[8] Cal Jillson, *American Government: Political Development and Institutional Change*, 5th ed. (New York: Routledge, 2009), 274.

[9] Alan C. Isaak, *Scope and Methods of Political Science* (Homewood, IL: Dorsey, 1975), 230.

transformation taking place in the world of communications portends important changes in the political process, which was already noted in our earlier discussion of political socialization.

We will close our discussion of political circumstance by looking at "Elections, Campaigns, and Voting". It seems fitting to conclude with these core activities of democratic politics, noting that although more and more sophisticated methods of projecting election outcomes have been developed, there are always some surprises.

CHAPTER 10

Citizen Participation and Public Opinion

In Chapter 1 we spent considerable time discussing the Ideal Principles of American Democracy, which represent the values that our nation aspires to achieve. What makes democracy really work, however, is citizen participation. By "citizen participation" *political scientists mean actions through which ordinary members of a community attempt to influence public policy.*[1] In terms of our basic concepts, this means average residents of the community (formal citizenship is *not* required) getting involved in authoritative decision making. While the specific methods used by citizens for doing that have significantly changed in recent decades, the different *basic types of citizen participation* throughout U.S. history have been:

- *Complaining:* Both personal observation and reports from colleagues covering several decades lead this author to conclude that the number one form of citizen participation is

complaining. Individually, through petitions or demonstrations, or through the media, citizens are not shy about expressing their dissatisfaction with public services or public policies.

- *Proposals and Recommendations*: The second most frequent form of citizen participation (again, based only on observation and reports) is contacting officials with suggestions for improving a public service or revising a current policy.

- *Attending Meetings*: Many complaints and recommendations are personally delivered at public meetings of governing bodies. With "Open Public Meetings Laws" (often called "Sunshine Laws") now the norm, communities must be advised when and where decision-making bodies will meet, including any schedule changes.

- *Commenting on Proposed Regulations*: The Administrative Procedures Act of 1946 established both the norm of, and the basic procedures for, having all proposed government regulations subject to public review

---

[1] Based on Ann O' M. Bowman and Richard C. Kearny, *State and Local Government: The Essentials,* 5th ed. (New York: Pearson, 2012), 69.

and comment. Admittedly, few individual citizens have the time or expertise to evaluate technical rules regarding public program implementation, so we rely on the staffs of our interest group associations and elected representatives to do this for us.

• *Advisory Bodies*: There are approximately 1,200 boards, committees, commissions, and so on, that provide advice and formal recommendations to various national government agencies on policy matters. Interested citizens can impact public policy by serving on these bodies and providing their perspective and specific input.

• *Volunteering*: Community members can enhance the delivery of some public services by volunteering their time and effort. These activities are often carried out in conjunction with community groups and associations such as senior citizens clubs, veterans' organizations, and local youth sports leagues. In a number of states, for example, communities rely on an extensive network of volunteer fire companies and rescue squads to provide these first-response emergency services.

• *Interest Group/Association Activity*: A variant of volunteering is political activity on behalf of an interest group or association. Individuals promoting environmental causes, supporting recreational activities, and supplementing social services through their voluntary efforts also raise awareness of related issues, impacting public policy.

• *Voting*: The most direct form of participation in authoritative decision making is individual voting, especially in those states that have initiative and/or referendum, the process by which citizens can place policy questions on the ballot by petition. Of course, it is by choosing representatives to serve as authoritative decision makers for specific terms of office that we make our system of indirect democracy work. Voting is discussed in Chapter 12.

• *Electioneering*: Whether a community holds partisan or nonpartisan elections, citizen participation is required to make them meaningful. Through party committees and campaign organizations, individuals perform the basic tasks through which we compete politically. Individuals who volunteer for particular campaigns will often be recruited by parties for local committees. These individuals are straddling the line between "ordinary community member" and political activist. Election campaigns are also covered in Chapter 12.

• *Running for Office*: The ultimate means that a citizen has for participating in the authoritative decision-making process for his or her community is running for office. When a citizen chooses to seek office, or is recruited to run for office, he or she clearly crosses the threshold from "ordinary community member" to political activist.

Each of these types of citizen participation involves communication, and it has been noted throughout our journey that the twenty-first century is a new era in political communication, with "E-government" as the new norm. Today, individuals (especially youth) anticipate being able to contact public officials quickly, receive timely feedback, obtain needed information, and complete basic transactions quickly and conveniently over the Internet. This has certainly enhanced opportunities for political participation for most Americans, but it is also putting some of the most disadvantaged members of our community at further disadvantage. The U.S. Census Bureau has collected data on Internet use since 1997 through its Current Population Survey, and over 30 percent of households surveyed reported not having Internet service in 2009, including much higher percentages of Black and Hispanic households than White or Asian ones.[2]

Having looked at how citizens participate, the next logical question is "Who participates more and why?" Some *factors that impact citizen participation* are:

- *Individual Factors*: "Stakeholders" in a community tend to participate more. Individuals who have established families, careers, or businesses in a community will tend to pay more attention to public issues and get more involved. Since we are hesitant to discuss "class" in the United States, social scientists formulated the concept of "Socioeconomic Status" (often abbreviated SES) to differentiate individuals and households based on a combination of income, education, and occupation. Those with higher SES usually participate more.[3] We will look at "demographic" variables more closely when we discuss voting in the Chapter 12, but will note here that older individuals have historically participated more, while women have steadily become more active than men in recent decades,[4] and African Americans

now participate at rates similar to Whites, while Latino and Asian Americans still tend to participate at lower rates.[5]

Based on this author's observations, the most important factor in individual participation is the particular interests each of us have. We all tend to have just a few specific interests that we really pay attention to, and this leads to sporadic or episodic participation. When people think one or more of those interests would be impacted, *and* other factors converge to allow or facilitate their input, people speak up. Participation is presented here as part of the circumstantial component of a community's authoritative decision-making structure because it is one of the most variable system inputs.

- *Community Features*: A community's *political culture* will certainly impact participation. An often quoted breakdown of political cultures in the United States distinguishes individualistic, moralistic, and traditionalistic subcultures,[6] and research using counties as the core unit of analysis identified ten distinctive regional subcultures in the early 1990s.[7] Moralistic communities tend to display higher participation rates, since they place a higher value on "civic duty" than do individualistic ones. Traditionalistic communities lean toward preserving the status quo, which tends to limit participation. Two other community features that impact participation are *political*

---

[2] Table 1. Reported Internet Usage for Households, by Selected Householder Characteristics: 2009.Current Population Survey (CPS) October 2009, http://www .census.gov/hhes/computer/publications/2009.html.

[3] Jennifer Jerit, Jason Barabas, and Toby Bolsen, "Citizens, Knowledge, and the Information Environment, *American Journal of Political Science,* 50 (April 2006), 266–282.

[4] Virginia Sapiro, *The Political Integration of Women* (Urbana: University of Illinois Press, 1983).

[5] Frederick C. Harris, Valeria Sinclair-Chapman, and Brian D. McKenzie, "Macrodynamics of Black Political Participation in the Post-Civil Rights Era," *Journal of Politics,* 67 (November 2005), 1143–1163.

[6] Daniel J. Elazar, *American Federalism: A View from the States,* 3rd ed. (New York: Harper & Row, 1984).

[7] Joel Lieske, "Regional Subcultures of the United States," *Journal of Politics,* 55 (November 1993), 888–913.

competitiveness and *size*. Lack of competition tends to dampen participation in politics, since it is human nature to be more motivated when one has an actual opportunity to win. Smaller communities have higher overall participation rates in all types of civic activities, including politics.[8]

PUBLIC OPINION

"Citizen participation" involves individuals attempting to influence public policy. Public opinion is *the current distribution of collected individual opinions on matters of public concern.* It is important to note how changeable public opinion can be, which is one of the key reasons it is presented here as part of the circumstantial component of a community's decision-making structure. The primary tool used to measure public opinion is telephone polling, which has become quite scientific when properly administered. Polling still represents aggregated responses to specific questions asked at a specific point in time. The use of answering machines and Caller ID, along with the proliferation of cell phones, has complicated the process, but professional pollsters have developed computer programs that take these problems into account.

One of the most basic uses of polling is to collect public opinion on various issues, and political scientists usually classify results as one of three basic types:[9]

• When there is *general public agreement on an issue*, there is said to be *consensus*. The higher

the level of agreement, the stronger the consensus.
• When *opinions are sharply opposed*, it is described as *divisive* opinion.
• When polls *show neither pattern clearly*, it can be described as *mixed*.

Motivation and methodology must be taken into consideration when evaluating polls. Polling conducted by candidates, political parties, or advocacy groups might reflect bias, and one particular practice deserves special note. "*Push polling* is among the black arts of politics," and is "not really intended to gather information about the respondent's opinions, but to use negative and often false information to push the respondent away from a particular candidate."[10] Unfortunately, push polls have become a regular feature of our elections. With respect to methodology, the following factors should be reviewed before accepting any poll results as valid:

Who conducted the poll? Professional polling organizations such as Gallup, Roper, Harris, and the Pew Research Centers can generally be trusted because their reputation is on the line. One should consider whether there is any basis for bias, and evaluate the results in that context.

What sampling method was used? Random or stratified random sampling is required to insure that the population is accurately represented. Randomness of a sample is a mathematical property reflecting that every element of a population had an equal chance of being selected. Randomness is most often achieved today using computer programs, and all polls should indicate a sampling error (for example,

[8] J. Eric Oliver, "City Size and Civic Involvement in Metropolitan America," *American Political Science Review* , 94 (June 2000), 361–373.
[9] Steffen W. Schmidt, Mark C. Shelley, and Barbara Bardes, *American Government and Politics Today*, 13th ed. (Mason, OH: Thomson Wadsworth, 2008), 192.

[10] Cal Jillson, *American Government: Political Development and Institutional Change*, 6th ed. (New York: Routledge, 2011), 98. Italics added.

± 3 percent). This tells you how accurate the sampling methodology was, and should be applied when interpreting poll results. For example, a poll with a sampling error of ± 3 percent showing Candidate A preferred by 45 percent of respondents should be understood to represent a range of support somewhere between 42 percent and 48 percent.

How were the questions asked? The problem of "push polls" noted above illustrates why the content of the questions asked is important. Professional pollsters strive for objectivity. A poll many readers have likely heard about is the one that tracks the president's "approval rating." It asks the simple question, "Do you approve or disapprove of the way (Fill in the name) is handling his (someday soon her) job as president?" Wording can impact results, whether this is done intentionally or not. Some research done in the heyday of telephone polling showed that "the way questions are phrased, the possible answers that are offered and the order in which comparisons are made can have profound effects on people's answers."[11] Recently, a research project in a state considering a referendum on same-sex marriage found 10 percent higher support for "legalizing" it "when the issue is framed as 'marriage equality' instead of 'gay marriage'."[12]

Who is being sampled? A sample of people eligible to vote is unlikely to help you accurately predict the result of an upcoming election, since many of them may not even be registered to vote. Professional campaign pollsters usually focus on "likely voters," those with regular voting histories. Do note that current television call-in polls and most Internet "polls" are not scientifically accurate because the samples are self-selected, which clearly cannot meet the requirement for randomness. Multiple responses are also often allowed. Interest groups/associations have been known to steer members to websites conducting "polls" and encourage them to respond multiple times to skew results in their preferred direction. It should be noted that efforts to develop scientific Internet polling techniques are making progress, but the problem discussed under citizen participation of the disadvantaged not having Internet service will also have to be resolved.

DOES PUBLIC OPINION AFFECT OUR POLITICAL PROCESS?

The basic answer to that question is yes, and some of the ways it does are:

It has become a source of power or weakness for political leaders: President Ronald Reagan was masterful at using public opinion (and citizen participation) to pressure Congress into passing legislation he wanted, while President George W. Bush was considered ineffective during his last few months in office due to record-low approval ratings. President Bill Clinton enjoyed high approval ratings until his impeachment. His acquittal restored his reputation somewhat, but it will always be stained.

It does actually impact public policy: In fact, one of the first political scientists to systematically study public opinion and its effects defined the term as "those opinions held by private persons which governments find it prudent

---

[11] *US News & World Report*, December 4, 1995, 55.
[12] David Radlawski, "Framing Matters," Rutgers-Eagleton poll Rutgers University, *The Star-Ledger*, February 12, 2012.

to heed."[13] Recall our discussion of the roles that legislators adopt; it appears very few apply a pure "Trustee" approach. Today all public officials use polling to identify what issues are most relevant to their constituents, and more sophisticated polls and focus groups are often used to measure how important each issue is to them and how intensely they hold those opinions. Changes in public opinion are certainly taken into account by authoritative decision makers. A major study of its impact found that when public opinion shows support for a change in policy, decision making moved in the direction of the desired change significantly more than it remained unchanged and twice as often as it moved in the opposite direction.[14] Sudden, intense shifts in public opinion, which are often the result of an unexpected, abrupt change in circumstances, certainly attract the attention of public officials and those seeking, or considering seeking, public office.

Most notably, public opinion serves as a restraint on public officials:[15] Authoritative decision makers at all levels of government most often are very well aware of the parameters within which they can operate. This is due to the basic fact that they must either face the public at the next election, or were appointed by and report to people who must. Early research on public opinion revealed that part of the general public regularly pays attention to public policymaking, and labeled those who do the "attentive public."[16] Later research refined that conclusion to reflect the fact that this tends to be restricted to issues or issue areas of particular interest to these individuals. That means that there are actually multiple "attentive publics" attracted by particular policy matters who are ready to react to any proposals for radical change. In this regard, one can see that public opinion operates similarly to citizen participation.

We will close our discussion of public opinion with two points. First, *notable shifts* in public opinion that grow and are sustained can create *cumulative effects that over time can change a community's political culture*, as different values (for example, new roles for women; religious, racial/ethnic—and most recently gender—tolerance) become more widely accepted. Second, *public opinion and citizen participation are the peoples' two major direct input mechanisms* into the policymaking process. They are certainly part of the agenda setting, evaluation, and feedback stages, and undoubtedly impact the policy decision and implementation stages. One of the key variables in the extent of the impact both have on any particular authoritative decision in the U.S. political process is the mass media, the next circumstantial factor we will explore.

---

[13] V. O. Key, Jr., *Public Opinion and American Democracy* (New York: Alfred A. Knopf, 1961), 14.

[14] Benjamin Page and Robert Shapiro, *The Rational Public: Fifty Years of Trends in Americans' Policy Preferences* (Chicago: University of Chicago Press, 1992).

[15] John W. Kingdon, *Agendas, Alternatives, and Public Policies* (New York: HarperCollins, 1995), 65.

[16] Jillson (see Note 10) describes them as "the 10% of Americans that knows a lot about politics" in contrast to "the 90% that pays no more than intermittent attention," 124.

CHAPTER 11

The Mass Media

SOME VERY BRIEF HISTORY

This author feels blessed to have lived in the United States of America during one of the most transformative times in world history (and thinks it can take a significant share of the credit, but that is really a topic for historians). Undoubtedly, one of the most amazing transformations has been in the area of communications. Having been one of the first children ever to grow up with television, its potential political power was very evident to me from the very beginning of my political science studies. Communications theory came in a close second to decision making when I was grappling for a focus for my graduate studies. Seeing the science fiction that I read as a 10-year-old boy come to life over the last few decades, including the telecommunications revolution, has been breathtaking at times. The impact on politics has been enormous, and may just be beginning.

The first great communications revolution, the very first mass medium, was the printing press, which certainly transformed politics. The telegraph has been described as the very first "information revolution," giving birth to the new age of electronic media. Radio and television both rather quickly became an important part of life in their times, and gradually transformed human life, including politics. The range of experience and information that they introduced into, eventually, the average life exploded the isolation of existence. This appears to be happening again via the Internet, but in more complex ways. This analyst's limited knowledge precludes any attempt at fully explaining the impact of the mass media on political behavior. The following overview of its roles and impact on the U.S. political process is intended to provide only a baseline of knowledge.

Radio set off the never-ending quest in reporting news to be right on the scene of an event. Science-fiction writer Arthur C. Clarke first envisioned the communications satellite in a short story around 1940, and I recall the launch of the first successful one, Telstar. Ted Turner's idea for a satellite-based television network that would broadcast 24 hours, 7 days a week was ridiculed by some when first proposed. When "24/7" news and weather channels were proposed, few understood the eventual significance. One illustration of the endurance of established media is how radio's influence was revived in the late twentieth century, when "talk radio" helped fuel the conservative revival in the United States. It remains an important political communication tool. Television's influence is still primary, it seems, including in politics, but the Internet is rapidly gaining ground.

We now live in a world that includes blogging, podcasting, and continuous social networking in both long-term and short-term, expansive and condensed (epitomized by tweeting) modes done using amazingly reliable, personally controlled devices we can carry in our pockets. A mixed communication structure has evolved, with even print outlets remaining (and influential in many communities), but intertwined with mass media in ways that are changing as we speak, both structurally and technologically. We will return to these important changes at the conclusion of this chapter.

THE MASS MEDIA'S POLITICAL ROLES

Recognizing that the main reason for the mass media's success in society, in the "bread-and-butter" economic sense, is its entertainment value, our focus here will be on its political aspects. The dominance of the private sector in the U.S. mass media is an important fact to keep in mind, especially when compared to the other developed democratic nations of our world. The mass media proliferated more for political than economic reasons first in the United States, but at its core is now a commercial enterprise. That blended back into the political realm when advertising techniques developed originally for marketing began to be used in political campaigns. In the current social milieu of our nation, wealth more

than skill in formulating and presenting ideas seems to be the difference between success and failure in politics, particularly in the electoral arena.

The idea that what we today call the mass media, taken together, form a distinct substructure in politics, particularly democratic politics, goes back to the discussions about the "fourth estate"[1] evolving in France. The importance of that substructure to democratic politics was recognized by the insertion of freedom of the press among the first asserted in the Bill of Rights. An excellent summary description of the general political role the mass media play in the U. S. political system is that of "principal intermediary and filter between politicians and government and the citizens they must lead."[2]

Some useful variables to keep in mind when studying political communication include the sheer quantity of it and its intensity as indicators of interest, participation, and activism within a democratic political system. Another would be any pattern(s) of structural bias, either formal (in regulation, for example) or delivery, such as how issues are framed. Again, organizational patterns and technology should be looked at. Among the *specific political roles* the mass media play in the United States are:

- *Reporting the News:* The simple act of transmitting information has political implications. In today's "24/7" news cycle world, public officials are expected to be ready to inform their constituents of important

---

[1] A classic dictionary simply defined "fourth estate" as "the public press." *Webster's Seventh New Collegiate Dictionary* (Springfield, MA: G. & C. Merriam, 1972), 331.

[2] Cal Jillson, *American Government: Political Development and Institutional Change*, 5th ed. (New York: Routledge, 2008), 116.

happenings instantaneously, and the mass media compete to be the first to break almost any story. While the quantity of political news available has grown exponentially, its quality has been diluted. How this occurred will be briefly explored below.

- *Research/Information Source:* This needs little explanation. The explosion of access and information availability, both free and commercially, is *the* sociological phenomenon of our age, and has really enhanced opportunities for political participation for most Americans. As we noted in Chapter 10, however, it is also putting some of the most disadvantaged members of our community at further disadvantage. The U.S. Census Bureau has collected data on Internet use since 1997 through its Current Population Survey, and over 30 percent of households surveyed reported not having Internet service in 2009, including much higher percentages of Black and Hispanic households than White or Asian ones.[3] While access may be available at schools and through libraries, having a service at home is the true measure of social—and political—penetration.

- *Identifying Public Problems:* To this political scientist, the most significant impact of the telecommunications revolution was the cementing of the takeover begun by radio and television of the agenda-setting apparatus of the nation by the mass media from political organizations. The significance of this role leads to concerns related to the dilution of political information that is accompanying its proliferation. Unfortunately, crises have always been one of the most effective ways to draw political attention. As the amount of information being circulated expands, it takes more serious situations to succeed in this.

- *An Oversight Mechanism:* Through their "watchdog" function, the mass media have always been one of the key components of the checks and balances process in the U.S. political system. From helping to foment the American Revolution, to the marvelous "muckraking" of the Progressive era, to the investigative reporting of today, the mass media's scandal mongering has served an important purpose. Even the more salacious tabloid side of this helps to awaken political awareness at times.

- *Providing a Political Forum:* The mass media have been one of the primary mechanisms for transmitting political information in the U.S. political process since its beginning. Recall that "Committees of Correspondence" were used to foment the American Revolution and *The Federalist Papers* to successfully campaign for ratification of the Constitution. In addition to such direct debates, advocacy and education functions are accomplished both directly and indirectly. The various forms include paid advertising, commentary, and outright electioneering, including good management of free media. The proliferation of political "debate" in its most general sense by the telecommunications revolution is showing signs of transforming the meaning of democracy. Tailoring of message and delivery are becoming available on wider bases in apparently accelerating ways. This is creating significant system turbulence, another topic we will return to in our conclusion.

---

[3] Table 1. Reported Internet Usage for Households, by Selected Householder Characteristics: 2009. Current Population Survey (CPS) October 2009, http://www.census.gov/hhes/computer/publications/2009.html.

- *Socializing New Generations*: We noted in chapter 4 that while its impact was not ignored, political scientists "relegated the mass media to secondary status among the agencies of socialization, assigning them a minor, primarily reinforcing role in the politicization process,"[4] but that this is no longer true. Research specifically designed to compare the impacts of different agents will be needed to definitively determine this, but it appears that the mass media may now be becoming the primary agent of political socialization in the United States—at least for new generations. Moreover, in addition to the direct influence that political news reporting and political commentary can have on audience perceptions, the indirect influence of subtle messages that are transmitted must also be considered.

THE MASS MEDIA'S POLITICAL IMPACTS

In addition to *facilitating political (often partisan) debate* in the United States, from the very beginning, our mass media also developed some patterns that need to be taken into account when considering their impacts. One stark reality is that, particularly with respect to government,

the mass media tend to focus on "bad" news. Unfortunately, good news is not very successful in drawing readers, viewers, or visitors to websites. Another clear pattern that developed in the twentieth century was the growing focus on national issues as the United States became a world power and cooperative federalism evolved. It was noted above that electronic media rather quickly established the "24/7" never-ending news cycle, which has placed a new burden of rapid responsiveness on government. In addition to these general impacts, the following *specific impacts* should be noted:

More, but more shallow, information: The explosion of information availability has been accompanied by the dilution of its quality. Some particular patterns worth noting are:

- *"Managed news,"* which one text defines as elected and appointed officials generating and distributing information "in such a way as to give government interests priority over candor,"[5] attributing its origin to George Washington. This ranges from simply timing the release of information to catch or avoid a news cycle to deliberately slanting or planting reports about public policy matters. The Reagan administration was considered the first to master the process, but with technology changing so quickly, will it even continue to be possible to control the flow of information?
- *"Spin,"* when candidates and public officials deliberately promote interpretations of events in a manner that is favorable to themselves or the faction or position they

---

[4] Diana Owen, "Political Socialization in the Twenty-first Century: Recommendations for Researchers," paper presented at "The Future of Civic Education in the 21st Century" conference cosponsored by the Center for Civic Education and the Bundeszentrale fur politische Bildung, James Madison's Montpelier, September 21–26, 2008. Downloaded from http://www.civiced.org/pdfs/GermanAmericanConf2009/DianaOwen_2009.pdf , 7/23/11. She cites W. Lance Bennett, "Civic Learning Online: Responding to the Generational Shift in Citizen Identity," *Around the CIRCLE*, 5 (2008), 1–2.

[5] Steffen W. Schmidt, Mark C. Shelley, and Barbara Bardes, *American Government and Politics Today*, 13th ed. (Mason, OH: Thomson Wadsworth, 2008), 328.

support. This is most heavily used during campaigns and after elections.

- *"Infotainment,"* when presentation style gains emphasis over reporting to enhance viewership. This should not be confused with political satire (using humor to express a political viewpoint), which often serves to draw youth into the political arena. While it may attract more attention to current events, it may also lower the seriousness with which public issues are taken.

Key tool for presidents and other leaders: Public support is the lifeblood of politics. We noted the general impact the modern mass media had of shifting the public's focus to national issues over the course of the twentieth century. Intertwined with that was growing attention paid to the president, particularly as he emerged as a world leader. President George W. Bush's ineffectiveness during his last few months in office was mainly due to the Great Recession, but poor media management made things worse. Bush had lost almost all credibility with the mass media after the Valerie Plame affair. President Reagan, on the other hand, was masterful at using the media to sway public opinion and citizen participation to pressure opposition Congresses into passing legislation he wanted. His media skills also helped him to minimize the fallout from the Iran-Contra Affair.

Reshaping of election campaigns: One of the first impacts of the spread of radio and television was that more public officials became household names. This coverage wound up strengthening the power of incumbents by facilitating their reelections. The president, in particular, draws daily attention. While debates have again become the norm for political races at all levels, the reality is that advertising now dominates election contests. Ineffective attempts to control campaign financing have fueled both negative and advocacy advertising, raising the cost of campaigns, increasing dependency on consultants, and shifting political "debate" from issues to personalities. Reporting on campaigns has assumed a sports-casting demeanor, featuring "horserace" coverage focused on candidates' positions in preference polls rather than on issues. Feeding frenzies are another feature of modern campaign coverage, with media sources stampeding to react to the latest unexpected development. The Internet is certainly reshaping election media campaigns again, with new goals like having your video go "viral" and using social networking to raise funds. Developments are moving rapidly and we can anticipate ongoing dynamism. The possibilities truly are wide open.

Voter behavior: The onslaught of information we all now face increasingly forces people to filter what they actually process. One manifestation in politics is that we tend to watch campaigns with "selective attentiveness," an inclination to pay more attention to ads and news stories that support candidates and positions we favor, reinforcing our existing views. This is a specific version of the broader filtering effect that the worldviews we all possess have on our interpretation of all events. As one might anticipate, there is a complementary effect whereby the media have the most influence on those who have not developed a firm worldview or formed strong opinions, those frequently labeled the "undecided."

"E-government" is transforming public administration: "E-government" is the new norm. Today, most individuals (especially youth) anticipate being able to contact

public officials quickly, receive timely feedback, obtain needed information, and complete basic transactions quickly and conveniently over the Internet. The standard term for "public service workers who interact directly with citizens in the course of their jobs" has been "street-level bureaucrat,"[6] but that is yielding to "screen-level bureaucrat." This should lead to greater efficiencies in the long run, but will disrupt established service patterns during the transition, epitomized by the troubles facing the Postal Service. The problem of further disadvantaging the disadvantaged is again an issue here.

GOVERNMENT REGULATION OF THE MEDIA

The Federal Communications Commission (FCC) was created in 1934 to regulate media "according to the public interest, convenience, and necessity." In contrast to the light touch the government has used toward the print media, electronic media have been *regulated* from the beginning *with respect to both ownership and broadcast content.* Originally, the regulation of ownership was geared toward preventing the development of monopolies controlling information in communities. Ownership of multiple types of media in the same community (the local newspaper, radio station and television station, for example) was restricted. That changed dramatically with the Telecommunications Act of 1966.

After 1966, a single corporation was allowed to offer both local and long-distance telephone service, cable and satellite television services, and Internet services, along with owning studios that can produce media content (music recordings, films, television shows, etc.) and distribution operations. The era of the media conglomerate was born. During our discussion of public opinion, we noted that most of the remaining print outlets have now partnered with electronic media firms, increasing the concentration of control over information flow. The counterargument is, of course, that the number of media offerings has exploded, greatly expanding the choices consumers have and precluding meaningful control by any single provider, even a conglomerate.

The other subject of government media regulation has been broadcast content, particularly for screening out "indecent" images and language. Since viewers originally had no control over what came into their homes over the radio or the television, the norm quickly developed that no offensive content should be allowed to be broadcast. What we now call a "zero tolerance" approach was adopted, with both heavy fines and informal career sanctions imposed on entertainers who violated the norm. The advent of subscription cable television opened the door to more risqué content on those channels, which eventually loosened the standards of acceptability for all broadcasts.

The success of "smart phones" and tablet computers has made all these services portable, meaning that anyone can be exposed to anything, anywhere, at any time. In keeping with its conservative ideology, the George W. Bush administration clamped down on what it considered to be indecent content, setting off a string of court battles challenging major fines levied

---

[6] Michael Lipsky, *Street-Level Bureaucracy: Dilemmas of the Individual in Public Services* (New York: Russell Sage Foundation, 1980).

on broadcasters. Given the spontaneous nature of communications today, television stations are seeking relief from being punished for "fleeting" violations involving the infamous seven banned words, for example.[7]

It must be noted that compared to the rest of the world, U.S. regulation of the mass media is very light. Even in most advanced industrial states, the government either owns or exercises significant control over all or part of the broadcast media. Concern arose in this country when President Bush authorized wide-scale monitoring of telephone and Internet communications after the 9/11 terrorist attack. This unease was increased when certain provisions of the Patriot Act seemed to expand government's surveillance authority. The recent renewal of that Act did not alleviate many of those fears, particularly since the technological capability for surveillance is becoming increasingly sophisticated.

CONCLUDING NOTES

The flow of information, particularly between government officials and the people, is the lifeblood of democracy. Why? Because "the scale and organization of politics are dependent upon how far and how fast information about people, policies, and platforms [meaning political party positions on various issues] can be moved."[8] The transformation of the mass media both structurally and technologically has important implications for the political process. With media conglomeration continuing, these technological and organizational changes seem to be intertwining, creating compound effects. The Internet has succeeded in mating with every other form of communication, creating both completely new forms of interaction (e.g., Twitter® and Facebook®) and new forums for conventional political debate (e.g., the "blogosphere" supplementing and intertwining with major newspapers and magazines).

The dominance of the private sector in the U.S. mass media is an important fact to keep in mind, especially when compared to the other developed democratic nations of our world. The mass media at its core is now a commercial enterprise, which is the dominant characteristic shaping its behavior. Debates about media bias usually focus on ideology, but they may miss the most important point: "In fact, the political coloration of the mainstream media comes less from the personal beliefs of reporters and managers than from the corporate structure of the industry. They are more cautious than they are either liberal or conservative."[9] For all media, a focus on "ratings," their revenue source, is the key to success.

The overall role of the mass media in our political system seems to be growing, and the implications of that are currently unknown. The new technology appears to have the mass media assuming the primary role in political socialization, for example, and the impacts on policy formulation, implementation, and evaluation will certainly continue and expand. Two trends are particularly worth noting. The first is *organizational message tailoring*. Compiling and analyzing all information about a user has become the norm for Internet service providers, and the "profile" developed is used to generate

---

[7] *FCC v. Pacifica Foundation*, 438 U.S. 230 (1978).

[8] Cal Jillson, *American Government: Political Development and Institutional Change*, 5th ed. (New York: Routledge, 2011), 102; brackets added.
[9] Ibid., 117.

advertising and other marketing activities customized to that user. This tactic has been used in political advertising for some time, but targeting was based on group characteristics (age, gender, etc.) or political positions (pro-life, pro-gun-control, etc.). It will be interesting to see how this shift to individualized marketing makes the transition to political campaigns.

A countervailing trend worth noting has been produced by the convergence of advancing technology and American individualism, *personal message filtering*. Those willing to learn how can customize their equipment to filter all content to which they are exposed. As described by the first analyst to sound the alarm about this phenomenon, one can create a "Daily me" information stream including only the content one wants to see or hear and nothing more. He "warns against 'information cocoons' and 'echo chambers,' wherein people avoid the news and opinions that they don't want to hear," and asks the critical question, "What happens to democracy and free speech if people use the Internet to listen and speak only to the like-minded?"[10]

That dynamic will be seen over and over again. Both private and public organizations will seek to use technology to manipulate people's behavior, but individuals will fight back. Given the ongoing structural consolidation, the seemingly unending stream of technological innovation, and the reality of human resistance, one can easily predict that ongoing, and possibly accelerating, system turbulence will be the key characteristic shaping the flow of political information for the near future. What should we be striving for? "Ideally, the media and public officials would cooperate to ensure accurate reporting on the issues demanding political decisions, on the options available, and the actual effects, good and bad, of existing policies."[11] We could add that all basic government information and services would be available to all citizens, but as we all know, we do not live in an ideal world.

---

[10] Cass Sunstein, *Republic.com.2.0* (Princeton, NJ: Princeton University Press, 2009), http://press.princeton.edu/titles/8468.html

[11] Cal Jillson, *American Government: Political Development and Institutional Change*, 5th ed. (New York: Routledge, 2008), 124.

CHAPTER 12

Elections, Campaigns, and Voting

ELECTIONS

Elections are the core activity of modern democracy. First among the *basic reasons why we have elections* is that they are the *source of legitimacy* for both our public officials and our political process. While elections might be primarily symbolic in a number of other "democratic" political systems, in the United States they are the actual method used for *popular selection of authoritative decision makers*. In addition to filling the various public offices in our communities, elections can also serve as *a policymaking or policy changing mechanism.* This can occur directly in those states that allow citizen initiative, but even in those that do not, the selection of public officials sets the direction that public policymaking will take, for the next term at least. Changing the party in power almost always results in significant policy changes; changing leadership within the same party often signals the ascent of one faction over another and subsequent policy shifts.

The basic power to organize, conduct, and regulate elections was retained by the state governments under the U.S. Constitution. Control of elections remains primarily at the state level, with the national government empowered to ensure that voting rights are not infringed upon by the Fourteenth ("equal protection of the laws"), Fifteenth ("race, color, or previous condition of servitude"), Nineteenth ("sex"), and Twenty-sixth ("age" for those 18 and older) Amendments, the Voting Rights Act of 1965, and subsequent legislation. As you might expect, a wide array of specific processes and procedures exist across the nation, and no attempt will be made to summarize and compare them for our overview. The basic qualifications for national offices are specified in the Constitution:

- *President and Vice President*: Natural born U.S. citizen at least 35 years of age with 14 years of U.S. residency.
- *Senator*: U.S. citizen for at least 9 years, at least 30 years of age, and "an inhabitant of that state for which he shall be chosen."
- *Representative*: U.S. citizen for at least 7 years, at least 25 years of age, and "an inhabitant of that state in which he shall be chosen."

TYPES OF ELECTIONS

Baseline knowledge that every member of a political community should have includes an understanding of the different types of elections that are held and the purpose of each:

- *Open Primary elections* are conducted to allow *all registered voters in a community to select candidates for public offices* to be filled in the next general election. Alternative methods used for candidate selection include party caucuses (meetings of all party members) or party conventions (meetings of elected delegates).
- *Closed Primary elections* are conducted to allow *only party members who are registered voters to select that party's candidates for public offices* to be filled in the next general election. Any voter wishing to change parties must usually do so well in advance of the primary election.

Some Notes About Primaries

Specific laws and procedures vary among the 50 states, and certain primaries are hybrids often labeled "semi-open" or "semi-closed." Some states allow individuals to switch parties on primary day, for example, while others allow registered Independents to declare a party at the polls on primary day. Any serious student of politics should learn about his or her state's specific election laws. It is also worth noting that open primaries provide the opportunity for political parties to try manipulating the choice of the opposition party's candidates. This tactic usually involves identifying the weakest potential opponent and urging your party's members to go out and vote for him or her. Some view this as a "dirty trick," while others simply consider it "hardball" politics.

- *General elections* are conducted to allow *all registered voters to choose public officials* in accordance with their state constitutions and laws and all relevant local ordinances.
- *Nonpartisan elections* are conducted with *no party labels used*. This does not mean, however, that political parties do not play a role. Depending on the local political culture, parties may be very active in the electoral process despite the absence of the specific labels.
- *Off-year elections* are those conducted *when no routine national elections are being held*. Presidential elections are held each leap year, and "midterm elections" refers to congressional races conducted at the two-year midpoint of each presidential term. Some states schedule their major elections (notably for governor) during off-year elections to minimize any fallout from national politics (often labeled the "coattail effect") on state and local races.
- *Runoff elections* involve *the top two vote-getters facing off* in a subsequent election. They are used in states or localities that require candidates to receive a majority of votes cast in order to win, as opposed to the standard winner-take-all plurality approach used in most elections in the United States. In an attempt to reduce costs and improve voter turnout, some communities are trying a new "instant runoff" process in which voters rank candidates in their order of preference. When no candidate receives a majority of first choices, those receiving the fewest are eliminated and the second choices of those voters tabulated. This continues until a candidate receives a majority of the total votes cast.
- *Recall elections* are those seeking *to remove public officials from elected offices prior to the end of their terms*, usually as a result of citizen

petition. State laws specify the requirements, which usually include a minimum percentage of valid registered voter signatures.

- *Special elections* are those conducted to *fill unexpected vacancies* in public offices due to resignation, removal, or death. Again, state laws specify when these are required and how they will be conducted. A special election can be conducted concurrently with a recall election.

- A *Referendum* is an election in which *citizens vote on proposed policies* (laws, budgets, bond issues, constitutional amendments) as opposed to choosing public officials or candidates. Especially when paired with direct "Initiative," the process by which citizens are allowed to directly place policy questions on the ballot by petition, referendum is often referred to as "direct democracy."[1]

CAMPAIGNS

As noted at the beginning of Chapter 7, the United States does not conduct *a* presidential election, but rather a collection of 51 state and district elections. The Electoral College is a unique mechanism created for translating the "Great Compromise" on representation into an election process that usually does not involve the other branches, which was necessary to maintain the independence of the Executive branch. Each state is recognized as a distinct political entity, while the realities of population and its shifts are accounted for. Concerns over the "undemocratic" nature of the Electoral College, revived by the closeness of the 2000 election, are genuine. Changing it would be extremely significant:[2]

The electoral college is the linchpin of the American political system. Any change in the existing winner-take-all system has sweeping ramifications for all aspects of our political system-presidential campaigns, political participation, electoral coalitions, congressional elections, and the two-party system.

Calls for a change to direct election of the president are unlikely to succeed, since it would be difficult to persuade enough of the smaller states to ratify the required constitutional amendment. Direct election would be a radical change to our political process, and would alter the delicate dynamics of U.S. federalism in ways we might come to regret.[3] Adoption of the approach currently used by Maine and Nebraska should satisfy critics of the Electoral College for the most part. Both choose their electors by congressional district, with the statewide winner awarded the two "Senate" electoral votes. This reform would both retain the state-based nature of the presidential election and better reflect the popular vote. It would also make the elections more competitive—and perhaps even more interesting. The author of the thorough academic analysis that warned of "sweeping ramifications" concluded:[4]

My own view is that the optimal presidential electoral system would encourage presidential campaigns to build broad electoral coalitions, stimulate citizen interest and

---

[1] A good source of information is the Initiative and Referendum Institute, www.iandrinstitute.org.

[2] Turner, Robert C. "The contemporary presidency: do Nebraska and Maine have the right idea? The political and partisan implications of the district system." *Presidential Studies Quarterly*, 35 (1) (2005): 116–136.
[3] Ibid. A good editorial example is Bill Whalen, "Hail to Thee, Electoral College," *The Star-Ledger* 10/6/2004, 18.
[4] Turner (see Note 2), 133.

turnout in presidential elections, produce a president who can govern, strengthen the two-party system, discourage electoral fraud, and be relatively neutral, I think the district system excels in meeting these criteria.

Before someone has to worry about planning an Electoral College victory strategy, however, he or she first needs to win his or her party's nomination. This is accomplished by garnering a majority of committed delegates to that party's national convention by competing in a state-by-state series of party primaries and caucuses and for the support of state and local party activists who go as "superdelegates." The process formally begins in early January of each leap year, but informally begins much earlier. Prospective candidates form exploratory committees of supporters and party notables and "float their names" in the mass media. Favorable initial responses lead to the true test, the quest for early financial support. Early competition for campaign support, particularly financing, has been called "the invisible primary."

Party nominating contests now receive national attention, especially the early ones in New Hampshire and Iowa. Primary elections are often hard-fought events, particularly when there is no dominant candidate, and they require extensive personal effort on the part of the candidate, sound organization, and significant resources. As noted in our discussion of the mass media, face-to-face debates are now a mandatory feature of all elections. Another feature of twenty-first-century election campaigns is the growing importance of Internet-based activities. The full benefit of the Internet as a campaign organizing tool is still being discovered, but its value in that regard and for fundraising was clearly demonstrated by the 2008 Obama campaign.

Campaign Financing

A proposed set of ingredients for a successful election effort that also outlines the major elements of a campaign will be offered below. Readers seeking more in-depth knowledge are urged to review the growing literature on campaign management.[5] The second item on that list of ingredients needed for success is money, although many of my colleagues, many other political analysts, and most students (based on responses given in class over nearly two decades) would list it first. Rising costs for television and radio advertising, technical equipment and the expertise needed to use it effectively, and travel have driven up the basic cost of election campaigns significantly.

Attempts by Congress to regulate the financing of election campaigns for national offices began almost 100 years ago with little effect. One major reform did succeed when The Hatch Act of 1939 led to the virtual elimination of partisan political activity among national civil servants. The Federal Election Campaign Act of 1971 and subsequent amendments spawned by the Watergate scandal tried to restrict both spending and contributions, but were weakened by court rulings that tended to treat such restrictions as limits on free speech and/or political activity. Some positive results were achieved, including creation of the Federal Election Commission and initiation of the disclosure of the amounts and sources of campaign contributions in formal reports. *Political Action Committees (PACs) as legal mechanisms specifically for raising and distributing political contributions* emerged from these efforts also.

---

[5] For example, Daniel M. Shea and Michael John Burton, *Campaign Craft: The Strategies, Tactics, and Art of Political Campaign Management* (Westport, CT: Praeger, 2000).

Originally created as a means of circumventing campaign-finance reforms, they have been integrated into the formal process.

Two consequences of these attempts were interesting shifts in political activity. Interest groups/associations soon discovered that restrictions on contributions to campaigns did not prevent them from spending money independently of campaigns in ways that indirectly benefited candidates they preferred. "Independent expenditures," spending by private groups that is not coordinated with any campaign, have become a regular feature of elections. State attempts to regulate these independent expenditures led to a 1990 Supreme Court ruling that upheld legal limits on independent expenditures on behalf of candidates, but was interpreted as supporting independent spending promoting issue positions.[6] So, fundraising strictly for "issue advocacy" has now become common also.

The evolution of independent expenditures and issue advocacy in response to efforts to legally control campaign contributions points out one of the stark truisms about government regulation. Whenever you tell someone what they cannot do, you are also telling them what they can do. Lawyers earn reputations within their field for discovering and exploiting loopholes. A legal distinction between two basic types of campaign financing created as part of efforts to regulate it seems to be the root source of a number of these loopholes, and clearly illustrates how past policymaking impacts current authoritative decision making:

- *"Hard money"* refers to funds contributed directly to a specific candidate for a specific campaign ("Smith for Senate 2012"). There

are significant controls on hard money, particularly with respect to limits on individual donations, what it can be used for, and information that must be collected from donors and compiled and reported to the Federal Election Commission.

- *"Soft money"* refers to funds contributed to private groups or organizations other than a campaign to be used to *indirectly* help or hurt candidates for public office or a political party with voter education, registration, and turnout efforts initially, but mostly through issue advocacy advertising recently.

The Bipartisan Campaign Reform Act of 2002 (commonly known as the McCain–Feingold Act) was the latest attempt to control campaign spending. With the goal of redirecting political donations back into actual campaigns, the law banned soft money contributions to national political parties (but not to state and local parties) and increased dollar limits on individual campaign donations, while restricting issue advocacy by private groups, including banning advertising targeting specific candidates just prior to an election. That restriction was ruled unconstitutional in 2006,[7] but most other provisions remain in effect. Removing restrictions on issue advocacy sparked the proliferation of "527" and "(c)(4)" organizations (so named based on the particular Internal Revenue Service Code sections that apply to them) and an explosion of independent expenditures in subsequent elections.

The redirection of soft money contributions to state and local political parties fueled increased campaign expenditures at those levels. Since they are the base components of our national parties, and the training grounds for our

---

[6] *Austin v. Michigan State Chamber of Commerce*, 494 U.S. 652 (1990).

[7] *Wisconsin Right to Life, Inc. v. Federal Election Commission*, 126 S. Ct. 1016 (2006).

national leaders, let us take a brief look at some of their campaign financing tactics that raise concerns:

- *"Bundling"* is collecting the maximum donation allowed from multiple donors and presenting them to the campaign "in a bundle" to increase one's influence.
- *"Wheeling"* is the movement of campaign contributions by party committees and leaders from surplus areas to areas where funds are needed to enhance overall party prospects.
- *"Pay-to-Play"* is making campaign donations to position oneself or one's firm to pursue government contracts.

All three of these tactics are also applied at the national level, and since both major parties can—and do—use them, one is hesitant to shout, "Unfair!" Recognizing that campaigns are battles for political control, one must accept the fact that people will fight hard to win. Elections are one of the arenas in which our Ideal Principles clash, moreover. How does one reconcile maximizing personal liberty as manifested by campaign contributions with the importance of genuinely competitive elections to our democracy? *Some possible remedies* for our campaign financing dilemma include:

Time Limits on Campaigns: Costs have risen in part due to the increasing length of campaigns. Since our system relies on fixed terms of office (subject to recall or impeachment), when an office would be open is public knowledge. It is difficult to envision an effective time limit being imposed that would not be perceived by the courts as a de facto limit on free speech.

Limit Total Expenditures: Spending over $1 billion to elect our president seems like a huge waste to many Americans. Realizing

that we spend more than 12 times that much each year on chocolate helps to put that total cost into perspective. Given the Supreme Court's historical linkage of political donations with free speech, recently reinforced by the *Citizens United* ruling that the use of soft money by corporations and unions cannot be limited,[8] an overall expenditure limit is unlikely to be accepted as constitutional.

Public Financing: Partial public financing of presidential campaigns was begun in the 1970s when individuals were allowed to designate $3 of their federal taxes to a special program created to provide matching funds for candidates meeting certain criteria. In order to receive those funds, however, a candidate had to accept a limit on the total amount of money he or she could raise for his or her campaign. This appeared to help, fueling the insurgent Carter and early Reagan campaigns within their respective parties. In recent elections, the lure of unlimited private contributions has led most presidential candidates to forgo the relatively small amount of matching funds provided. "Clean Election" initiatives in Maine and Arizona seem to be working, and deserve further study for possible replication and application at the national level.

Free Television Time: The largest single campaign expenditure is producing and airing television advertising. Since the airways are owned by the public, consideration should be given to providing some set amount of free television time to each candidate or party every night. While it is very unlikely that the Supreme Court would accept a ban on paid political advertising as constitutional, providing a

---

[8] *Citizens United v. Federal Election Commission*, 130 S. Ct. 876 (2010).

baseline amount of national television exposure to candidates could change the dynamics of the presidential selection process. Any such proposal would certainly be strongly opposed by both the media conglomerates and political consulting/marketing firms.

INGREDIENTS FOR SUCCESS

Political campaigns epitomize the circumstantial aspects of our political process. One mistake can counteract months of effort. This author's jaw literally dropped during the 1976 debates when President Ford responded to a question about Eastern Europe by stating it was "not under the domination of the Soviet Union." Given the opportunity to retract his response, he did not, and his attempts to clarify it failed when he repeated the same phraseology. Given the closeness of the final election results, that "unforced error" could well have been the difference between victory and defeat. With new technology allowing continuous recording and videotaping, candidates must literally take care with every word they speak.

Incumbents (current officeholders) have a distinct advantage over challengers due to the extensive free media coverage they receive, a distinct fundraising advantage, and the rewards reaped from constituent casework. Reelection success for House incumbents has fallen below 80 percent only twice since World War II, including the Tea Party insurgency of 2010. Senate incumbents face somewhat stronger odds, but their success rate also fluctuates around the 80 percent level. Circumstances in particular races (e.g., a hot issue, candidate error, political or party turmoil in a state) can easily blunt and incumbent's usual advantage, and "the drama of a singular event can supersede years

of policymaking,"[9] particularly for incumbent chief executives. The article from which that quote is drawn cites the assassination that set off World War I as "the biggest of all such wildcard events" in history, and the Tunisian fruit seller's self-immolation that triggered the 2011 Arab awakening in the Middle East as a major recent example.

Both incumbents and challengers must plan, organize, and run their campaigns to find the correct "recipe" by properly blending these *basic ingredients for success*:

Get Out the Vote: Elections are won with votes. Although money may be a necessary ingredient, it alone is not sufficient to guarantee victory. This has been illustrated by a number of campaigns in history, and most recently by former New York Mayor Rudy Giuliani's 2008 effort. This is when and how political parties prove their worth to candidates. While individual campaign operations are important, most campaign volunteers are local and state party activists, and their organizations provide both the "operational knowledge" of the community and the coordination of "ground game" activities that lead to victory. The Internet age may eventually change this, but getting voters registered and to the polls currently remain critical for success, particularly in close races.

Money: Fundraising is like breathing for political campaigns; failure to do enough of it means you will either die or are have diminished operating capacity that will likely

---

[9] Karl Ritter, quoting Director Philip Seib of the University of Southern California's Center on Public Diplomacy, "Leaders' policies still at the mercy of sparks set off by lone acts," *The Star-Ledger,* 3/29/12, 2.

lead to defeat. The rising costs for advertising, travel, staff, and so on, were noted above, so the amounts needed to be raised and spent well will likely increase. Good money management and proper accounting and reporting should be built into a campaign from the very beginning, usually by hiring experienced professionals.

Good Candidate: Undoubtedly, the capabilities of individual candidates are among the keys to electoral success. What are the qualities of successful public office seekers?

- They are usually *articulate* and *mediagenic.* The people want their leaders and representatives to be able to both communicate clearly and motivate them when appropriate. They also expect them to project a positive image at all times. Today that means looking and sounding good on both big and small screens. While charisma is not an absolute requirement, it certainly helps.

- Most voters also want their leaders and representatives to be *experienced.* The type and level of experience expected depends on the office being sought. A presidential candidate's range of experience should be wide and deep, with many voters preferring a successful record as an elected executive. Candidates for the House or Senate are expected to know the community or state they would be representing well and have significant coalition building skills. A judge should have specialized knowledge in the particular area of the law (civil, criminal or constitutional) over which he or she would be presiding.

- Their experience should also demonstrate *applied intelligence*, above average brainpower combined with knowledge of how to get things done. We want smart leaders and representatives, but not necessarily intellectuals. A record of professional achievement in a challenging field, including politics is usually expected.

- A critical ingredient is *people skills.* Public policymaking and administration require almost constant negotiation with both rivals and supporters. Interpersonal communications should be easy–even enjoyable–for political candidates. Getting people to like you increases the chances that they will vote for you.

- Last, but certainly not least important, is having a *role model reputation*. Even a hint of scandal can derail a presidential campaign, while the expectations for House and Senate candidates will vary with the political culture of the particular state involved. Tolerance levels regarding personal behavior seem to be rising, moreover, and serious "opposition research" into a candidate's personal history is now routine.

Good Team: As with any complex project, success requires a combination of special skills and sound general management. A successful election campaign usually requires an experienced campaign manager and other paid campaign staff; at least some consultants in specialty areas like polling, fundraising, voter analysis, and so on; and motivated volunteers whose activities are coordinated by experienced campaign, interest group/association, or party liaisons.

Good Media Management: One of the greatest challenges facing any candidate is maximizing the benefit and minimizing the damage to the campaign from dealings with the mass media. This includes both the free media outlets that report—and frame—the news and paid advertising. Today, political advertising involves not just television and radio, but also the new Internet-based media, and traditional media like direct mail and newspapers. An interesting new twist in advertising is *narrowcasting*, whereby electronic advertising can be very specifically targeted using cable television and social media.

Attractive Policy Proposals: Some voters actually do focus on the substance of the policy proposals that candidates put forth. People will judge an individual's leadership potential to a degree based on the ideas that they offer. Note that although the potential effectiveness of policy proposals should be the primary basis for their attractiveness to voters, personal perceptions based on ideology and the varied impacts of political socialization tend to be more important to them. This is the "selective attentiveness" mentioned in our discussion of the mass media in action.

VOTING

It seems very fitting that voting should be the last topic covered in discussing a democratic republic, since it is the most common and direct input mechanism that the people have into the authoritative decision-making process. We make our system of indirect democracy work by choosing qualified and capable individuals to serve as public executives and legislators throughout our Federal Republic, and as judges and a variety of other authoritative decision makers in some of our states. Only two basic points of historical perspective will be noted for our brief overview:

- *Expansion:* Although the U.S. Federal Republic started out with very limited suffrage (essentially only rich, white men), its history over the years has been one of continuous expansion. State governments began shedding property requirements in the 1800s, the Fifteenth Amendment eliminated race as a legal limitation, and the Nineteenth Amendment finally gave women the vote nationwide in 1920. Federalism's contribution should be noted in that some states, beginning with Wyoming and Colorado, granted women the vote decades earlier. One of the accomplishments of the anti–Vietnam War movement was getting the Twenty-Sixth Amendment extending the vote to 18-year-olds ratified in 1971. While the Americans with Disabilities Act of 1992 and its 2008 amendments mandate full access to voting for persons with disabilities, it remains to be seen whether that has actually been achieved.

- *National Intervention:* African Americans continued to be denied their voting rights until the post–World War II Civil Rights Movement of the 1960s succeeded in getting the Twenty-Fourth Amendment outlawing poll taxes ratified and the Voting Rights Act of 1965 passed with the support of President Lyndon Johnson. U.S. Justice Department scrutiny of voting laws, procedures, and practices is still in effect in several southern and southwestern counties, and a number of federal court cases dealing with discrimination questions raised by redistricting have been heard. The latest issue raising concerns over discrimination deal with new state laws tightening voter identification requirements. Minority communities feel they are being targeted, and arguments are being made that certain requirements, most notably a government-issued identification card with a photograph, amount to voter suppression efforts like those used in the days of Jim Crow.

FACTORS IN VOTING

One of the subfields of political science that lends itself to quantitative analysis is voting behavior, and it has been well researched by both academics and professional campaign consultants. The consultants focus on factors that enable them to identify voters most likely to support their clients, and one of the latest trends is using purchasing patterns and other personal behaviors. The academic literature is too extensive to even attempt a meaningful review here, so some of the key points that have been learned are summarized below. These are presented in three categories:

1. Individual Factors:

    Socioeconomic Status (SES) as the concept used by social scientists to differentiate individuals and households based on a combination of income, education, and occupation was introduced in Chapter 10. Those with higher SES tend to vote more, with level of education showing a clear progression.[10]

    Age: Older individuals have historically voted at higher rates, but the youth (18–24) vote increased notably in 2006 and 2008, but seems to have retrenched

in 2010. There is no clear trend on which to base future projections.

Race: African Americans now register and vote at rates similar to Whites, with some studies showing higher turnout for them when income levels are taken into account, while Latino and Asian Americans still tend to vote at lower rates.[11]

Gender: Historically, women voted at lower rates than men, but their turnout steadily increased over the decades, surpassed that of men in 1980s, and remains higher.[12] Some of this progress can be attributed to increased education levels and more women becoming individual stakeholders in society.

2. Institutional Factors: These are variables related to a community's political climate and formal process:

    The Political Culture: In more traditionalistic and moralistic communities, turnout tends to be higher since voting is treated as a civic duty as well is a right by more people. A range of shared community attitudes toward voting also exists; some encourage it, some are neutral, and the political atmosphere in some communities makes voting unattractive.

    Registration and Voting Procedures: One of the benefits of the spread of computer technology has been greater ease in maintaining the voting rolls and using these records in holding elections.

---

[10] Jennifer Jerit, Jason Barabas, and Toby Bolsen, "Citizens, Knowledge, and the Information Environment," *American Journal of Political Science,* 50 (April 2006), 266–282.

[11] Frederick C. Harris, Valeria Sinclair-Chapman, and Brian D. McKenzie, "Macrodynamics of Black Political Participation in the Post-Civil Rights Era," *Journal of Politics,* 67 (November 2005), 1143–1163.
[12] Virginia Sapiro, *The Political Integration of Women* (Urbana: University of Illinois Press, 1983).

Registrations can be processed more quickly, so deadlines for registering have been moved closer to election dates, enabling more people to vote. Restrictions on the use of absentee ballots have been lifted, and early voting has been instituted in several states, increasing turnout. In this regard, continuing the tradition of Tuesday elections, which dates back to our agricultural past, has been criticized for reducing turnout. Although voting online is still not possible due to security concerns,[13] voting by mail has been very successful in the state of Oregon, which began allowing citizens to vote by mail in the 1980s and has had an excellent experience with it.

Political Competitiveness: The level of competition between the major political parties or among political factions or particular interests in a community impacts voter turnout. Greater competition generates greater attention from the media, raising awareness of the upcoming election and motivating more people to vote. Conversely, the absence of political competition, including dominance of the community by one party or interest, reduces media attention and individual awareness, leading to lower turnout.

3. *Circumstantial Factors:* These are variables related to the situational realities of political contests near and at election time that affect the perceptions and motivations of potential voters:

Type of Election: General elections tend to draw more voters than primaries, since registered Independents can always participate, they receive greater attention in the media, and they are perceived as more important. Presidential elections always outdraw those held at midterm, while off-year elections tend to attract the fewest voters.

"Hot" Issues: Particularly with respect to statewide constituencies during national elections, issues that draw extraordinary notice from potential voters (often due to extensive media coverage) tend to increase turnout. These can range from national concerns like illegal immigration or abortion that happen to be receiving extra attention in response to state or local policy initiatives or local matters such as scandals or major policy mistakes.

Popularity of Candidates: Particularly popular, or *un*popular, candidates can draw more voters to the polls. Yes, the desire to keep someone *out of* office can motivate some individuals who would not otherwise vote to do so.

Closeness of Contests: The media love close races and give them extra attention, which raises both awareness and voter motivation. Elections that clearly appear to be decided tend to have the opposite effects, on the other hand.

Personal Motivation: As individuals, our particular interests shape our voting behavior. It is our individual interests that make each election more or less important to each of us. An issue that may not be "hot" for the general community may generate intense feelings in some people.

---

[13] The PBS *Newshour* explored this topic in "Internet Voting: Will Democracy or Hackers Win?" broadcast 2/16/12, and concluded it is still "a distant dream right now." Transcript downloaded 2/17/12 from http://www.pbs.org/newshour/bb/politics.

Our personal perceptions and ideologies impact what we do, as well as the basic realities we all must deal with. It seems appropriate to consider some of the reasons people give for *not* voting besides personal circumstances (e.g., illness, work or child care interfering, transportation problems):

- Do not know where to go to vote
- Do not think their vote counts or will make a difference
- Do not think they know enough
- Do not like/dislike any of the candidates enough to be motivated to vote
- Turned off by negative campaigning
- General cynicism about government

Most of those reasons, which reflect student responses during classroom discussions about voting over two decades, cannot be countered by government action. Mailing sample ballots with specific information about where to vote and when the polls will be open to every registered voter, as some states now require, would alleviate that problem. E-government could also render that problem moot, as more governments make more information available online.

Recognizing the central role that voting, as the only direct input into public policymaking that individuals have, plays in our democratic republic, we should continue removing procedural obstacles to voting and consider how we might raise the confidence of more potential voters. Until secure Internet voting becomes available, for example, more widespread use of voting by mail should be promoted. Moving elections to the weekend also deserves serious consideration. Maintaining and strengthening the most democratic element of our political process should be a priority we all share.

Conclusion: Still a Good Ship?

PUTTING THE PIECES OF THE PUZZLE TOGETHER

Our journey through the U.S. political system has admittedly been "cruise-like," using brief stops to complete an overview of our system's political culture, configuration, and major operational aspects that both create and reflect our political circumstance. While some connections have been pointed out along the way, our analysis has been of a piecemeal nature so far. To begin pulling the pieces of the puzzle together, let's review several themes that have continually arisen over the course of our journey:

- *Complexity:* Despite the deep human desire for simplicity, life and politics seem to prefer complexity. One of the great strengths of the U. S. Federal Republic is its capability of handling complexity. To gain a complete appreciation for the complexity of our system, one must also study state and local government in some detail. Recall that this involves approximately 88,000 distinct authoritative decision-making bodies, *not* including thousands of homeowners

associations, arrayed in potentially ten (10) levels of "government" authority over an individual or household (see Figure 5-1). Also, recall that a substantial portion of state and local intergovernmental relations occur horizontally, so Figure 5-1 only hints at the potential complexity one could encounter.

- *Custom and Usage:* Throughout our journey we have encountered custom and uage creating informal norms of behavior. American pragmatism leads to repetition of practices that work, and this is reinforced in our political system by the importance placed on legal precedents. Our willingness to adapt our formal structures and processes to accommodate the realities of life has been one of our great strengths. Formal structures are the "skeletons" that people turn into functioning social systems, and this interplay of the formal and informal aspects increases system complexity, making adaptability harder. With the proud tradition we have to build upon, as we head toward the midpoint of our third century as a democratic federal republic, the turbulence we are facing may require that we modify some traditional ways to preserve ourselves and resume prosperity.

• *"Subsystems"*: This monograph portrays the U. S. political system as a mosaic, a set of intricately intertwined and overlaid "subsystems" that both compete and cooperate, with the U.S. Federal Republic as its core structure. Figure C-2A is an attempt to portray that mosaic in an idealized manner, and will be discussed in detail below. It illustrates that the U.S. Federal Republic itself is a complex set of formal and informal "subsystems," the original "polyarchy" in which "subsystem autonomy and organizational pluralism are always marked features of the social and political order."[1] The development of informal policy subsystems (the "issue networks" that sprout around the "cozy triangles") both reflects the impact of custom and usage and further increases system complexity.

• *Technology*: Along with globalization (which has been taken note of when appropriate, and deserves more attention but will not receive it in keeping with our goal of a compact overview), technology has already reshaped, and is continuing to transform, our political process in the twenty-first century. The infusion of technology into every aspect of our social process is transforming that very process: "The means by which people receive and process information has been essentially altered. Communication takes place more through technological intermediaries than via face-to-face contact." This was discussed in some detail with respect to political socialization in Chapter 4, but the impact of

changing the "core mechanism" of how we communicate is having much wider impact in the political arena.[2] Technology both adds to and better enables us to cope with complexity as it supports subsystem development by facilitating new forms of organization. It has certainly become customary (an accepted–even expected–part of life), and has changed the "how" element in our essential definition of politics. The tugs-of-war taking place today are *very* different from what they were before the first personal computers rolled off the assembly line in the 1980s.

• *"Tugs-of-war"*: The back-and-forth nature of the competition among the various elements of the U.S. political system can be visualized as tugs-of-war between and among them. While oversimplifying the complex interaction that actually occurs, it is a useful way to visualize the basic competition. Envisioning multiple entities engaged in multiple tugs-of-war simultaneously may be difficult, but it comes closest to portraying the reality of the U.S. political process.

Many of these tugs-of-war involve more than two parties, moreover. "Cozy triangles" among congressional (sub)committees, interest groups/associations, and executive agencies have been recognized as important policy subsystems for decades, but there appears to be a broader

---

[1] Robert Dahl, "Pluralism Revisited," *Comparative Politics*, 10 (1978), 191–203.

[2] Diana Owen, "Political Socialization in the Twenty-first Century: Recommendations for Researchers," paper presented for presentation at "The Future of Civic Education in the 21st Century" conference cosponsored by the Center for Civic Education and the Bundeszentrale fur politische Bildung, James Madison's Montpelier, September 21–26, 2008. Downloaded from http://www.civiced.org/pdfs/GermanAmericanConf2009/DianaOwen_2009.pdf, 7/23/11.

pattern of triangular relationships. This application of the triad concept to political design questions beyond the "cozy triangles" was originally inspired by the work of Charles W. Anderson[3] and reignited by Jenna Bednar's recent work, which is discussed in detail below. Four examples are illustrated in Figure C-1 below.

Originally, the European calls for the separation of powers argued only for disconnecting the executive and legislative functions; the Constitution of 1787 created the first political system with the judicial function structured "as a third distinctive governmental task,"[4] creating a triangular tug-of-war among independent government branches. Federalism did the same for the three levels, since the Founders were well aware of the importance of local governments, and even technical definitions of federalism recognize that a local level is implied.[5] The political party structure that informally evolved is basically triangular (Democratic–Independent–Republican), representing a basically triangular ideological rivalry (Liberalism–Pragmatism–Conservatism). Perhaps this insight can serve as the basis for further, more systematic analysis, but here these triads are intended to serve as a

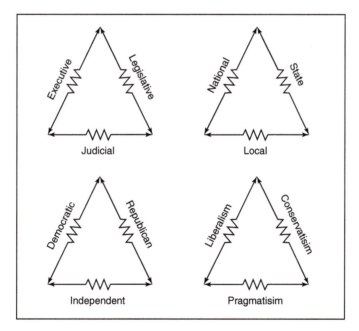

FIGURE C-1: Sample Triangular Tugs-of-War in the U.S. Political System

[3] Charles W. Anderson, *Statecraft: An Introduction to Political Choice and Judgment* (New York: John Wiley & Sons, 1977), 195–199.

[4] Cal Jillson, *American Government: Political Development and Institutional Change*, 6th ed. (New York: Routledge, 2011), 39.

[5] See, for example, Gregory S. Mahler, *Comparative Politics: An Institutional and Cross-National Approach* (Upper Saddle River, NJ: Pearson, 2008), 28.

heuristic device to help the reader visualize the complexity of the U.S. political process.

Figure C-2A is an *ideal* portrayal of the U.S. political system that attempts to link many of the elements and concepts previously discussed. A number of them are from specialty subfields in political science, and some useful research "hints" have been offered in footnotes along our journey for those of you who may be thinking of pursuing further academic study. The portrayal certainly does not depict the power relationships among the elements, which are heavily impacted by political circumstance, but does represent the basic structural frameworks that have been established or emerged over the last 225 years. The "cozy triangles" are shown at the base since they represent the usual core policymaking pattern. The judiciary is placed at the top not to imply that the courts dominate or direct the policymaking process, but rather to denote that they are the final interpreter and enforcer of the Constitution, the final stop for any specific question. Our national bureaucracy is placed at the center to denote its continuous role in converting the decisions of policymakers into operational public programs, along with its constant participation in the "cozy triangles."

Seeing the Presidency (the *institution*, not the individual) at the bottom probably seems odd to many readers, but note that this accurately shows that institution (1) at the top of the bureaucratic "pyramid" with his or her Cabinet, (2) close to the "People" subsystem, depicting its unique status as the only nationally elected office, and (3) continuously interacting with the "cozy triangles," a regular activity for White House staff. The chart is not intended to be a static portrayal, moreover. Each component triangle should be envisioned as growing or shrinking relative to the others based on the particular issue being decided and the particular political circumstances

shaping the decision-making process at any point in time. When envisioned as a fluctuating mosaic, similar to the images produced by a kaleidoscope, it can be seen as a useful rendering of the complex tugs-of-war that permeate the U.S. political process. A simple example would be when ratification of an international treaty is under consideration, the Senate triangle and the Presidency would be "larger," since they would be the principal decision-makers. For a revision of the tax code, the House triangle would be larger.

This attempt is certainly imperfect, and criticisms and recommendations for refinement are anticipated and will be welcomed. As an ideal portrayal, it *is* intended to convey a sense of cohesiveness and stability. Triangles tend to be stable structures, and interlocking triangles reinforce each other, generating more stability. The overall image that Chart C-2A is intended to present is rooted in the basic "gestalt" principle "that the whole is greater than the sum of its parts" and carries "a different and altogether greater meaning than its individual components."[6] That principle could likely be applied to many political systems, but that subject must be left for a different journey. Future political scientists will want to note that the "People" subsystem (Figure C-2B) reflects a rudimentary continuum incorporating Milbrath's typology of popular participation[7] with the "attentive public" concept.[8] With issue networking possibly being transformed by the

---

[6] From http://facweb.cs.depaul.edu/sgrais/gestalt_principles.htm, which credits Max Wertheimer, Wolfgang Kohler, and Kurt Koffka as "the prominent founders of Gestalt theory."

[7] Lester Milbrath, *Political Participation* (Chicago: Rand McNally, 1965).

[8] Donald Devine, *The Attentive Public* (Chicago: Rand McNally, 1970) originated the concept, and it has been applied in a variety of research.

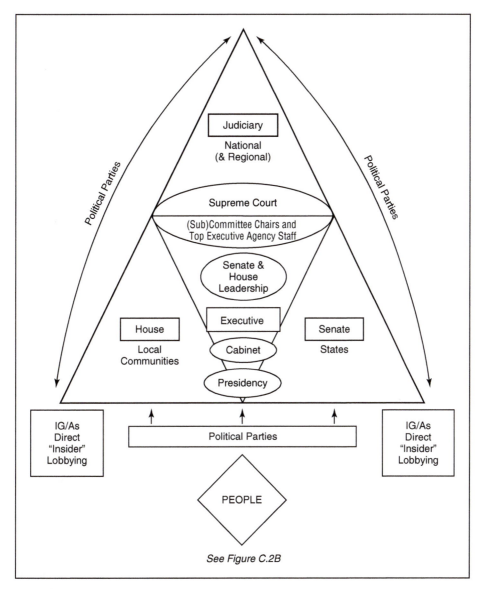

FIGURE C-2A: An Idealized Portrayal of the U.S. Authoritative Decision-Making Structure

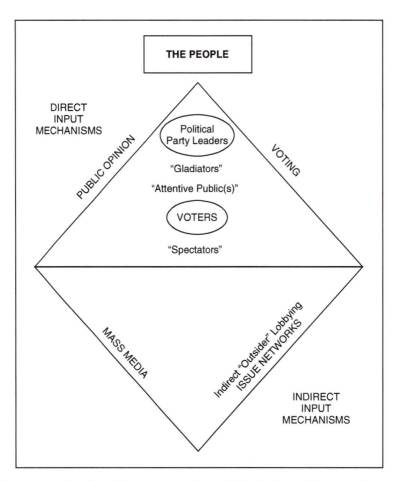

FIGURE C-2B: An Idealized Portrayal of the U.S. Political System "People" Subsystem

telecommunications revolution, we could be witnessing the beginning of the re-creation of direct democracy—or *1984* meets the twenty-first century and creates its *Frankenstein*.[9]

---

[9] With apologies to George Orwell and Mary Shelley. Some memorable recent manifestations of the "Cybernetics Gone Wild" theme (a science-fiction classic that has been around since at least the 1950s film *Colossus*) have been *Star Trek's* Borg, the *Terminator* movie villains, and television's Cylons from *Battlestar Galactica*.

For argued and defensible reasons, the "gestalt" principle can clearly be applied to the U.S. political system. Building on the innovative framework provided by our Founders, the United States has evolved something extraordinary, in the purest sense of that word. This is a thesis that has been argued by the "American exceptionalism" school of thought for some time, an argument wonderfully summarized in a recently updated comprehensive comparative analysis. Raymond Smith spotlights three key basic ingredients that helped shape our unique development. Fairly early in its history, the United States became "exceptionally large," while "also highly diverse and decentralized." These circumstances blended together to fortify the social and political forces molding its evolution to create "the only country that is large, highly populated, *and* wealthy. This is a combination that is wholly anomalous in the world."[10]

His analysis notes that in area the United States is about 14 times larger than the average country, and has about 10 times the average population of countries of the world. These factors converged with our relative geographic isolation to shape our exceptional economic and political history. Although technology has now essentially erased the basic protection from the rest of the world that isolation provided, the particular form of democratic federalism that it allowed to incubate remains as its bequest to future generations of Americans. It is our core political structure.

HOW WELL IS THE U.S. POLITICAL SYSTEM WORKING?

One of the grand theorems in social science today is that structure impacts function,[11] and with respect to governments, "capacity" is a typical concept used to study how well they function.

The operational definition of capacity taught by this political scientist was adapted from one of the prominent texts in use today about the state and local aspect of our political system: *"The ability of government(s) to respond effectively to circumstance, especially change, make authoritative decisions efficiently and responsively, and manage conflict equitably."*[12] Responding to circumstance involves much routine provision of services, with the true tests of a political system being those related to change and managing the inevitable conflicts that significant change entails. These are accomplished through efficient decision making by those in authority, and the overarching standard of success is whether decisions are effective. Are desired positive outcomes achieved and negative outcomes, including unintended ones, avoided? An additional standard used to evaluate public policymaking is equity, operationalized by this author as evenhanded treatment of all those involved throughout the policymaking process.

Applying this definition of capacity, with the themes highlighted above kept in mind, how well is the U.S. political system working? First, how effectively have we been responding to the problems that the first decade of the twenty-first century has thrown at us? The appropriateness and effectiveness of our responses to the 9/11 terrorist attacks will need to be debated for years before any valid conclusions could be drawn. Swift retaliation against the attackers and subsequent efforts to take apart the worldwide terrorist network have certainly had some positive impact, although their full long-term effects are still unfolding. The same can basically be said about our reaction to the Great Recession and

---

[10] Raymond A. Smith, *The American Anomaly: U.S. Politics and Government in Comparative Perspective,* 2nd ed. (New York: Routledge, 2011), 14.

[11] Gabriel Almond is usually credited with the first elaboration of structural-functionalism applied to politics. See the Introduction to *The Politics of the Developing Areas* (Princeton, NJ: Princeton University Press, 1960), which he edited with James Coleman. A more recent application is John R. Bowen and Roger Peterson, *Critical Comparisons in Politics and Culture* (New York: Cambridge University Press, 1999).

[12] Adapted from Anne O'M. Bowman's and Richard C. Kearny's definition in *State and Local Government: The Essentials,* 5th ed. (New York: Pearson, 2012), 3.

related financial crisis. Our response to Hurricane Katrina is viewed by this author as the greatest failure of U.S. public administration in our history, however.[13] Lack of leadership and coordination led to unnecessary suffering and death, while issues of equity and ethics are still being fully explored and resolved.

Our biggest domestic test to date in the twenty-first century is now underway, moreover. The U.S. political system has reached another crossroads at which we must clarify the role we expect our national government to play in our political system and individual lives. Raw—but peaceful—political conflict has been unleashed by the convergence of major demographic change, an economic crisis, and the rise on the political agenda of several issues that directly relate to our core Ideal Principles. A demographic "double whammy" is hitting the United States with the concurrent retirement of the "Baby Boom" generation and coming-of-age of the Millennials. The political gap between these two generations is clearly illustrated by their divergent views on gay marriage, an issue that stirs up many people's deep personal beliefs. The Great Recession and resulting "bailouts" and stimulus efforts triggered the most widespread and visible political movements this country has seen in 50 years, spotlighting both our growing national debt and widening income and wealth gaps. We will return to this scenario at the very end of our journey.

HOW ROBUST IS THE U.S. FEDERAL REPUBLIC?

Let's now return or attention to the core structure of our political system, the U.S. Federal Republic. In Chapter 5, the characteristics of successful federations proposed by Jenna Bednar in her recent, comprehensive theoretical work on that topic were introduced. A "robust" (healthy and vigorous) system of any kind is "strong, flexible, and able to recover from internal errors," she begins.[14] With respect to federations, she elaborates, "Robust system design has three properties: *compliance*, to dissuade "transgressions" [see below]; *resilience*, an immunity to design flaws and external shocks; and *adaptation*, an ability to adjust the rules to meet changing needs."[15]

These are needed to counter the basic problem that all federations face of all its component units sometimes seeking "to manipulate the division of authority to their benefit," which Bednar labels "opportunism" and examines in remarkable detail. The various "transgressions" that are "a normal part of federal practice" due to "inevitable" intergovernmental rivalry[16] take three basic forms. She portrays them, interestingly, as a triangular tug-of-war involving "shirking" and "burden-shifting" by subnational units and national government "encroachment."[17] It was this formulation that reignited this author's interest in the triad concept with respect to political design questions.

The United States has certainly experienced all three of these throughout its history. The long battle over basic Civil Rights for African Americans, described in Chapter 3 as the greatest failure of U.S. federalism in our history, epitomized state "shirking." "Burden-shifting" has taken many, many forms. Northern states and cities, for example, have long practiced "Greyhound

---

[13] An excellent , precise description of this failure is provided by Larry N. Gerston, *American Federalism: A Concise Introduction* (Armonk, NY: M. E. Sharpe, 2007), 105.

[14] Jenna Bednar, *The Robust Federation: Principles of Design* (New York: Cambridge University Press, 2009), 1.

[15] Bednar (brackets added), 13.

[16] Bednar, 63.

[17] Bednar, 68–69.

therapy,"[18] giving one-way bus tickets to southern destinations to some of their homeless to avoid the costs of providing shelter and social services to them for the winter. In our discussion of federalism in action in Chapter 5, we noted that preemption of state authority and unfunded mandates, which epitomize national encroachment in public policymaking, were key issues in that ongoing tug-of-war.

For a federation to have the three properties of robustness, Bednar then argues, it must contain a set of "safeguards" arrayed to achieve three specific design goals:[19]

- *"Coverage"*: "[T]he three types of opportunism must be resolved simultaneously."
- *"Complementarity"*: "Safeguards . . . are more than the sum of their parts; they make one another more effective."
- *"Redundancy"*: Since "safeguards are imperfect," there must be more than one in place to address each of the three types of opportunism at any time.

The basic safeguard built into all federations is any member government's ability "to strike back with retaliatory noncompliance and even threaten to secede," but that "alone is not sufficient to eliminate all transgressions," according to Bednar.[20] Other safeguards must exist and function as integral parts of its authoritative decision-making structure for a political system to achieve robustness.

Comparative politics tells us that for political systems to be successful they must be compatible with the community's political culture. When federalism was introduced as a theoretical concept in Chapter 1, it was noted that significant variation exists within this basic form. Doing what political scientists do (as described at the very beginning of our journey), Professor Bednar identifies four categories of "institutional features" of federations that provide a very useful framework for discussing the range of safeguards and how they work for federations: "structural," "popular," "political," and "judicial."[21] She explains each of the safeguard categories (which we will elaborate below) in significant detail, and then proceeds "to construct a system's theory of safeguards, where each is a unique component."[22] She does this by providing an amazingly comprehensive analysis of what each type of safeguard can contribute to the achievement of the three required system properties of a robust federation. In using the U.S. Federal Republic as her primary example in her theory building, she explains the theoretical underpinnings of its success in a way not previously accomplished by any scholar of federalism. This author must confess that he could not fully follow her mathematical arguments, but notes that they have been well received by her fellow political economists.

In the U.S. Federal Republic, judicial safeguards (most notably judicial review) cover all three forms of opportunism, as does intergovernmental retaliation, which has been enhanced in recent decades by the proliferation of formal structures, including the emergence of new levels of government (via regionalization at the old levels) being added to the competition. Bednar goes on to identify which transgressions are covered by each of the other three types of

---

[18] *Segan's Medical Dictionary*, 2011 (Farlex), http://medical-dictionary.thefreedictionary.com/Greyhound+Therapy.
[19] Bednar, 127.
[20] Bednar, 77–78.
[21] Bednar, 96.
[22] Bednar, 132.

safeguards, and then refines her assessment of the "coverage capacity" of all five by explaining the interplay of the frequency and severity of system sanctions in response to transgressions.[23] Appropriately balancing these two achieves complementarity, which improves compliance. Redundant safeguards also improve compliance, but that must not be overdone. All of this must be accomplished as "a delicate balancing act."[24]

The path to robustness for the U.S. Federal Republic was not an easy one. While the Madisonian Model gave us an excellent start by providing a strong base of structural safeguards, each of the other types had to emerge and evolve into what we have today. Many people do not acknowledge that the U.S. political system broke down twice in its history. After the failure of the Articles of Confederation, the Constitution of 1787 made our federation "much more robust,"[25] but it did not prevent the Civil War. In response to those who describe our system as broken now, and any others who fear that we are heading toward another breakdown, the following summary of our key safeguards is offered, including some highlights about how they have evolved:

- *Intergovernmental Competition/Retaliation*: The evolution of the tug-of-war between the national and state governments was summarized in Chapter 5, and it continues today as we grapple most notably with the issues of economic recovery, health care, and regulation. While, "by most accounts," the "Recovery Act stimulus effort was an extraordinarily successful collaboration

between all three levels of government,"[26] "in healthcare reform, greater centralization was instituted,"[27] leading a majority of states to challenge it in court. Both analyses conclude with uncertainty about the future of U.S. federalism, portraying the Obama approach to intergovernmental relations as a hybrid characterized by "a very unique mixture of collaborative and coercive strategies in dealing with states and localities."[28] This seems appropriate for an era of transition. Competition between the state and local levels seems to have intensified in recent years, moreover, and the emergence of regional governing structures has added a new level of complexity to this core safeguard. Recall our discussion above of how technology is reshaping the overall authoritative decision-making process. This includes intergovernmental relations. Today, successful public administration must incorporate technology, and those with the better technological resources and skills now have an advantage.

- *Structural*: The Madisonian Model, as presented in Chapter 2, was based on the concept of using structural safeguards so that "ambition must be able to counter ambition." Bednar explains "Madison's theoretical trick" as creating "antagonism within governmental parts" to generate "a self-regulating whole"[29] by combining fragmentation and partial interdependence. The basic *separation of powers*,

---

[23] Bednar summarizes these in Table 5-1 (134) and Table 6-1 (153).
[24] Bednar, 150.
[25] Bednar, 126.

[26] Peter A. Harkness, "What Brand of Federalism Is Next," *Governing* (January 2012), 16–17.
[27] Timothy J. Conlan and Paul L. Posner, "Inflection Point? Federalism and the Obama Administration," *Publius*, 41 (3) (2011), 443.
[28] Harkness, 16.
[29] Bednar, 100.

fortified with the addition of the *specific checks and balances* listed below in Table C-1, combined with the basic *sharing of formal decision-making authority between levels of government* that is the essence of federalism, provided an operational framework in which tugs-of-war among and within the components was inevitable. When the Supreme Court formalized the power of *judicial review* with the *Marbury* opinion, validated *Congress's implied powers* in the *McCullough* ruling, and *sanctioned extensive use of executive power in appropriate circumstances* in a series of cases related to the Civil War[30] the independent power of each branch was authenticated. The long history of judicial battles between the levels of government, from which key cases were highlighted in Chapter 5, has both certified the rise of national power and maintained a level of state power that keeps U.S. federalism alive and kicking.

- *Popular*: Bednar uses a classic American metaphor to describe the role of the people in the U.S. Federal Republic: "Madison envisioned federal dynamics as pulled by a joint team of national and state governments, but the people held the whip and reins."[31] Having multiple governments means having *more political offices* to fill, and *increases opportunities for popular participation* in the political process through elections. Since it creates a "hierarchy of offices," moreover, federalism *provides a "weeding out" process for public officials* through service at the lower levels. These officials are also responsible to *different groups of people*, who will *apply their different* individual and collective *perspectives to public issues and questions*. An interesting result of this safeguard at times is the choice of different parties to control the different levels of government, commonly referred to as "divided government." Several

Bicameral Congress provides a built-in "second look" at all proposed legislation
The Executive veto and congressional override authority
Senate confirmation of executive and judicial appointments
Senate ratification of treaties
Congress's budgeting powers (both authorization and appropriation)
Congressional authority to revise laws, most notably enabling legislation for Executive and Judicial branch operations, and to propose constitutional amendments
Presidential authority over implementation of legislation and judicial rulings, including the power to issue Executive Orders, commute sentences, and issue pardons

TABLE C-1: Specific Checks and Balances in the U.S. Constitution of 1787

---

[30] Notable examples are *Ex parte Merryman* (1861), *Ex parte Milligan* (1866), and *Mississippi v. Johnson* (1867), in which the Court ruled "that it had no jurisdiction to control the acts of the President." Robert E. Cushman, *Leading Constitutional Decisions* (New York: F. S. Crofts & Co., 1941), 164.

[31] Bednar discusses popular safeguards on pp. 109–112, from which all quotations in this paragraph are drawn.

theorists of federalism have argued that this "vertical balancing" expresses a desire for policy moderation on the part of the public.

The key to the people being a fully functioning safeguard in the political process is their ability to influence authoritative decision making. Note that federalism only increases the opportunities for popular participation. This validates concern over voter turnout, but one of the true strengths of *the U.S. political system* is that it *provides multiple avenues for citizen input*. In addition to *voting in competitive elections*, the people can—and do—use *public opinion* continuously to react to policies to which they object and to set boundaries on what policies governments at all levels can enact.[32] With technology giving the American people more and faster means of communicating their displeasure to public officials, this popular safeguard should actually grow in its influence as the twenty-first century unfolds.

In addition to what we labeled their *direct input mechanisms* of voting and public opinion in Section Three, people in the United States make excellent use of the *indirect input mechanisms* at their disposal. As stated back in Chapter 1, the key characteristic of a modern democracy is genuine competition among political organizations. Although it is fashionable to condemn the influence of "special interests" in our policymaking process, to do so ignores the realities of modern life. Using formal associations and professional lobbyists to promote public policies we want and oppose those we think will

hurt us—what has traditionally been called *interest articulation*—reflects, in this political scientist's view, the maturation of our political system in the form of the bureaucratization of pluralism. The U.S. political system is characterized by "an unusually large and decentralized universe of interest groups" whose activity "parallels the fragmentation of the U.S. governmental structure." Federalism, therefore, reinforces interest articulation as a safeguard by providing groups with the opportunity "to 'shop' (around for) the level of policymaking authority that will be most responsive to their needs."[33]

- *Political*: Interest articulation works best when complemented with active, effective *interest aggregation*, the filtering of the many interests into generalized, workable public policy proposals and platforms by political parties. Bednar summarizes the contrasting basic views on how political parties represent their members' interests, and concludes that "an integrated party system"[34] featuring ambitious politicians contributes to the success of a federation. How? The self-interest of politicians desiring higher office prods them to consider how their decisions will be perceived at the higher levels and within those larger communities. Political parties function as both the people's other indirect input mechanism, another popular safeguard,

---

[32] John W. Kingdon, *Agendas, Alternatives, and Public Policies* (New York: HarperCollins, 1995), 65.

[33] Larry N. Gerston, *American Federalism: A Concise Introduction* (Armonk, NY: M. E. Sharpe, 2007), parentheses added, 78.

[34] Bednar, 113–115. Her analysis and definition of "integrated party system" (one in which local, state, and national components depend on each other for success) is based on Mikhail Filippov et al., *Designing Federalism: A Theory of Self-Sustainable Federal Institutions* (Cambridge, UK: Cambridge University Press, 2004).

and as a political safeguard if their operations parallel the federal nature of the government. This is the case in the U.S. political system.

- *Judicial*: Bednar reverses the standard argument that judicial independence is the cornerstone of federal stability. While the judiciary "is incapable of single-handedly maintaining" system robustness, it can be "very useful" working in combination with other safeguards. Judicial safeguards are different, moreover. Both popular and political safeguards fulfill that role by pursuing "private interests or those unrelated to federal robustness," but that is *the* mission of the judiciary with respect to federalism. The main focus of its judicial review function is always the fundamental law under which the federation operates. By concentrating on the Constitution itself, the U.S. judiciary "overcomes some of the shortcomings of the other safeguards: it may be an umpire of federalism." She acknowledges that the courts depend on the other branches to impose penalties, and that the effectiveness of judicial safeguards builds over time; "the court's ability to intercede grows as the federation persists."[35] One of the distinctive characteristics of the U.S. Federal Republic is that "few other countries invest their court system with the scale and scope of power that the United States does," but how is this power used? Returning to Raymond Smith's thorough comparative analysis, we find "three major questions to consider":[36]

Are the courts impartial and independent? Are they a separate and coequal, or a subordinate, branch of the government? And do they have the power of judicial review?. . . As might be expected, in nondemocratic countries, the answer to all of these questions would be no. And the answer to all three of those questions in the United States is a definite yes.

But do these safeguards function effectively in the U.S. political system today? Based on over four decades of studying and working within that system (as outlined in the Preface), this observer has concluded that they do, although certainly not perfectly. Our system certainly appears to have redundant safeguards that complement each other and accomplish the coverage needed to achieve sufficient compliance, resilience, and adaptability to keep us afloat and moving, for the most part, in our desired direction. Bednar methodically analyzes the strengths and weaknesses of each type of safeguard and how they operate, reaching a similar conclusion. Recognizing the limitations of participant-observation as a basis for inference, her comprehensive effort provides a welcomed validation that the U.S. Federal Republic is working as it should.

Bednar's goal, which she clearly achieved, was to build "a logic of robust federal design."[37] In the end, however, she acknowledges that while good design can enhance the prospects for achieving robustness, a final ingredient is required for long-term success. The "necessity" for a federal political culture "if a federal union is to endure"[38] is one of the main conclusions of federalism studies. A shift in a community's shared core political values

---

[35] Bednar, 120–125.
[36] Raymond A. Smith, *The American Anomaly: U.S. Politics and Government in Comparative Perspective,* 2nd ed. (New York: Routledge, 2011), 101 and 91.

[37] Bednar, 1.
[38] Bednar (her italics), 186.

must occur. Only when members of a political community begin to value the federation itself as their basic authoritative decision-making configuration does that community become "a federal nation."[39] Political cultures are products of political history, so this is achieved over time through successful experience with federal politics.

The political history of the United States exemplifies the evolution of a robust federation, with trials and breakdowns producing reactions that strengthened the system in the long run. The failure of the Articles of Confederation led to the Constitution of 1787, and the Civil War both validated the Supremacy Clause and led to people calling themselves "Americans." Bednar cites the use of federalism's safeguards by Thomas Jefferson and James Madison to confront the Alien and Sedition Acts of 1798 as an early example of the U.S. "federal culture" beginning to evolve,[40] but it took considerable time. She concludes her analysis by noting that "this citizen expectation, this respect for the union"[41] had not taken hold when President Jackson publicly snubbed the Supreme Court's ruling against Georgia in 1832, but had been achieved by 1957, empowering President Eisenhower (who was no cheerleader for Civil Rights) to send troops to enforce the Court's public school desegregation decision in Arkansas.

IS THE U.S. POLITICAL SYSTEM DEMOCRATIC?

So, the conclusion that we have a robust federation is clearly defensible, but that is not our only criterion for success. Near the beginning of

this journey, we explored what a "democratic republic" was in theory, and stated that the United States appeared to be one. The people's very active use of political organizations, and our election of representatives and leaders to make our major authoritative decisions (plus appoint and oversee those who make the rest of them), with the expectation that those decisions would serve our needs and preferences were noted as the reasons why. Does that assessment hold up? Our discussions about the indirect input mechanisms of interest groups/associations and political parties provide ample evidence that our political organizations are functioning well. Some analysts, in fact, view our interest articulation process as excessive, even to the point where it can strangle our democratic process.[42] Bednar does warn that "a federal system of safeguards that works too well may stifle the very system it is designed to protect."[43]

Leadership was mentioned only briefly during our journey, in our discussion of the presidency. It is too complex a topic to take up here, especially public sector leadership, and there is a rich literature available for those who are interested.[44] A concise current consensus definition of *leadership* views it as *a process of moving people toward a mutually defined goal* that is "recognized as distinct because it:"[45]

1. Instills certain values in followers
2. Builds or upholds teamwork among followers

---

[39] Bednar, 190–191.

[40] Bednar, 202–204.

[41] Bednar, 218–219, citing *Worcester v. Georgia*, 31 U.S. 515 (1832), and *Brown v. Topeka Board of Education* 347 U.S. 483 (1954).

[42] Jonathan Rauch, *Demosclerosis: The Silent Killer of American Government* (New York: Times Books, 1994).

[43] Bednar, 170.

[44] An excellent comprehensive summary can be found in Robert A. Cropf and William Kummeracher, "Leadership in Public Administration," C10 of Robert A. Cropf, *American Public Administration: Public Service for the 21st Century* (New York: Pearson, 2008), 231–256.

[45] Derived from and based on Cropf, 235 and 239.

3. Motivates or inspires followers
4. Provides a clearly defined vision for the community
5. Keeps followers moving toward the vision established by the leader
6. Produces lasting change or innovation

Alas, political leadership, like beauty, is in the eye of the beholder. Most of us do not make objective assessments of our leaders, but tend to rally around those who support ideological and policy positions similar to our own. The "selective attentiveness" noted during our discussion of the mass media (i.e., our inclination to pay more attention to what reinforces our existing views and to filter out messages that challenge them) seems to be particularly active when we evaluate our leaders and potential leaders. The histories of our presidential campaigns and presidential approval ratings make it appear that this has always been the case, but it may be rising to new levels. The permeation of mass media throughout our society, converging with the dramatic rise in the importance of advertising in our electoral campaigns, seems to have fostered a swelling of partisan demonization of both our political leaders and candidates for leadership positions.

As unpleasant as this might get at times, it does tell us that the process of leadership selection is certainly active. Some studies even suggest that negative ads actually provide useful information to voters.[46] But is our process for selecting leaders and representatives democratic? History also tells us that the United States has always been a limited, indirect democracy, relying on social and economic elites to lead us in the early days, and on leaders and

representatives in modern times chosen through processes that have been notably circumscribed by both formal and informal factors.[47] The new "irony of democracy" in the United States is that our ingrained, deep commitments to free speech and citizen participation have combined to make sizable wealth—or access to it—the crucial ingredient needed just to pursue a major public office. The *Citizens United* decision[48] was the latest in a string of Supreme Court decisions over the last four decades that essentially equates the use of money for political purposes with free speech.[49] Its recognition of free speech rights for incorporated businesses and labor unions has stirred up significant opposition, including a movement promoting a constitutional amendment intended to reverse it.

That movement has been essentially Internet-based, moreover, along with a number of others currently seeking to reverse or modify other public policies. This illustrates both the vitality and adaptability of our citizen participation process, as well as demonstrating how our overall political process is being transformed by technology. The Bill of Rights is the foundation upon which all forms of popular participation are constructed in the U.S. Federal Republic. Despite fears about the erosion of our civil liberties that accompanied our nation's response to the 9/11 terrorist attacks, that foundation remains firm. The best evidence that can be cited

---

[46] John G. Geer and Ken Goldstein, "The Positive Effect of Negative Ads," *The Star-Ledger*, 3/21/08, 19.

[47] The classic presentation of this thesis was Thomas R. Dye and L. Harmon Zeigler, *The Irony of Democracy: An Uncommon Introduction to American Politics* (North Scituate, MA: Duxbury, 1971).

[48] *Citizens United v. Federal Election Commission*, 130 S. Ct. 876 (2010).

[49] An excellent overview of the evolution of campaign finance reform and the court decisions is provided by Steffen W. Schmidt, Mark C. Shelley, and Barbara Bardes, *American Government and Politics Today*, 13th ed. (Mason, OH: Thomson Wadsworth, 2008), 293–300.

is that within just the last few years we have seen two major populist movements take form and flourish to the point where they became factors in the authoritative decision-making process.

Fears that twenty-first-century technology gives governments the capability of truly controlling people are valid, but that same technology has made available the tools for increased information gathering, communicating, and organizing by individuals, groups, and communities that is transforming citizen participation. One of the hallmarks of American society has been innovation, and one of the great strengths of our political system has been its openness to new techniques. Shrewd use of the Internet appears to have been the key to the success of the insurgent Obama campaign in overcoming the fundraising and organizational advantages that the establishment candidates had in both the nomination contest and the general election in 2008.

To conclude our deliberation over whether or not the U.S. political system is democratic, let's return to the definition introduced back in Chapter 3: "Democracy is a competitive political system in which competing leaders and organizations define the alternatives of public policy in such a way that the public can participate in the [authoritative] decision-making process."[50] Based on what we have learned on our journey, this political scientist's answer is a qualified "Yes." The role of money in our political process must be clarified, since the advantage it provides those with access to wealth does dampen electoral competitiveness. With Internet-based technologies expanding opportunities for

political fundraising and campaigning, as well as political communication, debate, and political organizing in general, it does not appear to be blocking public participation, however. Since these technologies are particularly attractive to the Millennial generation, moreover, one can project greater participation through them in the future.

IS THE U.S. POLITICAL SYSTEM A DEMOCRATIC REPUBLIC?

Back in Chapter 3 we also identified the essential criteria for a political system to qualify as a republic: the authoritative decision-making process should produce policies that reflect the needs and preferences of the community as a whole, the general public, over those of any particular members of the community, especially the decision makers themselves. Government responsiveness to public needs is an issue primarily dealt with at the state and local levels in our political system, although the ongoing expansion of the scope of national policymaking since the New Deal has certainly increased that level's shaping of public service delivery. The interstate highway system led to changes in where and how people live; environmental regulation changed the air we breathe and the water we drink; and the push for alternative sources of energy is changing our landscape.

The issue of public preferences brings us back to questions of ideology and the very role of government in our lives, and therefore to the crossroads at which we currently find ourselves. President Obama chose health care reform as the defining domestic issue for his administration, and it may be the determining factor in the 2012 presidential election. The resulting legislation was challenged by 26 states regarding

---

[50] E. E. Schattschneider, *The Semi-Sovereign People: A Realist's View of Democracy in America* (Hinesdale, IL: Dryden, 1975), 138, with the bracketed information added.

two very basic issues in U.S. federalism.[51] Did the interstate commerce clause allow Congress to intrude in our economic and personal liberty in such a direct manner as an "individual mandate" to obtain insurance? The second issue was the latest serious episode in the tug-of-war between national and state government power: Can Congress mandate a major expansion of a program for which states must pay half the costs by threatening to withhold *all* program funding?

The Supreme Court's complex decision will keep constitutional scholars busy analyzing and debating it for years. It clearly continued the recent trend of limiting what Congress can do under the interstate commerce clause, but allowed the requirement that individuals have health insurance to stand since the only "penalty" is paying an additional tax. With respect to federalism, the ruling that the provision withholding all Medicaid funding was coercive was clearly a victory for the states. Of course, this ruling did not end the health care battle, but rather elevated it as a campaign issue. Adding that to the debate over how to improve our sluggish recovery from the Great Recession while addressing both our growing national debt and widening income and wealth gaps, and our international problems (most notably the ongoing Afghanistan-Pakistan War), the turbulence of the waters the crew of the "U.S. Federal Republic" is currently navigating becomes quite obvious.

Rather than formulating and adopting a rather clear and consensual path through this turbulence, however, it appears that our current crew has steered us into an ice field and gotten us stuck. It is gridlock over taxing and spending that has many claiming our political system is broken, but the opposite could also be argued. Since the United States is facing a rapidly and radically changing world, and the path it chooses now will likely set our policy direction for the foreseeable future, we should take our time and move cautiously. Recall that our Founders deliberately chose the protection from concentrated power provided by the Madisonian Model, and we have kept it while most of the world chose parliaments. The responsiveness to electoral will provided by the fused power of a parliamentary system now dominates. Our Founders preferred long-term to short-term thinking, however, and republican government to democracy.

Moreover, some political scientists claim that the "incremental" approach to policymaking, in which we move forward in small steps, provides the most genuine, permanent progress against public problems, and many recognize it as most descriptive of the U.S. policymaking process.[52] This author has always found the "mixed-scanning" model, which blends "incremental" decision making shaped by periodic "fundamental" decisions the most descriptive, however.[53] Given the extraordinary circumstances and the wide array of issues we are dealing with, an argument can certainly be made that we are at a fundamental decision point. One of the reasons for distinguishing the two types of decisions is to recognize when it would

---

[51] *Florida et al.* v. *Department of Health and Human Services et al.* The Supreme Court combined that case with *National Federation of Independent Business et al. v. Sebelius, Secretary of Health and Human Services et al.* and the Department's countersuit for hearing arguments and issued a consolidated ruling, 567 U. S. ___ (2012).

[52] One of the classic presentations of this model is Robert Dahl and Charles Lindbloom, *Politics, Economics, and Welfare* (Chicago: University of Chicago Press, 1952).

[53] Amitai Etzioni, "Mixed-Scanning Revisited," *Public Administration Review,* 46 (1986), 8–13.

be worthwhile to expend the time and resources attempting "rational" policymaking, which requires considerable research, analysis, and deliberation for success. For fundamental decisions to be democratic, moreover, they should also reflect significant public participation. These are usually marked by noteworthy formal actions, like constitutional amendments, important new laws or major court rulings accepted by the people, or by elections featuring what was called party realignment in the past, and today would feature a major ideological shift among swing voters.[54]

Given the amazing array of concurrent changes (technological, demographic, and economic) converging at this time, we may be at another turning point for the U.S. political system. Historians will have to determine that in the future. We are certainly at a "bending" point, clearly about to take another turn in the ideological "dialectical dance" described back in the Introduction. Moreover, that dance between the fluid national coalition that desires more government protection through national policymaking and the one that prefers personal freedom and state power may be the "secret ingredient" to the success of our democratic federal republic:[55]

> *What makes the U.S. political culture unrivaled is its peaceful dynamism. There are always competing patriotic forces arguing for their vision of America. Hamiltonians done you wrong for eight years? Cast your vote for the Jeffersonians for a change.*

And there appears to be a rhythm to this dance. The complex, fluctuating mosaic of ongoing tugs-of-war among our intertwined political subsystems accommodates these competing coalitions in a manner that seems to provide continuous representation of their core values and meaningful participation in the public policymaking arena. The apparent dominance occasionally achieved by one of the coalitions is always countered in some way somewhere within the system. Therefore, ideological "control" is always circumscribed, and actually shared by our two competing core "factions." A number of analysts, including some political scientists,[56] have proposed different "laws of political physics" to portray various action-reaction patterns encountered within various aspects of the process. Our Hamiltonian–Jeffersonian dialectical dance manifests such a pattern with respect to public policymaking. When one coalition gets voted out, it retains some residual power through its appointees who remain in key authoritative decision-making positions within the national structure or in at least some of the states.

The key pivot point seems to be the judiciary, particularly the Supreme Court, although there is likely some residual power retained in the bureaucracy, and even in Congress after one of the coalitions loses majority support. Its small size and important role as the umpire in our political process makes the Supreme Court the clearest manifestation of this phenomenon. The Supreme Court's staunch resistance to the Hamiltonian (pro-national government) New Deal throughout Roosevelt's first term is legendary. When

---

[54] See Steffen W. Schmidt, Mark C. Shelley, and Barbara Bardes, *American Government and Politics Today*, 13th ed. (Mason, OH: Thomson Wadsworth, 2008), 278–279 for an overview of party realignment and dealignment.

[55] *Newsweek*, June 8, 2009, 18, reviewing Simon Schama's *The American Future* (London: HarperCollins, 2009).

[56] For example, Deil S. Wright uses that term to describe some of the dynamics of public policymaking under federalism in *Understanding Intergovernmental Relations*, 3rd ed. (Pacific Grove, CA: Brooks/Cole, 1988).

the conservatives regained control of Congress and the Presidency in the 1950s, they faced "liberal" opposition from a Court led by Earl Warren (1953–1969), a Jeffersonian who advocated individual rights, but used Hamiltonian tactics to promote them. Warren Burger's appointment as Chief Justice (1969–1986) heartened conservatives, but a residual liberal majority kept the Court leaning left while the conservative New Federalism movement moved the Presidency and the Congress in the other direction, leading to further change in the Court.

The Rehnquist Court (1986–2005) brought the return of a Jeffersonian tilt, issuing key rulings favoring states' rights and narrowing Congress's authority to legislate under the interstate commerce clause. The current Roberts Court has been labeled "the most conservative in decades,"[57] but has been characterized by many 5-4 decisions. The "Obamacare" ruling is another split decision from a divided court giving both conservatives and liberals a basis for claiming victory on one of the major issues, which fits the transitional circumstances we are in Any future Obama appointees would be expected to move the Court leftward, leaving a Hamiltonian and liberal imprint. The 2012 presidential and congressional elections will hopefully at least move us out of the ice field. The strong partisan ideological divide underpinning our current policy gridlock will be resolved, if only temporarily, and perhaps even pushed aside by a strong reaction on the part of independent swing voters. It may take the next few elections for us to finally settle on a consensus course for our future, however. The dance continues.

The "ship of state" is a very old metaphor, but it still strikes a chord. To this political scientist, James Madison and his fellow Founders designed an excellent ship, and those political leaders who preserved it, repaired it, and improved it over the last two and a quarter centuries also deserve commendation. From what we have learned on our journey, together they developed an adaptive and resilient political system with the capacity to make authoritative decisions efficiently and responsively and manage conflict equitably. To this author, that describes a ship ready to go just when we need it! The test our political system is now facing is whether it can again respond to extremely turbulent circumstances.

Of course, questions about political design are never permanently answered. John Dewey was the first writer this author encountered who reminded us that each and every generation of Americans must reinvent our democracy. The Millennials will have to clarify the role of money in our political process, and deal with its continuing transformation by technology, including unexpected impacts that have yet to manifest themselves. But I think we are leaving them a darn good ship with which to sail those turbulent waters. One of the regular reminders I give my students is that there is no magic formula for good government. Governing is a continuous exercise in interactive social problem solving, which for this participant-observer has been most accurately described as "processes for moving toward a solution" that rarely, if ever, "wholly solves the problem." A realistic goal for those seeking to alleviate or reduce social problems, therefore, is to identify and take some steps "from here to a better there."[58]

---

[57] Adam Liptak, "Court Under Roberts Is Most Conservative in Decades," *New York Times*, 7/24/10, http://www.nytimes.com/2010/07/25/us/25roberts.html?pagewanted=all.

[58] Charles E. Lindblom and David K. Cohen, *Usable Knowledge: Social Science and Social Problem Solving* (New Haven, CT: Yale University Press, 1979), 26.

As we end this journey, the best advice this political scientist can offer for dealing with the future is to keep in mind that it is a fan. Humans tend to assume that the future will be basically the same as the present, but recent unusual events (e.g., tsunamis) should have reinforced the realities that (1) it is a variable, and (2) very low-probability events do occur. Within that context, the realistic goal noted above, which can be condensed to pursuing "progress," should be the primary focus of our efforts, and it was Alfred North Whitehead who best conveyed its essence: "The art of progress is to preserve order amid change and to preserve change amid order." So, it seems the future is another triangular tug-of-war (see Figure C-3). Is the U.S. political system up to the challenge? This political scientist concludes that, despite its imperfections, it is. But artistry is something only individuals can bring to a situation; the key to continuing our successful evolution as a democratic federal republic will be choosing the right crews.

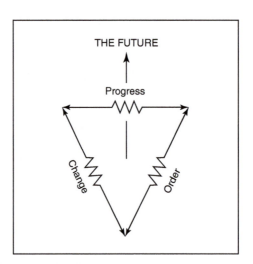

FIGURE C-3: The Triangular Tug-of-War

I N D E X

CPSIA information can be obtained
at www.ICGtesting.com
Printed in the USA
LVHW01s2040310817
547158LV00008B/64/P